Global South Asians

By the end of the twentieth century some nine million people of South Asian descent had left India, Bangladesh or Pakistan and settled in different parts of the world, forming a diverse and significant modern diaspora. In the early nineteenth century, many left reluctantly to seek economic opportunities which were lacking at home. In later decades others left freely in anticipation of better lives and work. This is the story of their often painful experiences in the diaspora, how they constructed new social communities overseas and how they maintained connections with the countries and the families they had left behind. It is a story compellingly told by one of the premier historians of modern South Asia, Judith Brown, whose particular knowledge of the diaspora in Britain and South Africa gives her insight as a commentator. This is a book which will have a broad appeal to general readers as well as to students of South Asian and colonial history, migration studies and sociology.

JUDITH M. BROWN is Beit Professor of Commonwealth History, University of Oxford, and Professorial Fellow of Balliol College. Her recent publications include *Gandhi: Prisoner of Hope* (1989), and *Nehru: A Political Life* (2003).

New Approaches to Asian History

This dynamic new series will publish books on the milestones in Asian history, those that have come to define particular periods or mark turning-points in the political, cultural and social evolution of the region. Books are intended as introductions for students to be used in the classroom. They are written by scholars, whose credentials are well established in their particular fields and who have, in many cases, taught the subject across a number of years.

Global South Asians

Introducing the Modern Diaspora

Judith M. Brown

Beit Professor of Commonwealth History,
University of Oxford

CAMBRIDGE
UNIVERSITY PRESS

Published in South Asia by

Cambridge University Press India Pvt. Ltd.
Cambridge House
4381/4 Ansari Road
Daryaganj, New Delhi - 110 002

First South Asian Edition 2007

ISBN-10: 81-7596-383-2 (Paperback)
ISBN-13: 978-81-7596-383-2 (Paperback)

ISBN-10: 81-7596-384-0 (Hardback)
ISBN-13: 978-81-7596-384-9 (Hardback)

This edition of *Judith M. Brown/Global South Asians: Introducing the Mod* *Diaspora* is published by arrangement with Cambridge University Press, Edinburgh Building, Shaftesbury Road, Cambridge CB2 2RU, UK.

Published by Manas Saikia for Cambridge University Press India Pvt. Ltd. and prir at Sanat Printers, Kundli, Haryana, India.

Contents

Illustrations

Acknowledgments

My first debt of gratitude incurred in this study of the South Asian diaspora is to those members of the diaspora who have knowingly, and sometimes unwittingly, contributed to my knowledge of their experience. I hope I may have repaid that debt in some small way if some of my readers are enabled to understand the diversity of the diaspora and the myriad issues with which its peoples have grappled for over a century and a half.

Marigold Acland, Senior Commissioning Editor at Cambridge University Press, first suggested that I might write this book, and encouraged me to engage formally with a topic which had interested me for decades, not just because of my work on South Asia itself, but because I used to teach at Manchester University which is located in an area of high South Asian settlement, and where some of the issues discussed here were a daily and present reality. To her and to Isabelle Dambricourt at Cambridge University Press I offer my thanks for all their help in the production of this volume. Several colleagues in Oxford have been generous in their time and advice, particularly Professors Steven Vertovec and Ceri Peach, and Professor Ian Talbot, now of Southampton University, who spent a year as a Visiting Fellow at Balliol College and engaged in many discussions with me on the diaspora as well as latterly reading the complete manuscript and making valuable suggestions. Nigel James of the Bodleian Library's map room was of invaluable help in the creation of maps. Stephanie Jenkins in the History Faculty was, as always, a fund of expertise and help in the process of producing a manuscript. From further afield I would like to thank publicly Professor Brij Lal, of the Australian National University of Canberra, who generously permitted me to use photos of his grandparents and of Indians engaged in sugar cultivation in Fiji, and whose own work helped to open my eyes to the reality of the indenture experience; and Dr Alleyn Diesel, who once took me on a tour of Hindu temples in Pietermaritzburg and has allowed me to use some of her exceptional photographs in this book. In the USA Rekha Inc. found for me two important photographs and gave me permission to use them here. Professor Renee C. Fox, Annenberg Professor Emerita of the Social Sciences at Pennsylvania University, and former visiting Eastman Professor at Balliol, most generously read my manuscript from the perspective of an American readership and from within a discipline other than my own, and I offer her my thanks for her encouragement in this project, as in so much else.

Finally my thanks, as always, go to my husband, Peter Diggle. He read the manuscript to ensure its accessibility and clarity, and helped me with photographic expeditions. But far beyond any specific assistance with this particular book, his constant support, fidelity and love make possible my academic work and my own global journeys.

Glossary

bhangra	form of Punjabi music
dukawalla	Indian trader in East Africa
fatwa	formal opinion on a point of Islamic law by a recognised Muslim authority
Gurudwara	Sikh place of worship
halal	meat butchered according to Islamic rules
hijab	headscarf worn by Muslim women
Hindutva	'Hinduness'
Imam	leader of prayers at a mosque
jati	caste; often quite localised endogamous group *cf. varna*
Jihad	Holy war (Muslim)
kangani	form of contract for labour in South East Asia
Kashmiriyat	the Kashmiri way of life
kosher	food acceptable to orthodox Jews
lascar	Indian sailor
madrassah	Muslim secondary school or college
Mandir	Hindu temple
pashmina	fine shawl
Pir	Sufi (Muslim) spiritual guide
puja	act of worship (Hindu)
purdah	forms of female seclusion or the wearing of a veil
raj	rule; thus the British raj in India
salwar kameez	Punjabi female dress of tunic and loose trousers
sirdar	Indian plantation overseer in context of indentured labour
varna	caste; one of the classical fourfold divisions of Hindu society
yagna	originally a central Hindu rite of sacrifice in the Vedas; specifically in Trinidad it means a variety of large-scale, socio-religious observances

Maps

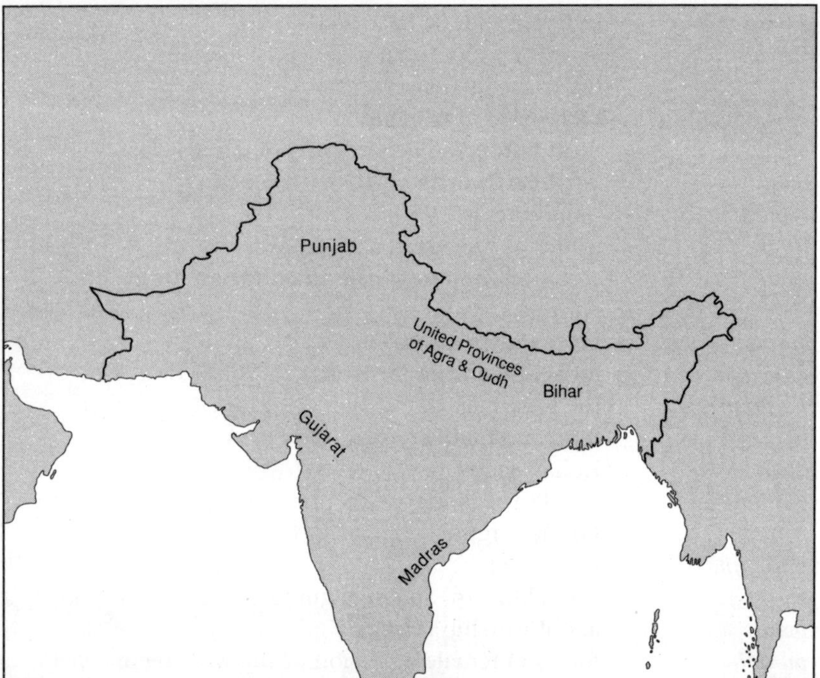

Map 1. India pre-1947, showing major areas from which emigrants went into the diaspora before independence and partition of the subcontinent

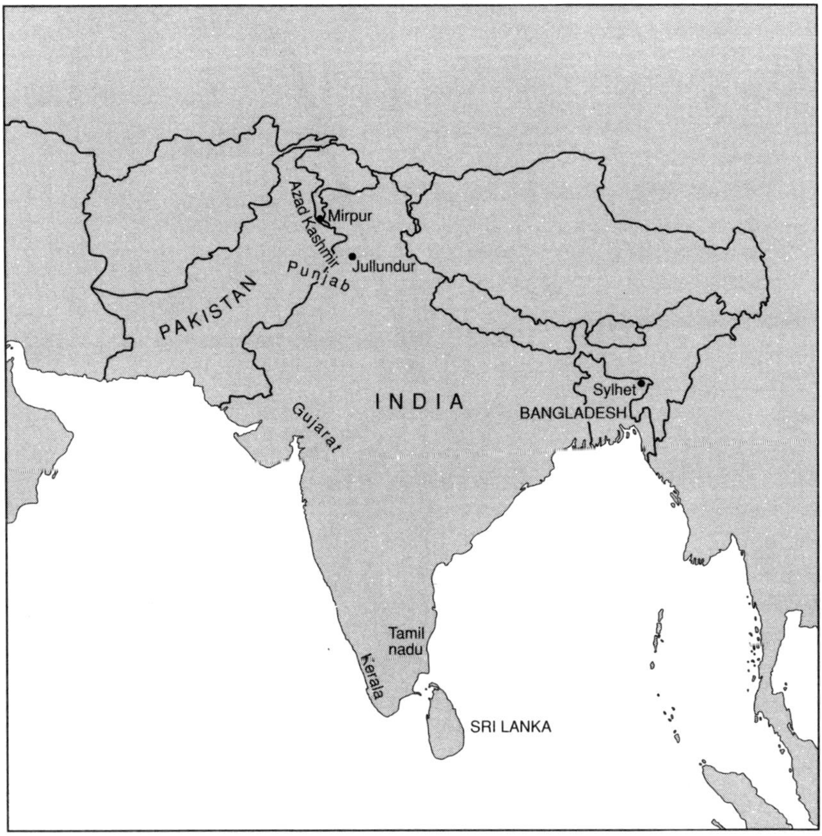

Map 2. South Asian subcontinent post-1971, showing major areas from which emigrants went into the diaspora

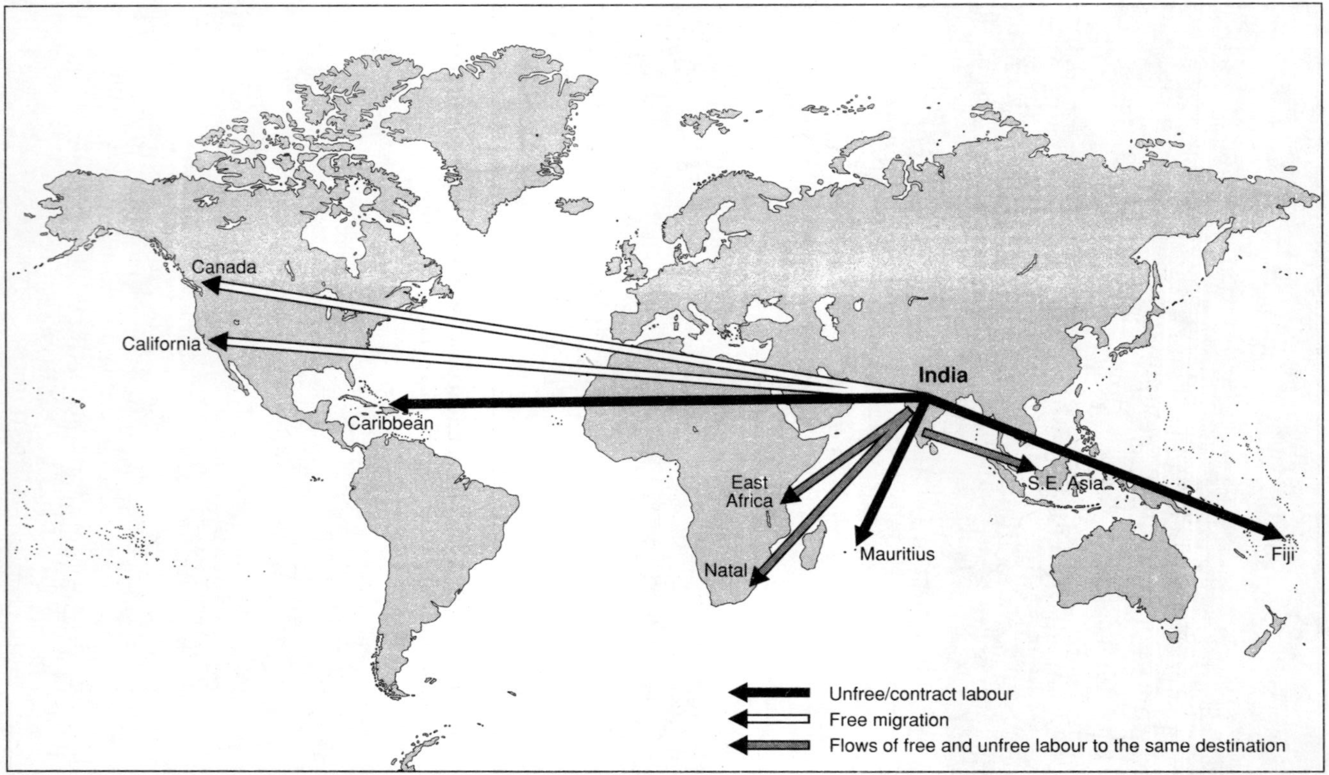

Map 3. Flows of migrants from India before 1947

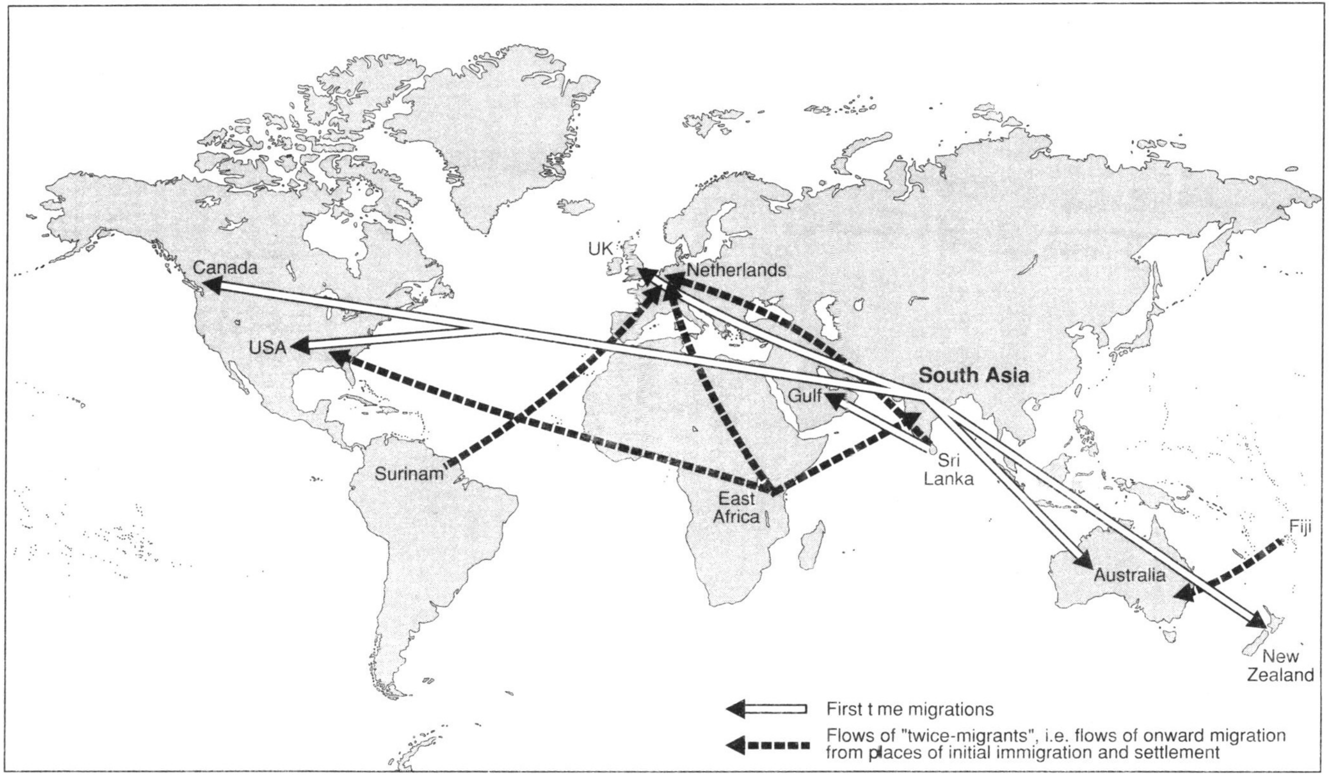

Map 4. Flows of South Asian migrants after 1947

Map 5. Major locations of South Asian settlement in the UK (late twentieth century)

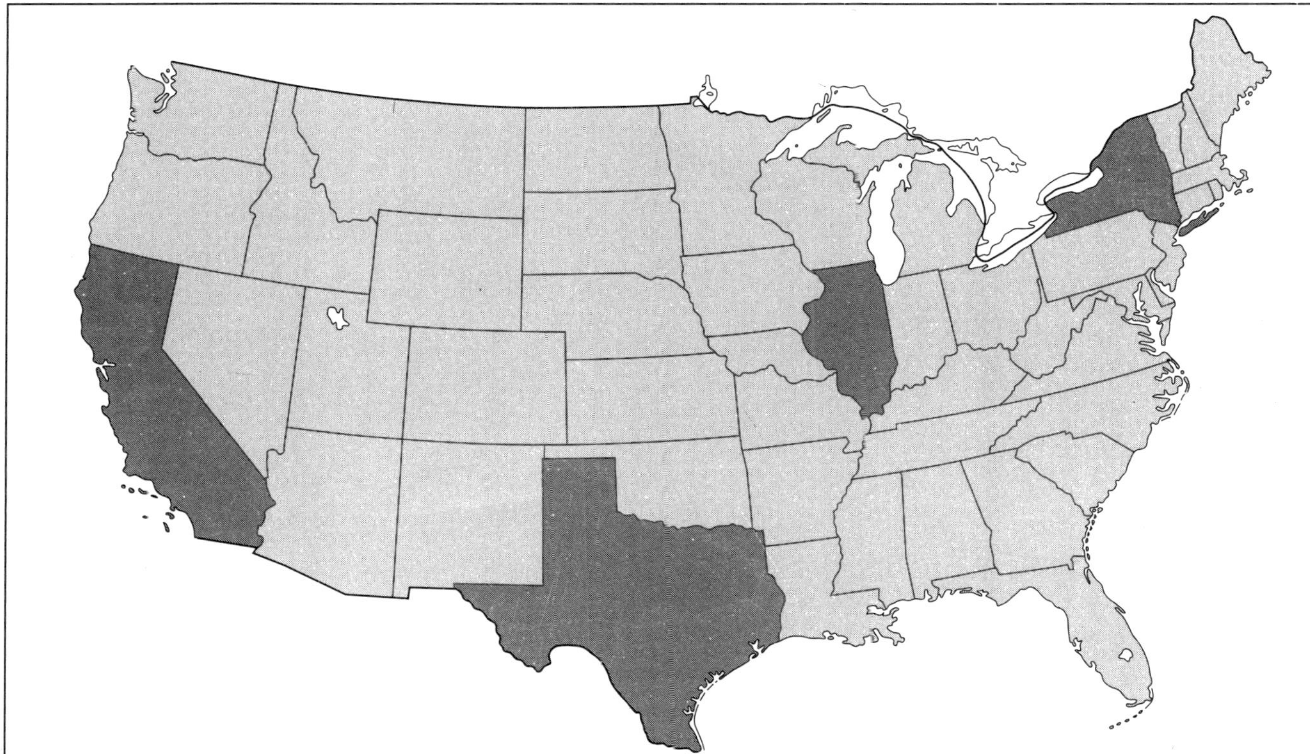

Map 6. US states with the highest concentrations of South Asian settlement (late twentieth century)

Introduction

Men and women have been on the move since the earliest beginnings of human societies. Migration in small and large groups, and the establishment of new homes, have been among the strongest creative forces in the peopling and settling of the world's land mass and the making of human history. However, in the last two and a half centuries, far larger movements of population have occurred than ever before, changing the face of many local societies and of the planet itself. Among the most dramatic of these relatively modern flows of people have been those who travelled as slaves from Africa across the Atlantic, the Chinese who journeyed overseas as labourers and traders, the Europeans who migrated to northern America and to temperate climates in southern Africa, Australia and New Zealand, and the peoples of the Indian subcontinent who have spread out around the world in significant numbers. Such major flows of people have been propelled by demographic pressures, the forces of economics, and politics. Some have left home of their own free choice, whereas others have been compelled, whether formally or not. Some have been lured by hope, others driven by fear. For all of them, the technology of swifter travel has been a critical factor, as metalled roads and the internal combustion engine superseded human and equine feet as the fastest mode of travel on land, and as the sailing ship gave way to the steam ship in the nineteenth century, and eventually to mass air travel in the twentieth, to enable movement between continents and across oceans.

The focus of this book is the overseas migratory experience of the peoples of the Indian subcontinent, or South Asians. The political map of their region of origin changed radically in the mid-twentieth century. In 1947 the British withdrew from their imperial rule of two hundred years, leaving a partitioned subcontinent and two independent nation states, India and Pakistan, followed swiftly by an independent Ceylon, later known as Sri Lanka. Pakistan was composed of widely separated western and eastern wings, and the eastern wing split away to form Bangladesh in 1971. To accommodate these changes the whole area is most conveniently referred to as South Asia, and its peoples as South Asians, except where the people of the particular countries of the subcontinent are referred to. Out-migration from South Asia was not the largest of modern migratory movements. By the last decades of the twentieth century, somewhere over 9 million people of South Asian descent lived outside the subcontinent, outnumbered by those of African, Chinese, European and Jewish descent who lived outside their homelands.[1] However, they had become widely spread – in Europe, Africa, Asia, the Middle East, the Caribbean, North America and the Pacific. Not surprisingly, given geographical proximity, other parts of Asia had the largest number of migrant South Asians. Malaysia had the largest South Asian population (nearly 1.2 million) but this was well under 10 per cent of the total population. However in some other places, though they were fewer in number, they now formed a very significant part of the local population. In Trinidad, for example, though their numbers were relatively small (just over 400,000) they made up about 40 per cent of the population, similar to the percentage of the population of African descent. In Fiji they had come to outnumber the indigenous Fijian inhabitants with a population of over 800,000. In the United Kingdom, the South Asian population was larger than that in any other European country, and indeed of any other country in the world except Malaysia. In 1991, according to the last UK census of the century, and the first which counted ethnic minorities, the minority population was just over 3 million (5.5 per cent of the total), and of these almost half were of South Asian origin. Of the South Asians the majority were Indians, followed by a much smaller group of Pakistanis, and by a yet smaller group of people whose origins lay in Bangladesh. A decade later the actual numbers of all three groups had risen considerably, though Indians still outnumbered Pakistanis and Bangladeshis grouped together and were the largest single ethnic minority in the UK. The three South Asian groups together accounted for 3.6 per cent of the total population and 45 per cent of the ethnic minority population.[2]

[1] C. Clarke, C. Peach and S. Vertovec (eds.), *South Asians Overseas. Migration and Ethnicity* (Cambridge, Cambridge University Press, 1990), p. 1.

[2] The actual numbers in the UK in 1991 were Indians (840,255), Pakistanis (476,555), and Bangladeshis (162,835). By 2001 the actual numbers were Indians (1,053,411), Pakistanis (747,285), and Bangladeshis (283,063). The 2001 figures are available on the internet at National Statistics Online – Population Size. The Censuses for 1991 and 2001 are published by the Office for National Statistics, UK.

For worldwide numbers in 1987 see Clarke, Peach and Vertovec (eds.), *South Asians Overseas*, p. 2. A further source to be found on the internet is the CIA World Fact Book. Although ethnic minorities are not always given in the same way for each country, it is useful because it is regularly updated. Patterns of overseas settlement and the reasons for these will be discussed in detail in subsequent chapters.

The absolute size as well as the distribution and concentration of people of South Asian descent outside the subcontinent makes their migratory experience of considerable interest and importance. South Asians have made a significant and distinctive contribution to the economies, societies and cultures of the places to which they have gone, whether as semi-free labourers on contracts of indenture on plantations in Natal, the Caribbean and Malaya; as traders and entrepreneurs in East Africa; as semi-skilled industrial labour in Europe; or as high-flying professionals in electronics and computing in the USA. Moreover, they have increasingly influenced the politics, economies and cultures of the places which they and their ancestors left, as they have gained in wealth and political articulation, and used modern technologies of travel and communication to fashion many kinds of close links with their former homelands. (This is particularly the theme of Chapter 5.) More broadly, this modern experience of migration is part of a far longer history of the interconnections between South Asia and a wider world. Movement and migration was no new experience in India by the start of the nineteenth century, as Chapter 1 shows. But it was rapidly and dramatically transformed by new modes of travel, within the political context of imperialism and decolonisation, and the economic environment created by the industrialisation of the western world. As the South Asian migrants' individual experiences showed, they were increasingly, if often unwittingly, players in a global world, moved by global forces which reached down to the villages from which they came. It was not until late in the twentieth century that commentators began to use the phrase 'globalisation' to describe and help to explain some of the transformations of the modern world and its growing interconnectedness. Increasingly flows of goods, investment, finance, services, people and ideas link the world together, compressing older ideas of space and separation, fashioning new types of economies, polities and societies. Among these flows, different types of movements of people are of great importance. South Asians overseas reflect many of these different types, from unskilled labourers to highly qualified professionals, from small-time peddlers and shopkeepers to multi-millionaire owners of modern industries. Their experience illuminates a key part of recent world history and deserves close attention.

But should we call this outflow of peoples from South Asia a diaspora? The word came into English usage in the late nineteenth century, as a borrowing from a Greek word (διασπορα), which meant to 'disperse' or literally to 'sow over', and was used to describe the scattered Greek communities of the ancient Mediterranean world. This was originally a neutral word merely indicating geographical dispersion, but in English it soon took on sinister and catastrophic overtones of forced expulsion of an ethnic and religious minority from its homeland, of persecution and exile. The Jews were the classic example. But in the later twentieth century, as scholars became interested both in older and newer forms of forced and free migration, the word acquired a far looser meaning, describing almost any group of migrants permanently settled outside their place of origin. Not surprisingly, there has been much scholarly literature on how the word diaspora should or should not be used.[3] For the purposes of this book I shall use it to denote groups of people with a common ethnicity; who have left their original homeland for prolonged periods of time and often permanently; who retain a particular sense of cultural identity and often close kinship links with other scattered members of their group, thus acknowledging their shared physical and cultural origins; and who maintain links with that homeland and a sense of its role in their present identity. This avoids any essential notion of compulsion and victimisation, (though compulsion may have been present in some cases), recognises the many reasons and contexts for migration, and emphasises the transnational nature of diasporic groups. It is also analytically useful as it points to different aspects of such migrants' lives and helps us conceptualise their experience, in particular social forms, connections and relationships, senses of place and self, and the ongoing processes of evolving culture in new contexts.[4] However, if this exploration of diaspora gives us a tool for understanding the experience of the millions of South Asians abroad, is it appropriate to speak of one South Asian diaspora? As subsequent chapters will show, South Asian migration involved great diversity – different kinds of people in socio-economic terms moving at different times for different reasons; people of different religions, reflecting religious diversity on the subcontinent, including Hindus, Muslims, Sikhs, Parsis and Christians; people from different regions and linguistic backgrounds; and latterly people from different nation states. So great is the diversity of origins, characteristics and experiences, that it is most realistic to see South Asians abroad as members of different diasporic strands, or even as different diaspora groups originating on the one subcontinent, who have created many transnational communities which share a sense of origin in that region of the world.

[3] See the series on global diasporas edited by Robin Cohen, in particular his introductory volume, *Global Diasporas. An Introduction* (London and Washington, University College London Press and University of Washington Press, 1997); and the discussion in N. Van Hear, *New Diasporas. The Mass Exodus, Dispersal and Regrouping of Migrant Communities* (London and Seattle, University College London Press and University of Washington Press, 1998).

[4] See a particularly helpful discussion on the Hindu diaspora by S. Vertovec in his *The Hindu Diaspora. Comparative Patterns* (London, Routledge, 2000), particularly chapter 7, 'Three meanings of 'diaspora'', pp. 141–159.

There are many sources available for students of the South Asian diaspora and its peoples, particularly in the different countries to which they have moved. Among these are government documents which chart the movement of peoples and policies toward such movements, as in the case of Indian indentured labourers in the nineteenth and early twentieth centuries, or the immigration policies of the countries of the developed world in the twentieth century. For most receiving countries there are decennial census reports which to an extent document the presence of ethnic minorities, though these vary in their usefulness, depending on whether and what sort of questions about ethnicity, religion and place of birth are asked. Where ethnic minorities are perceived to be in some senses problematic there may well also be official enquiries and reports on minority experience in housing, employment, health and education, and press coverage of particular issues and events. The voices of people in the diaspora are most often heard in situations where they are educated, articulate and participate in public debate. Where migrants were illiterate, particularly among the earliest unskilled labour migrants, evidence of their own understanding of their lives may well come less directly, through the processes of oral history mediated by professional historians anxious to capture the past, or through newspaper reports or records of court cases dealing with instances of trauma and law breaking.[5]

Literature is yet another way of listening to the experiences of migrant South Asians, and there is a growing body of work by authors of South Asian descent, writing in English outside the subcontinent, which provides entry into the world of diasporic South Asians. For the Indian experience in the Caribbean there is the writing of V. S. Naipaul, for example. Born in 1932 in a small town in Trinidad, his writings have explored the experience of being in some senses an outsider in the different places he might have thought of as 'home' – Trinidad, Britain and India. His most famous novel of Indian life in the Caribbean, *A House for Mr Biswas*, was published in 1961, and he won the Nobel Prize for Literature in 2001. David Dabydeen, born in 1955 in Guyana, has explored through fiction the life of the early Indian labourers there, as in his 1996 novel,

[5] See, for example, the collection of memories edited by Brij V. Lal in *Bittersweet the Indo-Fijian Experience* (Canberra, Australian National University, Pandanus Books, 2004). For the way individuals' experiences can be used by historians to recreate the experience of indentured labourers, see Brij V. Lal, 'Kunti's cry', and J. Harvey, 'Naraini's story', chapters 11 and 18 of Brij V. Lal (ed.), *Chalo Jahaji on a Journey Through Indenture in Fiji* (Canberra and Suva, Australian National University and Fiji Museum, 2000). See also the fascinating attempt to 'hear' women's voices from Mauritius: M. Carter, *Lakshmi's Legacy. The Testimonies of Indian Women in 19th Century Mauritius* (Stanley, Rose-Hill, Mauritius, Editions de L'Ocean Indien, 1994).

The Counting House. Moving on into the twenty-first century in Britain, Monica Ali invites readers of her *Brick Lane* (2004) to empathise with the challenges of a young Bangladeshi bride brought to East London, coping with a difficult older husband, rearing a family and grasping the opportunity of a cosmopolitan society she gradually and painfully comes to understand. The growing genre of films dealing with life in the diaspora is also a serious source, even when many of them are also excellent entertainment. *Bend it like Beckham* (2002), about a Punjabi girl in England desperate to play football, is both hilarious and instructive to the sensitive observer. Even more immediate than autobiographical and fictional literature or film is the vibrant world of the South Asian diaspora to be found on the internet, where a range of sites devoted to news, lifestyles, job opportunities and marriage arrangements, provide insight into the issues thought to be critical or troubling to younger South Asians, and brings them together across national boundaries to reflect on what it means to be Asian, Indian, Pakistani, Muslim, Hindu and so forth in a cosmopolitan and fast-changing world. It is not surprising that diaspora religious organisations have also made increasing use of the internet to connect with their followers, and to present themselves to the wider society. Hindu, Muslim and Sikh organisational websites are important sources, but ones which have to be used with care and some knowledge of which group or sect is behind them.

Such unconventional sources bring alive the evidence and analysis of the South Asian diasporic experience provided in the growing academic literature on South Asians outside the subcontinent. This comes from a great variety of intellectual disciplines, ranging from anthropology, sociology, human geography and history, while some contribute to new sub-disciplines specifically studying diasporas, migration, issues of hybrid identity and culture, or the growth of transnational families and communities.[6] Much of the academic work on the diaspora has taken the form of case studies of particular groups at a specific point in time, or of particular localities with high densities of migrant groups. Others are collections of essays which reflect on a particular theme in the diasporic experience, such as religion, work or kinship. Many of these will be cited during this book and listed in the select bibliography. It is partly because of the growing weight of case study literature on South Asians overseas that this present book is written. It is therefore worth briefly indicating its intentions. It is written for several different kinds of readers who want

[6] A convenient introduction to the theoretical debates on diasporas in general and their study, particularly within disciplines influenced by post-modernism, is to be found in J. E. Braziel and A. Mannur (eds.), *Theorizing Diaspora. A Reader* (Oxford, Blackwell Publishing, 2003).

an introduction to a complex but important topic which is of contemporary as well as historical interest, but with a particular slant towards students who want to progress from this to more advanced study of South Asians in the diaspora or other largescale movements of people. It cannot, in a relatively small compass, provide detailed coverage of the varied experiences of the many different strands in the South Asian diaspora. Moreover, primary evidence and secondary literature on the different diasporic strands is also very uneven and inhibits anything approaching total coverage. Understandably the evidence is most plentiful about areas and groups where there has been much official enquiry and collection of statistics about the arrival and growth of diasporic groups and their lives, by governments which have both motivation and the administrative ability to collect such material, as well as academic study by fellow citizens seeking to understand the dynamics of significant aspects of their own societies. Evidence from Britain therefore figures large in this work and it is clear that there are areas such as South East Asia where there is much work still to be done on the nature and experience of the South Asian communities there. However, the British case does also have particular significance because through it we can see the emergence of very varied diasporic strands in one country of destination, and track generational change over a lengthy period of settlement. The British experience is also one where the South Asian population is very significant in size and proportion of the total population, particularly in certain urban areas; and this offers evidence about interactions of significant minorities with the host society and political structure.

This volume seeks to offer a broad analytical way into the subject, first by sketching and contextualising the main flows of peoples out of the subcontinent since the early nineteenth century (the substance of Chapter 2), and then by focussing on the tasks which have to be done by each group of migrants and each generation of diasporic people. These 'tasks' are vital for establishing new homes and communities and taking advantage of new opportunities, for negotiating the way through the challenges of living in a different society and culture, and for retaining what are seen as essential links with kin and wider groups which share cultural norms, both in their new home and in the place from which they have come. They are discussed under the broad thematic headings of 'creating new homes and communities', 'relating to the new homeland' and 'relating to the old homeland', which are the titles of Chapters 3, 4 and 5. Another distinctive feature of this study is that it is written by a historian with a special interest in South Asia. My intention is to put 'South Asia' back into the story of migration, firstly by looking at the subcontinent from which migrants came, with its changing economy and society, and the traditions and experience of mobility which contributed to the larger overseas flows of population in recent times (see Chapter 1). Secondly, South Asia, which is itself not a static given but rapidly changing in the twentieth century, is seen as a constant backdrop or presence in the lives of the peoples of the diaspora, as a region which provides many aspects of their senses of identity and meaning, one to which they return for short visits with increasing frequency, one where they have kin and friends, where they invest goods and money, and one in whose politics they are often interested. South Asians abroad cannot be understood just as local 'ethnic minorities' in the countries to which they go, as so often they are compartmentalised for policy makers and journalists. They are involved in a dense network of local and global connections which make them truly transnational people, at home in several places and responding to opportunities and challenges both local and global, and keenly aware of the emerging role of South Asia in a changing world environment.

1 Traditions of stability and movement

This chapter sets the scene for the rest of this study, by looking at the subcontinent of South Asia and its connections with the world outside, over time. Although individuals and family groups made the decision to move abroad, and we need to understand their small-scale and local decisions, these were taken in the context of a widening environment, that of the British Empire in the nineteenth and early twentieth centuries, and of a world of independent nations bound together by new patterns of globalisation in the later twentieth and the present centuries. Particularly crucial in this widening environment was the impact of demand for various forms of labour and skill, and the political issues related to immigration of people with different ethnic origins from the majority in areas where they sought to go.

1 The subcontinent under British rule: the image of rural stability

The great land mass of the Indian subcontinent, equivalent to Europe in size, came under the political control of Britain in piecemeal fashion from the middle of the eighteenth century to the early nineteenth century. In theory, the ruling authority was until 1858 the East India Company (EIC), a trading company whose origins lay in a royal charter of 1600. But as it transformed itself in the early 1800s into an organisation for governance and military control, its trading activities declined as a component of its activities and profit. This was with the exception of opium, which alone constituted nearly half of the country's exports, shipped east to China and South East Asia. The EIC was finally wound up after the rebellions in northern India of 1857, and, as formal imperial rule was vested in the British government, India became the largest country in the British Empire. During the final fifty years of its existence the EIC had struggled with the problems of extending political and military control over such a vast area while still attempting to make a profit. It constructed a structure of civil administration over those areas it controlled directly, and where it seemed prudent it used a pragmatic system of 'indirect rule', keeping in place indigenous rulers who could be trusted as subsidiary allies to keep their areas peaceful and loyal. Even in the areas of its direct political rule it relied heavily on the many Indians who worked within its civil governmental structures, served in its huge army, and paid the taxes it levied. Increasingly, the British parliament and government found mechanisms for surveillance and control of the EIC's activities, so there was no radical change in practice when India came under the sovereignty of the British crown.[1]

The society over which the British came to rule was complex. By far the majority of Indians were to be found in the countryside, dependent upon agriculture. But there were significant differences according to region, in language, culture and the nature of the local economy and social order. In general there were some common patterns in rural society – the importance of the joint farming family, dependence on kinship networks and village communities, marriage with carefully defined hierarchical networks, and the comparatively low status of women compared with men. Across India as a whole there were significantly different religious traditions. The majority were Hindus, but there was a large minority of Muslims (mostly to be found in the north and west), a small group of Sikhs (clustered in the north-western region of Punjab), communities of Christians in southern India, whose origins lay almost at the start of the Christian era, and Parsis along the western coast, whose ancestors had fled from persecution in Persia. Such traditions had more implications than creating shared patterns of belief and worship. They created the boundaries beyond which marriages and close social interaction did not normally occur, and internally they could fashion hierarchies of status. This was particularly so in the case of Hindus, amongst whom the complex hierarchical patterns of caste society had emerged, built on ritual position reflecting Hindu ideas of purity and pollution, and socio-economic status, which in turn determined the nature of intra-Hindu social interactions and particularly of marriage networks.[2]

[1] On the extension of East India Company control over India see P. J. Marshall, *The New Cambridge History of India II.2. Bengal: The British Bridgehead. Eastern India 1740–1828* (Cambridge, Cambridge University Press, 1997), and C. A. Bayly, *The New Cambridge History of India II.1. Indian Society and the Making of the British Empire* (Cambridge, Cambridge University Press, 1988). P. J. Marshall also examines the extension of metropolitan British control over the company in *Problems of Empire: Britain and India 1757–1813* (London, George Allen & Unwin Ltd, 1968).

[2] The nature of caste and how it changed over time, and the difference between *varna* (a pan-Indian notion of ritual hierarchy) and *jati* (locally ranked endogamous groups), is the subject of considerable historical debate. Modern scholarship has shown how caste, in either of these meanings, was not immutable. Change occurred over time in people's

The British differed among themselves in their understanding of this society, and in what they felt they could or should be attempting to do in and with it. Some believed it was their duty and destiny to attempt radical change, either by converting Indians to Christianity, or by modernising India through the processes of good government, law and modern education. Others believed that they should respect 'Oriental' traditions and practices, and work within the assumptions and ideals of Indian society. In practice the early years of EIC rule served to make India more 'traditional', less able to change and respond to its new connections with a wider economic and ideological world. Most particularly, British concern to sustain Hindu law led to the formal elaboration and solidification of hierarchical society, as the new rulers took advice from the local Hindu 'authorities' on the nature of Hindu society, who were themselves at the apex of the caste system. As rulers anxious to maintain order and to collect taxation from those who owned or controlled land and its products, the British pressed Indian society into greater physical immobility, hoping to found their rule securely on a settled peasantry, by settling (and this is a telling word) the land revenue on farming groups in return for rights in land, and goading once nomadic rural groups into a settled lifestyle. A more homogeneous, flattened peasant society was coming into being, a trend strengthened by a long-term economic depression from the 1820s which dampened economic opportunity. At the same time population growth meant that there was less chance for personal physical movement into new agricultural land.[3]

It is not surprising that later British commentators considered India's society to be essentially static, and its people to be immobile, though historians can now see how far the new rulers were themselves responsible for creating barriers to movement. Part of the later British image of Indians was of people who were deeply averse to moving from their natal district, away from the securities of the village and kin group. William Crooke, a retired civil servant, writing at the end of the nineteenth century on the North-Western Provinces (later known as United Provinces, and source of many indentured labourers) wrote eloquently of the 'fact' that 'the Hindu has little of the migratory instinct, and all his prejudices tend to keep him at home'. Security in one's home village, known caste

understanding of caste, as did the position of groups in the context of local areas with changing socio-economic opportunities. An excellent discussion is to be found in S. Bayly, *The New Cambridge History Of India IV.3. Caste, Society and Politics in India from the Eighteenth Century to the Modern Age* (Cambridge, Cambridge University Press, 1999).

3 On the trend towards a more traditional and settled society, see C. Bayly, *Indian Society and the Making of the British Empire*, chapter 5; and D. Washbrook, 'India, 1818–1860: the two faces of colonialism', chapter 18 of A. Porter (ed.). *The Oxford History of the British Empire. Volume III. The Nineteenth Century* (Oxford, Oxford University Press, 1999).

standing, and the support of kinsfolk and neighbours, as well as the services of a family priest and the comfort of knowing he would be able to arrange his children's marriages in a familiar environment, all appeared to conspire to prevent him from leaving home.[4] Even at the beginning of the twentieth century those who compiled the decennial Census reports wrote in the same vein. In the 1911 Census, the caste system and dependence on agriculture were said to 'account for the reluctance of the native of India to leave his ancestral home'. In 1921, J. T. Marten of the Indian Civil Service wrote of 'the home-loving character of the Indian people, which is the result of economic and social causes, and of the immobility of an agricultural population rooted to the ground, fenced in by caste, language and social customs and filled with an innate dread of change of any kind'.[5]

However, there was evidence of considerable mobility within India and abroad well before the nineteenth century, and the subcontinent clearly had traditions of movement as well as stability. Within India there were well-established patterns of trade sustained by indigenous credit networks, which took merchant groups long distances, by water along the coasts of the country or down the great riverine routes inland, and by land along established caravan routes. Considerably less affluent than the established merchant communities of India were those whose very life was nomadic – horse breeders and traders, elephant catchers, cattle herders, and rural folk willing to travel miles for agricultural work, as well as religious mendicants who secured a livelihood from the charity of the Hindu faithful. Many of these wandering people were, of course, the objects of suspicion and control as the colonial state took root in the early nineteenth century. Before land became a scarce commodity there was also rural migration in search of cultivable land. As one Punjabi, writing in the 1960s, noted, the family genealogy maintained for religious purposes at the holy Hindu city of Hardwar enabled him to trace the family's movements over many generations. They were farmers and sometimes soldiers. 'Our family were Khatris from the West Punjab countryside. For

[4] W. Crooke, *The North-Western Provinces of India. Their History, Ethnology and Administration* (London, Methuen, 1897), p. 326.

[5] *Census of India, 1921 Volume 1. India. Part 1 – Report* by J. T. Marten (Calcutta, Government of India, 1924), p. 88. See also *Census of India, 1911 Volume 1. India. Part 1 – Report* by E. A. Gait (Calcutta, Government of India, 1913), p. 91.

Even in the middle of the century a demographer could write that the Indians had 'long been famous for their attachment to their native locale', attributing this to the predominance of agriculture, the caste system, early marriage and the joint family, the diversity of language and culture in India, and lack of education. K. Davis, *The Population of India and Pakistan* (Princeton, Princeton University Press, 1951; reissued 1968, Russell and Russell), p. 108.

two centuries we had been moving along the banks of the Jhelum river, sometimes on its eastern and sometimes on its western bank, and for a while in the Himalayan foothills where the river drains into the plain.'[6] The history of another Punjabi village, studied in detail from 1848 to 1968, shows that even in 1848 nine men from the village were living elsewhere with their families, even though they were from the Sahota caste, agriculturalists with a claim to village land.[7] A further sort of rural movement was that of women, particularly in north India, where girls moved out of their natal village and away from their close kin to marry within the larger endogamous group. Although this was permanent internal migration, young brides would return to their own family, for example for the birth of a first child, and such journeys and the networks of kinship set up over generations by marriage created social networks spanning considerable distances.[8] Another form of internal mobility was the practice of pilgrimage. Hindus travelled to the great temples of southern India or to the holy cities of the north such as Banares or Hardwar. Some of the great bathing festivals on the holy river Ganges attracted large numbers, as they still do today. Muslims, despite a horror of idolatry, would travel to pay their respects and gain the blessing of Muslim saints, particularly the saintly figures of the Sufi movement, at whose shrines they were often joined by people of other religious traditions.

Evidence also suggests very considerable Indian movement outside the subcontinent over a long period of time. Religion was one dynamic force. Indian Muslim learned men were involved in networks of scholarship and devotion which spanned the Muslim world to east and west. The presence of Hindu temples, art and architecture in South East Asia also testifies to movement by Hindus outside India over a long period. India occupied a key geographical position in the maritime world of the Indian Ocean, at the heart of multiple trade routes stretching from the eastern coast of Africa to South East Asia, and eventually to Europe. Given the natural barrier of the Himalayan mountain range, and the difficulties of land travel, water-borne movement of people and goods was by far the easiest and quickest mode of movement. It is not surprising, therefore, that Indian merchants participated in trade across the region as well as up and down India's own coastlines; and when foreigners from Europe first engaged in trade – in spices, tea, cottons, and other materials – alongside Indians, they were very much the junior partners, working within systems

[6] P. Tandon, *Punjabi Century 1857–1947* (London, Chatto & Windus, 1963), p. 9.

[7] T. G. Kessinger, *Vilyatpur 1848–1968. Social and Economic Change in a North Indian Village* (Berkeley, Los Angeles and London, University of California Press, 1974), p. 90.

[8] British officials noted this female migration with some curiosity in their writings and Census reports: see, for example, W. Crooke, *The North-Western Provinces of India*, pp. 327–8.

which long pre-dated them, and increasingly in alliance with Indian merchants and financiers.[9] One result of this Indian involvement in the wide arc of Indian Ocean trade was the development of Indian settlements on the further shores of the ocean. Southern Indian merchant groups such as the Chettiars developed strong links with parts of Asia east of India, while Indians from western India travelled to and settled along the East African coast and in Zanzibar as traders and financiers. Clearly there were traditions of movement among India's peoples, as well as patterns of long-term stability in the locality of birth and family origin, well before the British established an imperial presence on the subcontinent, and on many of these, later patterns of migration were to be founded.

2 India and a larger imperial world

Major changes in patterns of movement within but particularly outside India occurred from the mid-nineteenth century as India was more tightly incorporated into the British Empire and, through that political linkage, drawn into a rapidly changing world economy. As the British economy led the way in industrialisation, world trade and international finance, it dominated a new world economic order, drawing in raw materials to feed its industries and its people, while exporting huge quantities of capital, manufactures and people. As a result of these processes fewer and fewer parts of the world were left untouched by the symbiotic processes of industrialisation and imperialism. India was at the heart of this deepening global interconnection,[10] and became increasingly significant for Britain as a source of raw materials, a market for manufactured goods, a destination for capital investment, and a source of labour for other parts of the Empire. Moreover, until the 1920s the Indian tax payer financed the world's largest standing army, which could be used around the globe to support the Empire in times of crisis.

Swifter travel and communication was part of the later nineteenth century pattern of imperial incorporation into a world economy, and had a profound influence on the personal mobility of people, including Indians.

[9] See P. J. Marshall, 'The British in Asia: Trade to Dominion, 1700–1765', chapter 22 of his edited volume, *The Oxford History of the British Empire. Volume II. The Eighteenth Century* (Oxford, Oxford University Press, 1998).

[10] Deepak Nayyar calls the period 1870 to 1914 an earlier period of globalisation: see his chapter 6, 'Cross-border movements of people', in his edited volume, *Governing Globalization. Issues and Institutions* (Oxford, Oxford University Press, 2002). This is an excellent broad introduction to understanding the wider environment of migration. On the British imperial economy see B. R. Tomlinson, chapter 3, 'Economics and Empire: the periphery and the imperial economy' in A. Porter (ed.), *The Oxford History of the British Empire. Volume III. The Nineteenth Century.*

In India itself roads and railways were seen as vital for security, as they enabled the rapid transport of troops as well as civilians and goods. Major roads began to be metalled in the 1850s. But far more important was the new railway network, begun in 1853, built mainly by private companies but backed by the government through a guaranteed rate of return on their investments. By 1910 India had the fourth largest network in the world. The length of track had risen from 1,349 kilometres in 1860 to 25,495 kilometres in 1890, and had doubled again by 1920–1921.[11] The carriage of freight and people escalated dramatically. Some people had predicted that Indians would not use the railways, but they were proved comprehensively wrong. In 1871 19 million passengers travelled, and by 1901 the figure was 183 million. Just before independence over 1 billion were buying tickets annually. As the 1911 Census commented, 'A journey of a thousand miles is easier than one of a hundred miles a century ago.'[12] Equally important developments occurred in international travel in this imperial age, connecting the subcontinent with a wider world. Steam began to give way to sail, shortening travel times, though sailing ships remained profitable on very long-distance routes almost to the end of the nineteenth century. The London government effectively subsidised the Peninsular and Orient shipping line (P&O) to India with the valuable mail contract, and the regular P&O service connecting Britain and India started in 1840. The opening of the Suez Canal in 1869 also significantly reduced the distance travelled by sea from Britain to India, as well as the time taken. Plymouth to Bombay was 10,450 miles round the Cape of Good Hope, but only 6,000 via Suez; and the Plymouth to Calcutta route dropped from 11,380 miles via the Cape to 7,710 via Suez. A network of coaling and repair stations was built along the major shipping lanes of the Empire, as were the telegraphic linkages which similarly connected the imperial world and its peoples.[13]

As a result of these changes in transportation, Indians began to move within India and across the seas in far greater numbers and in response to more opportunities. The 1911 Census enumerated just over 27 million Indians who had left the district where they were born: this constituted 8.7 per cent of the population. In 1921 the figure was 30 million or 10 per cent of the population.[14] Many of these people were living in districts

[11] On the railways see the section by J. H. Hurd, pp. 737–761 in D. Kumar and M. Desai (eds.), *The Cambridge Economic History of India. Volume 2: c. 1757–1970* (Cambridge, Cambridge University Press, 1983).

[12] *Census of India, 1911 Volume 1. India. Part 1 – Report* by E. A. Gait, p. 91.

[13] A. N. Porter (ed.), *Atlas of British Overseas Expansion* (London, Routledge, 1991), pp. 144–152.

[14] *Census of India, 1911 Volume 1. India. Part 1 – Report* by E. A. Gait, chapter 3; *Census of India, 1921 Volume 1. India. Part 1 – Report* by J. T. Marten, chapter 3.

next to the one where they had been born, but others had moved much further away. For men the opportunity which triggered internal migration was normally some new form of work. Many left their home localities in search of agricultural labour, particularly in areas where there were tea plantations. It was partly for this reason that Assam had the largest number of 'foreigners' of all areas of India, and they came from relatively near (Bihar and Orissa, Central Provinces, and United Provinces) and from far away in Madras. Bihar and Orissa and United Provinces were by far and away the largest sending areas, reflecting the fragile nature of agriculture and population pressure in those areas. Others left for work in the growing industrial towns such as Bombay and Calcutta. Bengal and Bombay Presidency (where these two cities were located) had 4% and 3.9% respectively of outsiders when the 1921 Census was taken. In Bombay City, which was expanding rapidly on the back of industrial growth, particularly in the cotton industry, the cotton mill workforce came mainly from areas up to 200 miles away. In Calcutta and its environs the jute industry also became a magnet for migrant workers and, in 1921, of a workforce in the jute mills of 280,000, just under a quarter were local Bengalis while over half came from Bihar and United Provinces.[15] Such migrant labour moved out of necessity, but more prosperous groups also followed new economic opportunities. The Marwaris were one of the most obvious economic success stories of the period. A merchant community originally from Rajputana in western India, they fanned out across the north of the subcontinent to reach Calcutta, and also moved south to Bombay City. In Calcutta they became traders in a wide span of commodities, from cotton piece goods to unprocessed commodities such as jute, oilseeds and grain, and they also became deeply involved in credit and banking. It was from this community that one of India's greatest industrialists of the twentieth century was to emerge – G. D. Birla.[16]

Others who moved away from home but within India did so in direct response to opportunities provided by the new imperial government. Most obviously there were those who enlisted in the new Indian army, officered by British men but manned entirely by Indian soldiers, known as

[15] See M. D. Morris, *The Emergence of an Industrial Labor Force in India. A Study of the Bombay Cotton Mills, 1854–1947* (Berkeley and Bombay, University of California Press and Oxford University Press, 1965), chapter 4 and particularly p. 63; on Bengal see D. Chakrabarty, *Rethinking Working-Class History. Bengal 1890–1940* (Princeton, Princeton University Press, 1989), p. 9.

[16] See M. M. Kudaisya, *The Life and Times of G. D. Birla* (New Delhi, Oxford University Press, 2003), particularly chapter 1.

sepoys. It was made up almost entirely of rural men who fell into the imperial categories of 'martial races', groups thought to be by physique and character particularly suitable for military service. Particularly notable was the high proportion in the army of Sikhs from the Punjab, now classified as a 'martial race'. By the First World War about 150,000 were soldiers, about one quarter of all armed personnel on the subcontinent. The reasons for Indian enlistment were varied but included familial strategy for maximizing family prosperity, as the pay was regular and good, as were pensions, while agriculture was subject to the vagaries of nature and land was becoming scarce. Some groups were proud of their long-established military traditions and merely continued them under new masters.[17] Service in the army could take men across India and beyond its borders. Another group who responded to new opportunities offered by the British were those farmers who migrated to the new canal colonies in the Punjab in the later nineteenth and early twentieth centuries in a remarkable exercise of internal migration and social engineering. The government hoped to create new model village communities to relieve the pressure on existing cultivated land, to increase local revenue and exports, to build groups of supporters and to provide homes for existing allies such as old soldiers and government servants. New forms of canal irrigation enabled the cultivation of several million acres of once arid wasteland, and the government was anxious only to welcome into these model agricultural colonies peasant groups thought to be of 'the best class' of agriculturalist. Thousands moved in response to this remarkable chance of access to land relatively near to their original homes.[18] After Burma came under the British Indian government in mid-nineteenth century, Indians also moved there for many different kinds of work – from manual and semi-skilled labour (particularly in the docks and factories of

[17] See D. Omissi, *The Sepoy and the Raj. The Indian Army, 1860–1940* (Houndmills and London, MacMillan, 1994). Chapter 2 deals with enlistment.

[18] See D. Gilmartin, 'Migration and modernity: the state, the Punjabi village, and the settling of the canal colonies', chapter 1 of I. Talbot and S. Thandi (eds.), *People on the Move. Punjabi Colonial and Post-Colonial Migration* (Karachi, Oxford University Press, 2004). See also the impact of the canal colonies on one village in the most densely populated district of Punjab, in T. G. Kessinger, *Vilyatpur*, pp. 90–92. By 1901 the district of Jullunder, where Vilyatpur was located, had produced over 56,000 settlers in the colonies.

The view of the canal colony experiment from the perspective of an admittedly paternalist member of the Indian Civil Service (ICS) is to be found in chapter 7 of Sir Malcolm Darling, *The Punjab Peasant in Prosperity and Debt* (1925; reprinted with a new introduction by C. J. Dewey, New Delhi, Manohar, 1977). An account of the work settling one of the canal colonies by another ICS man, Malcolm Hailey, later to become an international imperial figure, is chapter 2 of J. W. Cell, *Hailey. A study in British Imperialism, 1872–1969* (Cambridge, Cambridge University Press, 1992).

Rangoon), to jobs in the lower echelons of the civil service, and as money-lenders and traders. By 1901 Indians made up nearly half the population of Rangoon.[19]

Indians who had taken advantage of new forms of higher education in English and professional trainings also began to move in the service of the British raj and its institutions. Some moved out of their home provinces as imperial officials in the lower levels of civil government. This was the origin of some of the Bengali communities to be found in northern India. As education spread so did the rapid response of local groups to its implications for their status and fortunes. Increasing numbers became professionals of various kinds, particularly lawyers, and moved to towns and cities where they could find employment. The Punjabi author quoted earlier recorded the move to professionalisation in his own family in his grandfather's generation, who were born 1840–1850.[20] The Nehru family which gave India three Prime Ministers in the first half century of independence, was a classic example of upwardly mobile migrants who originated in Kashmir and via Delhi came to Allahabad in the United Provinces, where Jawaharlal's father made a fortune and a reputation as a civil lawyer. He came to count the Lieutenant-Governors of the province as personal friends and drinking companions, and he was the first Indian to buy a substantial house in the exclusive part of the city conventionally reserved for the British.[21] At a far lower social level there were those Indians who went into the personal service of British people and families, and moved with them as cooks, bearers and *ayahs* (nursemaids) when their employers were posted to new places in the subcontinent, often to be handed on in turn to other British employers by personal recommendation when their former employers returned to Britain.

However the most remarkable aspect of movement among Indians as India was incorporated into the British imperial economy was the dramatic increase in the numbers who now travelled abroad. This was particularly significant among higher caste Hindus, for whom travel across the sea had been thought of as ritually polluting. As late as 1902, when the Maharaja of Jaipur went to London to attend the coronation of Edward VII, he resolved the issue of pollution by chartering a whole ship, the SS *Olympia*, which was cleansed and consecrated so that he could effectively

[19] K. S. Sandhu and A. Mani (eds.), *Indian Communities in Southeast Asia* (Singapore, Times Academic Press, 1993), chapter 25. The journey to Burma was generally made by sea, but I include Burma and Ceylon as part of the subcontinent compared with destinations which involved a longer sea crossing to a different cultural world.

[20] P. Tandon, *Punjabi Century 1857–1947*, pp. 15–18, 25–29.

[21] J. Nehru, *An Autobiography* (London, Bodley Head, 1936), chapters 1–3. See also the autobiography of Nehru's sister, V. L. Pandit, *The Scope of Happiness. A Personal Memoir* (London, Weidenfeld and Nicolson, 1979).

travel across the water while still in India, eating and drinking only those things which came from India. This involved shipping cows and fodder for them, so that he could drink fresh 'Indian' milk daily. Lesser mortals could not afford such expensive attention to older beliefs, and for many who travelled overseas there were considerable qualms of conscience, and often major problems with their families and castes on their return home. Nehru commented on the storm within the Kashmiri Brahmin community of northern India when his father, Motilal, and others of the older generation travelled across the sea. Motilal refused to perform a purification ceremony on his return, but many others did so for the sake of peace, albeit without any real sense of religious obligation.[22] The young M. K. Gandhi was also officially outcasted by his own community when he travelled to England to study law in 1888.[23] The trajectories of many of these overseas migrants will be followed in the next chapter. Here it is significant just to note the range of people who went abroad both on a temporary and permanent basis, to indicate just how the links between India and a wider world were developing from the later nineteenth century.

By far the largest group of those who left India, many on a permanent basis, were those who served the Empire in some way, using 'service' here to denote many forms of paid work which sustained the imperial enterprise. By far the largest number were those who went as unskilled labour under a contract of indenture to work throughout the Empire in plantations and to a far lesser extent in mines, helping to provide the raw materials which were vital to feed Britain's population and fuel the process of industrialisation. Few of those who worked in Natal or Trinidad, for example on sugar plantations, would have recognised their position as cogs in an imperial machine, but they were essential to Britain's worldwide power and standing. For them labour overseas was most often perceived as the chance of temporary work abroad with assured pay, whatever the reality they eventually encountered. The system lasted from 1830 to 1916 and in this period hundreds of thousands of Indians moved overseas under its aegis, over half a million to the Caribbean, similar numbers to Mauritius, and over 152,000 to Natal, to take just some of the main destinations.[24]

More obviously in the service of the Empire were Indians who travelled overseas in the Indian army. Indian sepoys saw service in the later

22 Nehru, *An Autobiography*, p. 13.

23 M. K. Gandhi, *An Autobiography, The Story of My Experiments with Truth* (first pub. 1927: paperback ed., London, Jonathan Cape, 1966), pp. 34–35.

24 Indentured labour will be discussed in the next chapter. A good introduction to the subject is D. Northrup, *Indentured Labor in the Age of Imperialism 1834–1922* (Cambridge, Cambridge University Press, 1995).

nineteenth and twentieth centuries throughout the world, from China to the Middle East to the Western Front in the First World War.[25] The Brighton Pavilion on the south coast of Britain, an exotic oriental fantasy and former royal residence, was given over during this war to become a hospital for Indian soldiers recovering from their wounds in Europe, presumably in part because it was felt they would feel at home there. For some soldiers the end of military service brought the rewards of a pension and land back in their natal region in India. For others travel with the army opened the opportunity of further travel and work abroad. Sikhs, who had become a major group within the army, following their military service, moved on in significant numbers and inspired kin and friends to venture abroad to become guards, police and security personnel in many areas of the Empire. They were to be found in this type of work in Hong Kong, Malaya, and in British colonies in East Africa. The Hong Kong police was heavily Sikh and Punjabi Muslim from the 1860s into the twentieth century. The East African Rifles, established in 1895, also drew on Sikhs. Others found work in the new imperial railway systems of East Africa. The military experience also drew old soldiers, again mostly Sikhs, even further away from India to the western coast of northern America, particularly to Vancouver and California.[26] Smaller numbers of Indians who served the Empire abroad included Indian sailors or *lascars*, who worked on ships running between Asia and Britain. Many of these spent some time in British ports awaiting further work. Their conditions attracted official notice from the early 1800s, but it was not until Henry Venn, London clergyman and secretary of the Church Missionary Society (which sent missionaries to India as well as other lands), took up their cause in 1857 that a home for 'Asiatic' and African sailors was opened in London: it lasted until 1937. Similarly, personal servants of British people who had worked in India found themselves in England, often destitute when their employers abandoned responsibility for them. Some of the better organised were *ayahs*, female servants who were often nannies, who had an *Ayahs'* Home in London by the end of the nineteenth century, where they waited for employers who wished for their services on a voyage home to India. In the early years of the twentieth century there

[25] A selection of letters from Indian soldiers who reached Europe in 1914–1918 is found in D. Omissi, *Indian Voices of the Great War. Soldiers' Letters, 1914–18* (Houndmills, London and New York, MacMillan and St. Martin's Press, 1999).

[26] See D. S. Tatla, 'Sikh free and military migration during the colonial period', in R. Cohen (ed.), *The Cambridge Survey of World Migration* (Cambridge, Cambridge Univesity Press, 1995), pp. 69–73; T. R. Metcalf, 'Sikh recruitment for colonial military and police forces, 1874–1914', chapter 13 of his *Forging the Raj. Essays on British India in the Heyday of Empire* (New Delhi, Oxford University Press 2005).

were around 4,000 Indians in England and Wales, and 177 were women, presumably many of whom were *ayahs* in transit.[27]

The opportunities for work overseas offered by India's incorporation in an empire which was rapidly expanding its territorial sway in the later nineteenth century, also encouraged other sorts of free migrants who were willing to make long-term or permanent homes away from India. Many commercial communities saw and took the new chances open to them, such as those who went to East and South Africa, mainly from western India. They were known as 'passenger Indians' because they paid for their own sea passages, in contrast to indentured labourers, and sometimes as 'Arabs', reflecting the numbers of western Indian Muslims who travelled further west to Africa. It was for such a commercial firm of Muslim Gujaratis from Porbandar on the western coast of Gujarat, trading in South Africa, that Gandhi went to work as a struggling lawyer in 1893, after he had failed to make his way in India on his return from studying law in London. The Shia Ismailis were a distinctive Muslim trading group from the west coast of India who prospered in Zanzibar in the nineteenth century and then moved inland into Uganda after the establishment of British rule. Yet other Indians took up work in the civil employment of the governments of new imperial territories of East Africa.

A final and expanding group of overseas Indian travellers were those who went for higher education, professional training, and what might be called missionary or publicity work on behalf of Indian religious and social causes. Although few of these made their homes abroad their travels formed yet another strand in the many which increasingly knit India into a worldwide web of interconnections, and their experiences spread knowledge of that wider world among those at home who met them on their return, or heard and read about their experiences. Among them were the growing numbers of students who travelled mainly to England for higher education and professional training, particularly in law. Obviously they came from comparatively wealthy families who could afford the fees and costs of travel. Many found the experience at times lonely and bewildering, as both Gandhi and Nehru noted in their very different autobiographies. Nehru from his wealthy cosmopolitan background fitted into public school and Cambridge with considerable ease in the years

27 The vast majority of the Indians who were counted in England, Wales, and Scotland were aged 20–34 – an age when they were likely to be students or in work. See appendix, p. 111 in *Census of India, 1911 Volume 1. India. Part 1 – Report* by E. A. Gait. There are discussions of Indians in Britain during the whole period of East India Company activity and British rule in M. Fisher, *Counterflows to Colonialism. Indian Travellers and Settlers in Britain 1600–1857* (Delhi, Permanent Black, 2003); and R. Visram, *Ayahs, Lascars and Princes. Indians in Britain 1700–1947* (London, Pluto Press, 1986).

just before the First World War. A few years earlier the young Gandhi from a far more provincial and conservative background found the cultural adjustments of the voyage and of life in London deeply perplexing. He was too shy to eat in public on board ship, not knowing how to use a knife and fork, and fearing to ask what dishes contained meat. On arrival in England the business of finding proper vegetarian food continued to be a problem, as did numerous cultural issues such as admitting that he had married as an early teenager according to Indian custom.[28] But the experience of education and training in England was the springboard for the later professional and political careers of both Gandhi and Nehru, as it was for many of their contemporaries. Indeed, the British government was greatly concerned about the experience of Indian students at the heart of the Empire, commissioning reports on their lives in 1907 and 1922, and it was particularly watchful for radical tendencies among them. In time even some Indian women travelled to Britain to study, including Cornelia Sorabji (b.1866) who became India's first woman lawyer, and Nehru's own daughter, Indira (b. 1917) who became India's first woman Prime Minister. Both studied at Oxford.[29] A rather different Indian woman traveller to England was Pandita Ramabai Saraswati, a young Hindu Brahmin widow who came to see herself as both Hindu and Christian. She travelled to England for study in the early 1880s and then went on to America, where she became something of a sensation with her talks pleading for help for Indian women, particularly high caste widows. In 1889 she wrote for an Indian audience a fascinating and at times hilarious account of her American visit, covering the system of government, living and domestic conditions, learning, religion and charity, the condition of women, and trade and business.[30] Whereas Ramabai sought to elicit understanding and financial assistance, others who travelled west with an ideological agenda sought to preach reformed versions of the varied traditions which made up what came to be called 'Hinduism'. One reformist tradition was the Ramakrishna Movement, originating in

[28] On Gandhi's experiences travelling to and living in England, see his *Autobiography*, chapters 13–24.

[29] See the autobiographical work of Cornelia Sorabji, *India Calling*, first published in London in 1934, new edition by C. Lokuge (New Delhi, Oxford University Press, 2001). Benjamin Jowett, a famous Victorian Master of Balliol College, Oxford who was deeply interested in the Indian empire, befriended Cornelia, who was at Somerville College, introducing her to many notable figures in British public life. Balliol became famous for admitting Indian male students and also for training future members of the Indian Civil Service. Fascinating information on Oxford's many connections with the Empire is to be found in R. Symonds, *Oxford and Empire. The Last Lost Cause?* (Oxford University Press and MacMillan, 1986; revised paperback edition, Oxford, Clarendon Press, 1991).

[30] R. E. Frykenberg (ed.), *Pandita Ramabai's America. Conditions of Life in the United States* (Grand Rapids and Cambridge, William B. Eerdmans, 2003).

Bengal, whose leader, Swami Vivekananda, travelled to the USA in 1893 to speak at the World Parliament of Religions. He stayed for four years, gaining a body of western disciples, and founding a number of Vedanta societies to spread his reformist ideas. A somewhat different brand of Hindu reform movement was the Arya Samaj, strongest in western India, which called for a purified Hinduism based on the Vedas. Apart from its religious, educational and social work in India it also sent missionaries to many of those places, including the Caribbean and Natal, where Hindu indentured labourers had gone, to rectify what they saw as their degraded religious state.

The evidence suggests that during the period from the mid-nineteenth century to the First World War, many Indians left the area where they had been born to make new lives for themselves on the subcontinent or across the seas. India became involved in a dense and varied network of connections which linked its peoples and economy to many other parts of the world, as a result of the incorporation of the subcontinent into the British Empire at just that historical juncture when Britain dominated the world economy, and was culturally of global significance through its imperial institutions and its language. However, in the early years of the twentieth century the pattern of outward movement from India was dampened down for a variety of reasons. The system of indenture was abolished after the war, not least because of intense hostility towards it among educated Indians, just when their opinions were beginning to be taken seriously by their imperial rulers in the context of major constitutional reform. Then the Depression, which engulfed the world economy in the interwar period, precipitated a slump in the price of primary goods and the global demand for labour. Meantime, domestic politics in large parts of the English-speaking world led to changes in immigration policies, designed to keep out immigrants of ethnic origins not deemed desirable. Australia for example adopted a 'white Australia' policy, and the USA also devised immigration rules which kept out Indians. Globally people now needed passports to travel, compared with an earlier relaxed era where little or no documentation was needed to cross international borders. These changes proved, however, to be only temporary barriers to Indian overseas migration.

3 The opportunities of a post-colonial world

The Indian subcontinent achieved independence from British rule in 1947, and its inhabitants faced a new domestic environment which had considerable implications for the possibility of overseas migration. The most immediate impact of independence was felt in the north-west, particularly in Punjab, where the partition of the country into India and Pakistan led to massive and violent upheavals, including large-scale migration of people across the new international border in desperate fear of their lives, often having witnessed or been implicated in murder and other forms of physical savagery. Hindus and Sikhs trekked into India while Muslims fled to Pakistan. Probably about 12 million people left their homes, leaving behind what they could not carry, including houses and land. Those who fled from Pakistan vacated about 9.6 million acres of land, while Muslims fleeing India left behind 5.5 million acres. The former groups also left around 400,000 houses and 1,789 factories. The human misery involved can never adequately be told, though historians are at last beginning to plumb some of its depths.[31] What is clear is that it had a marked impact on Punjabis in particular and their attitudes to personal mobility, adding to the traditions of movement already firmly established in the region.

With political freedom came expectations of major economic transformation and rising standards of living, not least because of the rhetoric of nationalism and anti-colonialism. But the rulers of the new states on the subcontinent found that such benefits were virtually impossible to deliver, at least in the shorter term, given the magnitude of the task to be done, and the pressure of a rising population. From 1950 the region began to experience growth rates of over two per cent annually, as death rates fell under the impact of modern medicine, while birth rates remained constant. To take India, for example, the population just after independence was, according to the 1951 Census, just over 360 million; by 1971 it had risen to 547 million, and by the last decade of the century was over one billion, standing at 1,027,015,247 at the 2001 Census. This gave India the largest population in the world after China. In 2004 the populations of Pakistan (159,196,336) and Bangladesh (141,340,476) were smaller, but whereas India's birth rate had dropped to 1.44 per cent, Pakistan's was still 1.9 per cent and that of Bangladesh 2.05 per cent. It takes little imagination to see the pressure such population increase

[31] There is a growing literature on many aspects of the partition, including the politics behind it, the personal impact on individual lives, the experience of women, and the longer-term impact on India and Pakistan. See, for example, Part 2, 'Partition' of Talbot and Thandi (eds.), *People on the Move*; M. Hasan (ed.), *India's Partition. Process, Strategy and Mobilization* (New Delhi, Oxford University Press, 1994) and *Inventing Boundaries. Gender, Politics and the Partition of India* (New Delhi, Oxford University Press, 2000); I. Talbot, *Freedom's Cry. The Popular Dimension in the Pakistan Movement and Partition Experience in North-West India* (Karachi, Oxford University Press, 1996); U. Butalia, *The Other Side of Silence: Voices from the Partition of India* (New Delhi, Viking, Penguin Books India, 1998); T. Y. Tan and G. Kudaisya, *The Aftermath of Partition in South Asia* (London and New York, Routledge, 2000). An eye-witness account is P. Moon, *Divide and Quit* (Berkeley and Los Angeles, University of California Press, 1962).

puts on all social facilities, and particularly the impact on areas where land is the major resource and means of livelihood. It was not surprising that hard-pressed rural families would look abroad for alternative occupations and access to wealth from new resources. A further aspect of the post-independence domestic experience of the subcontinent, and particularly of India, was the growth of higher education, using English as the medium, and the expansion of the modern professions. This led over the decades to a major up-skilling of a growing elite, producing men and women with highly desirable and portable skills, for example in medicine and latterly in information technology, who were poised to take advantage of job opportunities abroad when these became available.

Politics and economics in the wider world environment were important factors encouraging or curtailing migration abroad from South Asia. In the immediate postwar years, of the developed economies of the western world and the neo-Europes of the antipodes, only Britain permitted open access to inhabitants of South Asia, by virtue of their status as citizens of countries within the Commonwealth which emerged out of the old Empire. The USA, Canada and Australia still closed their doors to Indian migrants. In the 1960s the politics of immigration, race relations and the need for skilled labour swung the pendulum the other way, as Britain rapidly curtailed primary migration for South Asians and others from the so-called New Commonwealth states, and as the USA, Canada and Australia loosened their controls and gave access to people with relevant skills and/or existing family already settled. The pattern of movement into America, for example, changed markedly after the 1965 legislation abolishing national origins quotas. Immigration from Europe sank between 1970 and 1990 from 32.2 per cent to 11.7 per cent, and Asian immigration (from all Asia not just South Asia) rose from 5.2 per cent to 15.2 per cent in the same period.[32] A further political change in the later part of the century which profoundly influenced overseas Indian settlement was the hostility to established Indian overseas populations from indigenous peoples in the aftermath of decolonisation. This led to the flight or expulsion of most Indians from the newly independent East African countries in the late 1960s and early 1970s, to Europe and north America; and from the 1980s onward of Indians from Fiji to Australia in particular.[33]

[32] D. Nayyar, *Governing Globalization*, p. 147.

[33] J. Connell and S. Raj, 'A Passage to Sydney', chapter 18 of B. V. Lal (ed.), *Bittersweet the Indo-Fijian Experience* (Canberra, Australian National University, Pandanus Books, 2004). The experience of East African Indians will be dealt with later in the book but a good introduction is V. Robinson, 'The Migration of East African Asians to the UK', in R. Cohen (ed.), *The Cambridge Survey of World Migration* (Cambridge, Cambridge University Press, 1995), pp. 331–336.

As important as politics in determining the flows of out-migration from South Asia and the onward migration of existing overseas groups, making them 'twice migrants', were wider economic trends which affected the demand for different kinds of labour. Immediately after the Second World War Britain not only had an open door to people from the countries of the Commonwealth, but an urgent need for labour to participate in the reconstruction of the economy, and the creation of social services such as the National Health Service and public transport. South Asians were among those who came in large numbers, mainly engaging in unskilled manual labour in the country's large industrial centres, but increasingly moving into self-employment. Twenty years later in the 1970s the most dramatic labour demand began to come from the Middle East, from countries made suddenly rich as the price of oil rose, but where local labour was scarce for various demographic and cultural reasons. Asia provided the people needed to help these oil rich states with their oil industries, construction, and many of the services these modernising economies required. By 1980 Saudi Arabia and the Gulf States had an immigrant workforce of 2.2 million, increasing to 5.1 million in 1985. Many of these immigrants were temporary, on short-term contracts, but the salaries were very attractive, as was the chance of sending home money. In the 1970s India and Pakistan between them provided the lion's share of Asian migrant labour into the Middle East, ranging from 97.3 per cent in 1975 to 45.5 per cent in 1979. Thereafter South East and East Asia provided more labour, and Bangladesh also began to contribute a significant number. By 1991 Bangladesh and Sri Lanka between them provided 22 per cent of migrant labour compared with 36 per cent from Pakistan and India.[34] The most recent demand for workers which has drawn South Asians, and particularly Indians, abroad has been the demand in the West, Canada and in the United States particularly, and in Australia and New Zealand, for highly skilled people in what are becoming post-industrial societies.[35] These range from medical personnel to engineers and those with skills in electronics and information technology. Moreover, international companies have no national barriers to recruitment, and skilled employment with them is a passport to international personal mobility.

Just as transformations in the technology of travel had enabled larger outflows of people from South Asia in the later nineteenth century, so a century later the technology of communications has transformed the

[34] M. I. Abella, 'Asian migrant and contract workers in the Middle East', in R. Cohen (ed.), *Cambridge Survey of World Migration*, pp. 418–423.

[35] The number of Indians in the USA has risen dramatically in the last quarter of the twentieth century, reaching over 800,000 by 1990.

possibility of relatively frequent long distance travel and also of international awareness and networking. From the 1960s travel by jet radically shortened travel times between South Asia and the rest of the world, compared with the earlier days of air travel when constant refuelling was required. In the 1930s Europe to India took three days by air, compared with eight or nine hours at the end of the century. Costs, too, had been slashed, making air travel no longer the preserve of a wealthy elite. In 1990 air transport costs per passenger mile were less than half of what they had been in 1960, and of course far cheaper still compared with 1930. Similarly the cost of international phone calls dropped (to less than one-tenth in 1990 compared with that of 1970), as did the price of computers (to less than one-twentieth in 1990 compared with that of 1970), making access to e-mail in the 1990s a relatively common possibility, at least among professionals and students.[36] This meant that where an older generation of people wishing to make contact with South Asia from Europe had had to rely on the post taking up to a week, or a laborious, booked international phone call with poor reception, by the end of the twentieth century their children and grandchildren could easily make instant contact with families and friends around the world by phone, e-mail and the internet. The consequences of these technological developments have transformed the experience of living in a new home, with the ability to communicate on a daily basis making physical absence less of a break in relationships. It has quickened the flows of information about possible opportunities abroad. It also makes many migrants re-think their social and political identities as they become truly transnational people, and in a new sense belong to several different homelands.

*****

This chapter has sketched the broad political and economic parameters within which migration took place on the South Asian subcontinent and from it overseas to create the contemporary South Asian diaspora. Despite British imperial images of India as a static society, and of Indians as immobile people constrained by social, religious and economic bonds to their natal villages, the evidence indicates that for centuries Indians had moved away from home even if in small numbers, whenever there had been a serious reason to do so. As India became incorporated into the global relationships created by the British Empire in the nineteenth century, so there was more incentive to move and many more Indians did so. The experience of physical mobility within the context of empire, or knowledge of its possibility, often became the foundation for later patterns of migration. But it was not until major changes in domestic and

[36] These statistics are taken from D. Nayyar, *Governing Globalization*, p. 162.

international politics, and the dramatic transformation of the world economy and the technology of transport and communication in the second half of the twentieth century, that the wider environment encouraged the development of more multiple strands in a worldwide South Asian diaspora. It is to these strands that we now turn, to provide the core factual evidence of migration on which an understanding of the diaspora must be based.

2 Making a modern diaspora

The modern South Asian diaspora, as it exists at the start of the twenty-first century, is a very complex human phenomenon. It has been fashioned by many different migratory trajectories of distinctive groups of people out of the subcontinent over at least a century and a half, which have created multiple strands in the diaspora. Chapter 1 sketched the changing environment over this period that enabled the movement of people out of South Asia, in terms of local and international economic change, political power and public policy, and the changing technology of transport and communication. This chapter charts the major historical flows of South Asian people from the early nineteenth century to the present. (See maps 1–6 of journeys and settlements.) It deals primarily with the initial stage of overseas movement, whether this was a first or a second migration, as in the case of some South Asian groups who were forced to move onwards often decades after their original journey, becoming 'twice-migrants'. It sets the scene for the following three chapters, which analyse how migrants dealt over time with the many challenges facing them as they made new homes on arrival and in subsequent years. Becoming a diaspora is a long-term business of managing change and continuity, and of negotiating old and new senses of identity as people come to terms with their new environment, and as they raise succeeding generations who in turn look critically at the position and achievements of an older generation of migrants and make their own decisions about who they are, how they should fit into their new homeland, and how they should relate to the land from which their parents, grandparents or even more remote ancestors came. Here we focus on patterns of movement: who journeyed, from where and to what destinations, for what reasons and with what resources. Resources include attitudes as well as money and skills. It is sometimes crudely assumed that migrants are 'problem people', particularly where there is public hostility to incomers of different ethnic origins. But it would be wrong to see South Asians who went abroad as failures, or as the helpless flotsam and jetsam of their societies, or as inherently problem people, either on the subcontinent or where they settled. It takes courage, energy, a vision of broader horizons and an awareness of the positive potential of change, and often connections, information and some material resources, to make the decision to move thousands of miles, to uproot oneself and often one's family.

1 Movement in the age of empire

The first large-scale movements out of the Indian subcontinent occurred in the nineteenth and early twentieth centuries when India was part of the British Empire. It was largely the dense networks of imperial connections binding India to a wider imperial world that drew Indians overseas, and led to the creation of settled populations of people of Indian origin around the globe. Three main distinctive types of movement occurred in this period, marked by different elements of choice and freedom.

Indentured labour

The recruitment of labourers under a contract of indenture for a specified number of years developed from the 1830s in response to the abolition of the slave trade and of slavery in the British Empire and in other European Empires. The owners of sugar plantations in particular faced a dire shortage of labour as slaves were freed and, understandably, few former slaves showed any inclination to continue on the plantations as free, paid labourers. To take just one example, in Mauritius, virtually all former slaves had left the plantations for good by the mid 1840s. In 1838 in Jamaica, sugar cane rotted in the fields for lack of people to harvest it, and the following year only limited planting was done.[1] Indentured labour was recruited from several different sources, but the Indian subcontinent provided the greatest number. About 1.5 million people left India under this system between 1834 and its ending in 1917, with the largest numbers going to Mauritius, British Guiana, Natal and Trinidad.[2] When they signed their contracts before leaving home, few knew where they were going or the reality of the conditions they would experience. None would have understood how they were a tiny part of an unprecedented pattern of economic globalisation sustaining the worldwide British Empire in particular, and that their labours fuelled British economic growth and also helped to feed the peoples of the Empire.

[1] D. Northrup, *Indentured Labor in the Age of Imperialism 1834–1922*, (Cambridge, Cambridge University Press, 1995) pp. 20–21.

[2] The statistics for the different regions and their subsequent Indian population by 1980 are in C. Clarke, C. Peach and S. Vertovec (eds.), *South Asians Overseas. Migration and Ethnicity*, (Cambridge, Cambridge University Press, 1990). p. 9. Mauritius received 453,063, British Guiana 238,909, Natal 152,184 and Trinidad 143,939.

Although the numbers of Indian indentured labourers were so large, they shared significant characteristics and were by no means representative of the subcontinent as a whole. Far more men than women were recruited, despite the humanitarian and social concerns of the British and Indian governments, and an attempt to insist on a female quota per batch of recruits. Probably overall the proportion of women migrants during the decades in which the system operated was just under 30 per cent of the whole. This created immigrant communities with a serious gender imbalance in the early years, before the birth of a new generation of Indians abroad helped to redress the shortage of girls and women. More Hindus that Muslims were recruited – probably somewhere between 80 per cent and 90 per cent. Although some came from south India, particularly to Natal, far more came from a small region of northern India in the region that is now eastern Uttar Pradesh and Bihar, but was then the United Provinces, Oudh and Bihar. Among indentured labourers travelling to Fiji, for example, for which destination there is a full set of emigration passes, United Provinces provided 46.5 per cent, Oudh 29 per cent and Bihar 10.5 per cent. Not surprisingly then, of India's three major ports, Bombay, Calcutta and Madras, Calcutta was the one from which most indentured labourers embarked on their new life.[3] What was it that persuaded people from such specific areas to leave India? Obviously ignorance was a factor, but so was poverty, landlessness and the hope for a better future. The districts from which labourers went were ones of high population density, where there was fragmentation of landed holdings, fragile agriculture and lack of alternative opportunities. In a considerable number of cases the situation had already driven recruits outside their district of origin in search of alternative work within India itself, most often to regional urban centres or to the indigo plantations of Bengal. Most of those who went abroad under the system had agricultural origins, but this was not a movement just of the lowest castes. Although they constituted the largest single group, there were also artisans and higher castes among those who left, a significant factor in subsequent years when Indians started to reconstruct free communities in the places where they had come to work under indenture.

The system of indenture was authorised and controlled by the governments of Britain, India, and the colonies to which labourers went. Indian recruiters in India had to be licensed, and recruits were brought to a registration officer, usually a magistrate, who had to see that the indenture contract was understood and entered into freely before they left for the

[3] Fig 3.2, Northrup, *Indentured Labor in the Age of Imperialism*, p. 66. For the Fiji evidence see B. V. Lal (ed.), *Chalo Jahaji on a Journey through Indenture in Fiji*, (Canberra and Suva, Australian National University and Fiji Museum, 2000) chapter 5.

coast. There were medical checks in the port of embarkation, and the ships on which they travelled were authorised, while conditions aboard were regulated. Once at their destinations the conditions of work were broadly regulated, as were those governing the way they were permitted at the end of their indenture to stay on as free workers or to return to India. Protectors of Immigrants were also appointed locally, as it became clear that many employers had few moral scruples at driving their new employees as hard as possible. This was the theory. Evidence from a wide variety of sources including official reports, court cases, and surviving memories, suggests that the system was generally harsh, at times punitive, and so tightly controlled the lives of labourers that some historians argue that it was little more than a new system of slavery.[4]

The degree of regulation of the system means that we know in considerable detail about the journeys of indentured labourers, their lives on the plantations, and their destinations when their indenture was completed. The whole experience of moving to a big port city, of being medically examined, and coming into contact with Europeans, must have been culturally perplexing to country folk whose social world would have been circumscribed by tradition and the conventions of caste and religion. Even more alarming and confusing would have been the voyage itself, with its regimented existence, lack of personal privacy, and disregard for social distinctions, as well as the sheer fact of spending weeks at sea for people who had probably never seen the sea before. Conditions on board authorised ships were by no means as bad as on the slave ships which crossed the Atlantic. The ships were generally well equipped by the standards of the times, and with the coming of steam the voyages were shorter and safer. (The journey from India to Fiji took an average of 73 days by sail but only 30 by steam ship.) Even so illnesses such as cholera, typhoid, smallpox, dysentery, measles and whooping cough could strike, which taxed the power and skill of the ships' surgeons. In 1859 one ship bound for Guiana lost 82 of its immigrants to cholera, while another ship four years later lost 124 to a severe fever. Other disasters could also occur, such as fire or shipwreck. The *Syria*, for example, was wrecked off Fiji in May 1884, and 56 immigrants drowned: many more would have done so without the rescue operation mounted by the chief medical officer and acting colonial secretary of Fiji, Dr William MacGregor, who was awarded medals in Britain and Australia for his attempts to save lives. One of the worst disasters was on the Mauritius route, when in

[4] The main advocate of this view was H. Tinker, author of the classic book, *A New System of Slavery. The Export of Indian Labour Overseas 1830–1920* (London, Oxford University Press, 1974).

1859 the *Shah Allam* burnt and only one out of over 400 immigrants survived.[5]

Once at their destination, the experience of immigrants was unfamiliar and harsh, and they were often subjected to considerable violence at the hands of the plantation owners and their overseers or *sirdars*, themselves Indians, who were in daily contact with the labourers. Their pay was minimal, and their accommodation in large barracks spartan and often unhygienic, without regard for social decency and privacy, particularly for couples and families. Their health was often poor, despite some provision on plantations for medical care. They were at the mercy of their employers, whose attitude was often minatory or actively punitive. Women were subjected to harassment at the hands of their male employers and overseers, who exploited them sexually or failed to understand their emotional and health problems, particularly those caused by childbirth and the death of children.[6] Records of court cases involving labourers point to the violence with which they were treated, and the difficulties in bringing employers to justice; while labourers themselves were often punished for even quite trivial misdemeanors. Health records indicate a high level of disease, particularly diseases attributable to poor living conditions and lack of medical care, such as dysentery, anaemia, diarrhoea, tuberculosis and chest infections. Moreover there were high death rates, from disease, accidents (particularly drowning and burns), and violence – the last category including murder and suicide. Suicide rates were alarming when compared with what might be generally expected in any given population. They were particularly high in Fiji and Natal among indentured labourers. In 1900–1903, for example, Fiji had a suicide rate of just under 7.3 per cent and Natal a rate of 6.3 per cent. These were probably attributable largely to poor conditions of work and living, but also to a sense of despair and helplessness in a new situation.[7]

Given the conditions of their lives under indenture it is perhaps surprising that comparatively few chose to return when their contracts had

[5] See B. V. Lal, *Chalo Jahaji*, Part 2 for chapters on various aspects of the journeys taken by indentured labourers. On pages 138–141 there is a unique description published anonymously in Edinburgh in 1909 of such a journey, entitled 'The Coolie Emigrant'. A detailed study of recruiting for work in Natal is in T. R. Metcalf, 'Hard hands and sound healthy bodies: recruiting "Coolies" for Natal, 1860–1911', chapter 12 in his *Forging The Raj. Essays on British India in the Heyday of Empire* (New Delhi, Oxford University Press, 2005).

[6] A classic study of the particular problems of women is B. V. Lal, 'Kunti's Cry', published in 1985 and reprinted as chapter 11 in Lal, *Chalo Jahaji*.

[7] On disease and death on the Fiji plantations see Lal, *Chalo Jahaji*, chapters 12, 15, 16 and 17. On suicide in Natal see S. and A. Bhana, 'An Exploration of the psycho-historical circumstances surrounding suicide among indentured Indians, 1875–1911', pp. 137–188 of S. Bhana (ed.), *Essays on Indentured Indians in Natal* (Leeds, Peepal Tree, 1991).

expired. Their persistence in their new homes was probably a reflection of the memory of what had driven them to indenture in the first place, a sense of having lost touch with kin and home in India, and also a sign of the fashioning of new kinship ties and families in the new homeland. About 28 per cent returned from Natal between 1860 and 1911, 35 per cent from Mauritius between 1836 and 1910, and 20 per cent from Trinidad between 1845 and 1918. Returning to India could be hard even though some went back to their villages, were well received, and bought land with their savings. An indication of the problems faced by returnees was the establishment of an Indian Emigrants' Friendly Service Committee in Calcutta in 1921 to give official and private charitable aid to returned indentured labourers in the form of housing, medical care and help to find employment. A moving force behind this was the Revd C. F. Andrews, a close friend of Gandhi, who had particularly concerned himself with the problems faced by indentured labourers.[8] Some who returned to India were unable to make a new life for themselves and re-indentured and returned to the colony from which they had returned or elsewhere.[9] Here was a pattern that recurs in the formation of the diaspora: the experience of movement whether on the subcontinent or outside it creates an attitude which assumes that physical mobility is an option for an individual and a family, and encourages further migration for individuals and others in their social circles.

Contract labour

The interlocking forces of imperialism and economic development also provided opportunities for work for many other Indians under contract for a specific period, in conditions which were freer and less arduous than those suffered by the indentured. Some of these opportunities were within South Asia itself, and between the early 1850s and the mid 1930s probably about 2.5 million Indians went to work in Burma and 1.5 million to Ceylon. Outside the broad parameters of the subcontinent Malaya was a major destination for contract workers. In the same period probably 2 million went, particularly to work on the sugar, coffee and tapioca plantations, and in the twentieth century on the rubber plantations which were of growing significance to the imperial economy. Many of those who went

[8] On the career of Andrews see H. Tinker, *The Ordeal of Love. C. F. Andrews and India* (Delhi, Oxford University Press, 1979).

[9] On the experiences of those who returned to India see Northrup, *Indentured Labor*, pp. 129–139; and M. S. Ramesar, 'The repatriates', chapter 9 of D. Dabydeen and B. Samaroo (eds.), *Across the Dark Waters. Ethnicity and Indian Identity in the Caribbean* (Houndmills and London, MacMillan, 1996).

on short-term contracts returned home to India, but sufficient remained to establish a long-term resident community. Those who went to Malaya were mainly Tamil speakers from south India, under a recruiting system known as *kangani*; but from the 1920s most of those who went for plantation work there were free labourers. Another element in the Indian mosaic in South East Asia was the fact that for some decades in the mid-nineteenth century Singapore was a penal colony for Indians, and prisoners learnt craft skills which were put to use building the colony's infrastructure. One of the public buildings Indian prisoners helped to erect was Singapore's Anglican cathedral, completed in 1861.

Further afield Indian contract labour helped to build the infrastructure of British rule in East Africa. The East African railways were a crucial link in imperial rule and most of those who built them were Indians, many of whom came from the Punjab. Very significant numbers of labourers were imported in the late 1890s, and by 1903 nearly 32,000 had been imported for railway construction. The highest point of Indian employment on the railways was in 1901 when nearly 20,000 Indians were employed, compared with 2,500 Africans. Although Indian labourers were called 'coolies', as were indentured labourers on plantations, many of these temporary workers were in no sense unskilled labourers but masons, carpenters, and even draughtsmen and surveyors. Most of these were repatriated when their construction work was done, but considerable numbers of those who had come by 1903 were invalided home (20.2 per cent) or died (7.8 per cent) – a serious reflection of their working and living conditions. Fever, diarrhoea, and respiratory diseases were the major killers, while bubonic plague and man-eating lions were a lesser if more dramatic threat. But again a significant number – possibly up to 19 per cent – remained, some still working on the railways, to form part of the emerging permanent Indian communities in East Africa. In Kenya, for example, by the 1921 census there were over 45,500 people of Indian origin, and some of these were Sikhs who had originally come to work on the railways.[10]

Free Indian movement

Given the growing economic opportunities of this period and the improvements in sea and rail transport, it is not surprising that Indians also travelled widely overseas and into the hinterlands of foreign countries

10 R. G. Gregory, *India and East Africa. A History of Race Relations within the British Empire 1890–1939* (Oxford, Clarendon Press, 1971), pp. 50–61. (These labourers were actually indentured but as their work and terms of service were so different from that of plantation indentured workers I have classified them as temporary contract labour.)

for varieties of trade and commerce, sometimes to places where there was a long-standing Indian commercial presence, as in East Africa, and sometimes to places where Indian communities were being built for the first time. Many took up permanent residence overseas or at least stayed for many decades, creating the core of a settled diaspora. They were often known as 'passenger Indians' who paid their own way, in contrast to those who arrived under indenture or some other form of labour contract. As Gandhi noted in South Africa, despite these clear social distinctions among Indians (and the fact that wealthier Indians had no social relations with indentured Indians) some white people used the word 'coolie' for all Indians; he himself was known as a 'coolie barrister' and sometimes treated with the rough contempt shown to labourers despite the fact that he was a London-trained lawyer.[11]

Some Indian traders continued long-standing patterns of commerce with South East Asia, often settling in Malaya, Singapore and as far away as Hong Kong, where they were heavily involved in the opium trade between India and China. Parsis were particularly prominent and successful from the first half of the nineteenth century; and they had their own cemetery there from 1854 and a Zoroastrian Centre from 1857. In 1901 the Hong Kong Indian population was 1,453 and by 1931 it had reached 4,745, by which time its members were engaged in a wide variety of occupations.[12] East Africa was also a significant commercial destination, following on from a long tradition of Indian commerce on the coast and on Zanzibar. Parsis were present in the nineteenth century on the coast, as were large numbers of Shia Muslim sects (particularly those following the Aga Khan). They were joined in the twentieth century by large numbers of Gujaratis, also from western India, where the long coastline naturally encouraged movements westwards across the Indian Ocean, particularly in times of drought and famine. In Africa trade clearly followed the railway. Many who had worked on the coast now travelled inland, serving Indian construction workers and then supplying Africans and white settlers. Known as dukawallas, they became essential to the East African economy and the daily lives of its peoples. Some made significant wealth, such as the founder of Hasham Jamal and Company who came from western India and engaged in a large produce trade through East Africa; or a Karachi Muslim, Rehmanji Mohemed Ali, who established a

[11] M. K. Gandhi, *An Autobiography. The Story of My Experiments with Truth*, (London, Jonathan Cape, 1966) pp. 89–90, 107–109.

[12] See B.-S. White, *Turbans and Traders. Hong Kong's Indian Communities* (Hong Kong, Oxford University Press, 1994); on South East Asia see the many essays in K. S. Sandhu and A. Mani (eds.), *Indian Communities in Southeast Asia* (Singapore, Times Academic Press, 1993).

large potato plantation and also brought in the first Indian films. Indians also began to rent urban land which they then subdivided and let to other Indians. As one District Commissioner commented in 1911, 'The profit on such plots must comparatively speaking be enormous.'[13] It is telling that by the end of the nineteenth century the Indian rupee had become the major currency of trade throughout East Africa. Passenger Indians also came in large numbers to South Africa, and particularly to Natal: by 1911 there were nearly 20,000 in Natal alone, despite considerable white hostility towards them and attempts to curtail their numbers and capacity to trade. They came mainly from a very limited area near the coast of what is now Gujarat – from the districts of Surat and Valsad and from Kathiawar. A few came to Natal from Mauritius, but had been born in Kathiawar, like Aboobaker Amod, a Memon originally from Porbandar, who opened a store in Durban in 1875 and also invested in urban property. By the early twentieth century virtually every urban area and large village in Natal had its Indian traders and store-keepers: by hard work and the use of family labour they undercut white competition by as much as 25 to 30 per cent.[14]

The expansion of British imperial rule round the rim of the Indian Ocean also provided opportunities for Indians who took up varieties of imperial employment, particularly in colonial police and security services and in civilian administration. Sikhs were, for example, recruited into the security services in Malaya and became the core of the new colonial police force. Similarly in Hong Kong Punjabis were recruited from India to become colonial policemen, largely at the instigation of a former Indian Police Officer, C. V. Creagh, who had served in the Punjab police before being transferred to Hong Kong in the 1860s. Indians went on being recruited through kin connections and Indian newspaper advertisements and were a major part of the police force well into the twentieth century. Punjabi Sikhs and Muslims were also recruited into the colony's prison services.

Indians also served the Empire in a civil capacity. They were recruited in large numbers into subordinate clerical and technical posts in British Malaya, not least because of the advantage they had in knowing English. By 1930, 655 Indians had posts in the clerical service of the Federated

[13] Gregory, *India And East Africa*, pp. 61 ff. One case study of groups of western Indians who migrated to East Africa, and for whom this was one migration in the middle of several, which eventually brought them to Leicester, UK, is M. Banks, 'Why move? Regional and long distance migrations of Gujarati Jains', chapter 6 of J. M. Brown and R. Foot (eds.), *Migration: The Asian Experience* (Houndmills and London, MacMillan, 1994).

[14] S. Bhana and J. Brain, *Setting Down Roots. Indian Migrants in South Africa 1860–1911* (Johannesburg, Witwatersrand University Press, 1990), particularly chapters 1 and 3.

Malay States, just over 65 per cent of the total, whereas Chinese held nearly 26 per cent and Malays only 9 per cent.[15] In Hong Kong at the same time many of the 3,000 Indians there were in government service, primarily in the army and police but also in the civilian services as doctors, vets, engineers, teachers, clerks, and telegraph workers. Similarly, Indians moved into government employment in East Africa, and by 1911 almost as many were government employees as they were traders of various kinds. In Uganda, for example, they were firmly entrenched in the civil service, the railways and postal service by the First World War. Goans in particular had a high level of education before they migrated to Africa, and gravitated particularly into government and private service rather than into trade.

A final and unusual strand in the free migration flows out of India in this period were the small numbers, particularly of Sikhs, who found their way to the Pacific coast of America and Canada. Many of these were former soldiers in the Indian army, and often had seen service in the Far East. It was from there that some went to Vancouver and others to San Francisco. Between 1904 and 1908 about 5,000 Indians, mostly Sikh Punjabis and almost all men, entered Canada and found work in railway construction, in forestry and in lumber mills. They clustered in Victoria and Vancouver. In 1908 stringent immigration rules curtailed this flow, and stopped primary male immigration, despite the attempt in 1914 of a group of nearly four hundred Indians to beat the ban in a specially chartered ship which complied with the new rule that migrants should come on a continuous voyage from their native country, thus effectively barring Indians as there was no direct steamship service from India to Canada. The *Komagata Maru* and its human cargo languished for two months in Vancouver harbour, to no avail. Only gradually were women and children allowed in, leading to family reunion. It was not until the 1960s that Indian migration was possible into Canada in any strength.[16] Significant numbers of Indians also made their way into California at this time, where there was high demand for labour in an area of intensive agriculture, where irrigation enabled the commercial cultivation of fruit and vegetables. By 1890 the size of the Indian community there was nearly 72,500. Between 1899 and 1914, 6,800 Punjabis had arrived, mainly from higher castes who sent sons into the army or abroad because family land was insufficient for their support. Many had already seen service

[15] M. Puthucheary, 'Indians in the Public Sector in Malaysia' chapter 13 in Sandhu and Mani (eds.), *Indian Communities in Southeast Asia*.

[16] An attempt to catch the flavour of the life of these early Indians in Canada is in S. S. Jagpal, *Becoming Canadians. Pioneer Sikhs in their Own Words* (Madeira Park and Vancouver, Harbour Publishing, 1994)

overseas in the army or police forces of the Empire. As all immigration from Asia was stopped in 1917, and Indians were denied citizenship and therefore the right to own land from 1923, they had to adapt to a very hard situation, often by marrying local women, mainly Hispanics, as local laws forbad marriage to white women. This was a social pattern almost unique in the diaspora, as South Asians have rarely married outside their own social groups, let alone outside their ethnic group. But it was not until 1949 that South Asians were allowed to bring wives and brides from the subcontinent. Despite these problems Indians struck deep roots in California and became known as good farmers and reliable neighbours.[17]

South Asians had moved abroad in an imperial age for a variety of reasons, armed with different skills with which to make a new life. By far the greatest number were from rural backgrounds and such migrants possessed little but their agricultural knowledge and capacity for hard labour. (In the course of time many of these labouring communities in the diaspora began to develop new skills and to move into new types of work, as will be seen in the next chapter. Here we have been concerned only with the initial pattern of movement.) By contrast, from the mid-twentieth century very different types of population flows occurred out of the subcontinent, leading to the creation of different types of diaspora community, as men and women from South Asia responded to the problems experienced in now independent nation states, and to many new kinds of opportunities overseas in an age first of decolonisation and then of globalisation.

2 Movement in an age of decolonisation and globalisation

The movement of people out of the subcontinent slowed down after the First World War, once the system of indenture was stopped, largely in response to Indian hostility to it, and as economic recession and new legal barriers to Indian migration were erected in places such as the United States and Canada. New Zealand and Australia had already closed their doors at the turn of the century, in 1899 and 1901 respectively. But in the second half of the twentieth century new flows of migrants left to make their mark across the world, often in places and societies where there had been virtually no permanent South Asian presence before. It was this second set of large-scale movements that made the South Asian diaspora a truly global phenomenon, visible and significant in every continent. There were four main and very distinctive kinds of migratory flow.

[17] J. M. Jensen, *Passage from India. Asian Indian Immigrants in North America* (New Haven and London, Yale University Press, 1988); K. I. Leonard, *Making Ethnic Choices. California's Punjabi Mexican Americans* (Philadelphia, Temple University Press, 1995).

South Asian migration into the United Kingdom

The first new flow out of the subcontinent came soon after the end of British imperial rule, at the time when Britain was reconstructing its economy at home after the devastations of the Second World War and offered considerable opportunities for employment for the unskilled as well as the skilled. South Asians were part of a larger movement of people from the New Commonwealth (i.e. people not from the older 'white dominions', who were therefore immediately recognisable and different from the majority of the British population by virtue of their ethnic and cultural backgrounds). Citizens of Commonwealth countries, including those such as India and Pakistan which had become independent, had free right of access into Britain at this stage. Caribbean immigrants came first, often fluent in English and offering desirable skills in transport and health. They were soon followed in the 1950s and 1960s by people from India and Pakistan, whose eastern wing became Bangladesh in 1971. (People from East Pakistan will be called Bangladeshis here for ease, although clearly many of them were born or lived in the area and migrated from it when it was part of Pakistan immediately after independence.) The flows from South Asia were only slowed when from the early 1960s successive governments enacted legislation restricting New Commonwealth immigration, out of concerns about social tension where there were large and distinctive 'coloured communities', the pressure immigration placed on housing in certain areas, and latterly to ward off a massive influx of Indians from East Africa.[18] Political parties were in large part responding to domestic political pressures, and behind these controls lay a degree of serious racism in many sections of British society. However, many MPs from the main parties were also deeply uneasy at the need to impose controls which appeared to raise humanitarian concerns and also threaten the nature and standing of the Commonwealth as it emerged out of the ending of the British Empire.

Despite increasingly stringent controls the size of the UK's South Asian population increased rapidly in actual terms and as a percentage of the total population. In 1961 it stood at 106,300 (0.23 per cent of the population). This had risen in 1971 to 413,155 (0.85 per cent of the population); in 1981 to 1,215,048 (2.52 per cent of the population); in 1991 to 1,431,348 (3.04 per cent of the population) and in 2001 to 2,083,759 (3.6 per cent of the population). Throughout these four decades those

[18] On the interlinked issues of British citizenship and immigration control, see R. Karatani, *Defining British Citizenship. Empire, Commonwealth and Modern Britain* (London and Portland, Or., Frank Cass, 2003). Chapters 4 and 5 deal with the making of the crucial 1962 and 1968 Commonwealth Immigrants Acts and the 1971 Immigration Act.

from or with ethnic origins in India have been the largest group, followed by Pakistanis, and then by people from Bangladesh. Figures for the later decades of the century of course reflect natural population increase, as more people from these ethnic groups were born in the UK, rather than there being an increase in the numbers of migrants. But in 1961 when the figures do reflect mainly immigrants rather than those locally born, there were 81,400 Indians compared with 24,900 of Pakistani origin. By 2001 those with origins in Pakistan and Bangladesh together numbered 1,030,348 compared with 1,053,411 with ethnic roots in India. (Significant numbers joined this South Asian ethnic group from East Africa in the late 1960s and 1970s, as will be discussed below. Consequently some of those counted by the Census as Indians will have roots in India by way of Africa.)[19]

Those who migrated directly to the UK rather than via East Africa or elsewhere came from several distinctive regions. These regions tended to have particular past histories and present problems which made migration overseas an attractive option for many, despite the great expense of saving for air fares. It should be remembered that all those who came at this time were financed by themselves or their extended families, and that air transport, used by most migrants from the early 1960s, was, comparatively, much more expensive than at the end of the century. Consequently the decision to make the journey was a huge undertaking. This was one reason why initially migration was often by males alone, and family reunions occurred later when there was a certainty about settlement and enough money to pay for wives and possibly children to travel to the UK. Further, in these particular areas of the subcontinent there was often experience of earlier mobility which had widened the horizons of local people far beyond their village or home region.

One of these regions lay in Punjab, a province of British India which had been divided in 1947, and where there had been a huge demographic upheaval as a result. In Indian Punjab the geographical core of out-migration to the UK was the area of the Jullundur Doab. This was one of the most heavily populated regions of India, where land was increasingly in short supply, and pressure increased with the influx of refugees from the area of the province which had become Pakistan. It was also the part of the province which had provided very large numbers of soldiers, particularly Sikhs, for the imperial army, and given them opportunities to travel within the Empire before and after military service, creating a

[19] A convenient source for many of these population statistics for the UK is a website on 200 years of migration into the UK entitled 'Moving here'. It is well illustrated, has individual histories, and scholarly texts: www.movinghere.org.uk. See also the decennial Census websites.

culture conducive to migration. Migrants from the region were by no means those at the base of rural society. One study of a Punjabi village in the Doab which sent many Jat Sikhs, known for their fine agriculture, to England, suggests that of a total village population in the middle of the century of over 1,600, 515 had migrated, 99 within India and 402 to the UK. Pressure on land was one cause for this demographic pattern, as was an exaggerated idea of the wealth which could be made abroad, to enhance a family's wealth and prestige at home. Some wealthy families also sent several children abroad as a defensive strategy, fearing the impact of legislation to place upper limits or 'ceilings' on landholdings in an independent India where socialist values officially drove economic legislation. Many of these Sikhs migrated to Gravesend on the Kentish outskirts of London.[20] Across the city in Southall, another area of large South Asian settlement, Jat Sikhs again came mainly from Jullundur. Other migrants came from the Pakistani side of the border which now bisected Punjab. Again many of these had experienced earlier movement as a result of migration to the new canal colonies or because of the partition of 1947. Many Pakistani families who settled in Oxford from the 1950s came originally from Jullundur and at partition had moved to Jhelum in Pakistan Punjab.

Another distinctive region of out-migration from the north of the subcontinent was Mirpur in what was Pakistani-controlled Kashmir after 1947. This, too, was an area where there was an acceptance of long-distance movement for work to compensate for lack of local opportunities and poor agricultural prospects. Before the railway transformed transportation on the subcontinent in the late nineteenth century, Mirpuris had been boat-builders and sailors on the great rivers of the area, and then, when river transport declined, they transferred their skills to the British shipping industry, monopolising the jobs of stokers in British merchant ships operating out of Karachi and Bombay. Then in 1966 much of the best land in the district was flooded by the building of the Mangla Dam, increasing the migration flow. About 250 villages were submerged and 100,000 people were displaced by the dam. Those with friends and relatives in the UK used their compensation money to migrate there.

Across the subcontinent in what became Bangladesh in 1971, yet another area produced a disproportionate number of migrants to the UK. These were people from Sylhet, another district with traditions of

[20] A. W. Helweg, *Sikhs in England. The Development of a Migrant Community* (Delhi, Oxford University Press, 1979). More broadly on migration out of Punjab over time see D. S. Tatla, 'Rural roots of the Sikh diaspora', chapter 5 of I. Talbot and S. Thandi (eds.), *People on the Move. Punjabi Colonial and Post-Colonial Migration* (Karachi, Oxford University Press, 2004).

movement in search of work related to seamanship. Before 1947 it had been in the British Indian province of Assam, and the land revenue settlement there had produced a society of small landholding farmers. Many of those above the level of the poorest preferred not to labour on the land themselves, and chose to work on boats which transported rice and jute down to Calcutta. There they encountered people, often their own kin, who encouraged them to work as *lascars* or sailors. Often the first Sylhetis to go to England were sailors who stayed for a short time to work in the UK. When the British immigration system made such easy movement in and out of the UK impossible in the 1960s many of them stayed permanently and took up industrial, labouring and other forms of work, including the ubiquitous 'Indian restaurant', which was often not Indian at all! Key Sylheti brokers who owned boarding houses in London helped to mediate this migration.[21] A final group of people from the subcontinent who migrated to the UK were Gujaratis, again from a region that faced seaward and had long been a source of movement beyond South Asia. However, most of them came to the UK via East Africa and their migratory experience to the UK in the 1960s and 1970s will be discussed when we consider the groups of South Asians overseas who were forced to engage in a second migration, to become those who are often known as 'twice-migrants'.

The nature of South Asian migration to the UK changed markedly over time. The earliest arrivals were generally single males, who came off ships, worked as pedlers, or took up industrial work often with the intention of only a limited stay. If they were married they left their wives and children at home on the subcontinent and lived a spartan bachelor life, often in houses which were little more than dormitories for a large number of single men. There were often stories of men engaged in shift work who left their beds in the mornings to be filled during the day by those who were doing the night shifts! Almost always this was 'chain migration' – people from kin and village groups who knew each other and spread news of work and accommodation by word of mouth and through these chains of social connection. This was as much the reason for the heavy representation of particular areas on the subcontinent in the migrant population in the UK, as was the local economic pressure and historical experience in the sending region. Many who have studied particular migrant communities in different urban areas in the UK have teased out the working of such chains. One particularly interesting example, which illuminates several aspects of the migration process, was

[21] K. Gardner, *Global Migrants, Local Lives. Travel and Transformation in Rural Bangladesh* (Oxford, Clarendon Press, 1995).

initiated in the 1950s by a British man who had commanded a unit of Punjabi Sikhs during the war. His family firm, Woolf's Rubber Company in Southall, needed labour to make car accessories. Drawing on his old servicemen's networks he recruited rural Sikhs from Jullundur. The patriarch of another chain of migrants living in east Oxford was also a former soldier.[22] Ironically in the 1960s during the period when South Asian migration was subjected to a voucher system, British attempts to control immigration further encouraged the development of chains, particularly those of kinship, as those who were already established sponsored and acquired vouchers for younger male brothers, cousins and friends. The growing restrictions also encouraged family reunions just as the primary migration of male workers virtually stopped. Not only did migrants want to bring in their wives and children while they could: wives and families back on the subcontinent encouraged this for fear of the effect of the single life abroad on the morals of their menfolk. The courage of these migrant women needs to be remembered. Although there had been considerable public and private investment in education on the subcontinent during the years of British rule, the availability of education was geographically and socially uneven and far more common in urban areas. Coming from rural backgrounds, where educational levels for girls were far lower then for boys, female literacy in a vernacular was still uncommon, and literacy in English was highly unlikely for young married women. Even in 1981 illiteracy among rural women in Bangladesh was 96.9 per cent and in Pakistan 92.7 per cent; and in India in 1971 it stood at 87 per cent.[23] Consequently, young women who flew to Britain to join their husbands faced enormous problems of adaptation in a strange environment, often initially unsupported by the network of female kin who would have surrounded them at home in South Asia. This was the beginning of permanent settlement and the development of stable ethnic communities in the UK. The issues to be addressed in this new phase of the migration process are discussed in the next chapter.

Many of those who came directly to the UK from South Asia in the 1950s and 1960s were rural people of some local standing in their original homes and none were abjectly poor. However, few had specialist skills which they could immediately deploy in their new home, unlike the more

[22] G. Baumann, *Contesting Culture. Discourses of Identity in Multi-ethnic London* (Cambridge, Cambridge University Press, 1996), p. 54; A. Shaw, 'The Pakistani community in Oxford', pp. 35–57 of R. Ballard (ed.), *Desh Pardesh. The South Asian Presence in Britain* (London, Hurst, 1994).

[23] F. Robinson (ed.), *The Cambridge Encyclopedia of India, Pakistan, Bangladesh, Sri Lanka, Nepal, Bhutan and the Maldives* (Cambridge, Cambridge University Press, 1989), p. 381. (Punjab had a rural female literacy rate of 19.9 per cent which was higher than many states in India, but this would not have been literacy in English.)

educated East African South Asians who came in subsequent decades. Consequently most of them found unskilled or semi-skilled jobs in factories and with a variety of urban employers. Southall Sikhs, for example, worked in a rubber factory and then branched out into local food processing factories. Gravesend, another popular Sikh destination, had paper mills and engineering works. Pakistanis were lured to Oxford in the 1950s when the City of Oxford Motor Services could not find cleaners and conductors for its buses, as white labour gravitated to higher paid jobs at Morris Motors. Many more South Asians found work in the great Northern and Midland industrial conurbations, where unskilled work in heavy industries was plentiful at this time. This led to a heavily urban pattern of settlement – striking in view of these migrants' rural roots – and also strong spatial clustering. The 1971 Census discovered that 65 per cent of Pakistanis and 58 per cent of Indians were concentrated in Greater London, West Midlands, Greater Manchester, Merseyside, Tyneside and West Yorkshire. London was the major centre for both groups but particularly for Indians, while for Pakistanis the West Midlands and West Yorkshire were also very important. Twenty years later these patterns persisted: by far the greatest number of Indians were to be found in Greater London, as were Bangladeshis, whereas Pakistanis were almost equally heavily concentrated in London, the West Midlands and West Yorkshire.[24]

Second time migrations

The impact of politics and of national policies on migration has already become clear, as we have seen how immigration law in many places denied access to South Asians at different times in the twentieth century. Nowhere was political influence more obvious than in those places where established groups of South Asians in the diaspora were forced to move on from the places where they had made their homes after their first overseas movement. Most of these second migrations occurred in the aftermath of the European colonial empires, particularly the British Empire, in places where South Asians had become significant groups of incomers who now for various reasons were seen as a threat to the new nation state and its indigenous peoples, and denied citizenship in their new homelands. Two of the most significant of these movements occurred in South Asia itself as people of Indian origin went 'home' to India from

[24] V. Robinson, 'Boom and gloom: the success and failure of South Asians in Britain', chapter 12 of Clarke, Peach and Vertovec (eds.), *South Asians Overseas*; A. H. Halsey and J. Webb (eds.), *Twentieth-Century British Social Trends* (Houndmills, London and New York, MacMillan and St. Martin's Press, 2000), pp. 140–141.

Burma and Sri Lanka. The Second World War led to the flight of probably half a million Indians from Burma in the face of the Japanese advance through South East Asia. When Burma gained independence in 1948 the national policy was to restrict Indians' access to citizenship, and eventually in 1962 those remaining were expelled, though some remain on the fringes of society, disguised by Burmese dress and names, and lacking any formal citizenship status. Similarly, independent Ceylon (later known as Sri Lanka) made most of its Tamil Indian residents non-citizens. Negotiations between the Sri Lankan government and the government of India did not completely resolve the issue, though under a series of agreements some were allowed to take Indian citizenship, and others Sri Lankan citizenship, while some thousands were repatriated to India. Ironically, probably more Sri Lankan Tamils fled the island to India when the civil war on the island broke out in the 1980s than the numbers of Indian Tamils who had been repatriated.

Outside the subcontinent there were a series of acute crises facing once-migrant South Asians who were now forced to move again in the post-colonial era. One of the most dramatic and publicised was the fate of Indians who had migrated to East Africa and now found themselves under pressure and sometimes acute threat from the policies of the new nation states of East Africa. Most of those who had gone to East Africa were from western India, and particularly the area which is now the Indian state of Gujarat. They had taken with them higher levels of technical and commercial skills and better educational qualifications than their compatriots who had left with little but their labour to offer. In Africa they had capitalised on these and they and their children had by the 1960s secured key and highly visible roles for themselves in the economies of these areas, as traders, managers, technicians and artisans, and also in the civil services. But it must be remembered that they were a tiny minority – 2.3 per cent in Kenya and 1 per cent in Tanzania and Uganda. Denied the right to buy land, by imperial policy, they were now primarily resident in urban areas, and tended consequently to cluster residentially. They also continued their tradition of marrying only within their own communities, and they had little social contact with black Africans. Clearly they had prospered under colonial rule and it was not surprising that Africans often viewed them with suspicion as colonial collaborators. As independence came Indians faced the prospect of an uncertain future and also the specific issue of citizenship in a post-colonial Africa. Some began to take defensive measures, for example by moving capital out of Africa to Britain, sometimes illegally, or by taking British rather than local African citizenship. In Uganda by 1969 just about half of local Indians had taken British citizenship, under one-third Ugandan citizenship, and under one-seventh Indian citizenship. In Kenya Indians were equally reluctant to take local citizenship. The exception was Tanganyika, where the Aga Khan directed his followers to apply for local citizenship. The Indian government was reluctant to believe that in a post-colonial era other newly independent nations would actively discriminate against Indians in their territories, and the only advice it gave to Indians was to integrate locally and become good citizens of African states, advice which Indians found unrealistic and even threatening.[25]

All these aspects of their presence made them easy targets for new leaders in struggling post-colonial states, who had numerous client groups needing visible and tangible proof of the benefits of independence. In particular, emergent African trading groups and African intellectuals anxious for government jobs would reap benefits from policies of Africanisation or from the more extreme case of the departure of Indian communities. Indians began to be squeezed out of jobs in all three East African countries. In Kenya for example an Immigration Act and a Trade Licensing Act in 1967 began to exclude Asians from the public services and many commercial positions, while the need to gain a licence to trade in certain areas was aimed at the Asian commercial concentrations in Nairobi and Mombasa. By 1968 the number of Asians in the public services stood at 8,000 compared with 12,200 in 1961. Not surprisingly a growing stream of Kenyan Asians headed in panic for Britain in the mid-1960s. In 1965 5,000 arrived, 6,000 in 1966 and 12,000 in 1967. It was thought that in the first two months of 1968 alone another 12,000 arrived; and in March Britain banned the entry even of British passport holders, unless they had what were called 'patrial' links with Britain. In Tanzania Julius Nyerere's African Socialism programmes put pressure on Asians, particularly those in the rural retailing sector. Here, too, South Asians began to move on, and Dar-es-Salaam experienced the same clear change as had Nairobi. Once an Indian-dominated city with 29 per cent of its population Indian in 1960, by 1969 Indians were only 11 per cent of the population.

However it was in Uganda that the most dramatic exodus of Indians took place – under threat of force – though it occurred slightly later than the mass departures from Kenya. In 1969 the Ugandan government followed Kenyan example with Immigration and Trade Licensing Acts which threatened the large number of Indians who had taken British citizenship (c. 36,600). A considerable number – over 24,000 – left between 1969 and 1971, most to the UK while smaller numbers went to

[25] See V. Robinson, 'The Migration of East African Asians to the UK', in R. Cohen (ed.), *The Cambridge Survey of World Migration* (Cambridge, Cambridge University Press 1995), pp. 331–336; an excellent collection of essays is in M. Twaddle (ed.), *Expulsion of a Minority. Essays on Ugandan Asians* (London, Athlone Press, 1975); H. Tinker, *The Banyan Tree. Overseas Emigrants from India, Pakistan and Bangladesh* (Oxford, Oxford University Press, 1977), particularly chapters 4 and 5.

the USA and Canada, and some, particularly the retired and elderly, returned to India and Pakistan. At this stage many found it possible to bring out their capital, despite the limits on what could officially be exported. The crisis for the Ugandan Asians finally erupted when Idi Amin took over power in January 1971. By the end of the year it was clear that this meant no respite, and in August 1972 he announced that Asians would be expelled from Uganda in 90 days, and that they were guilty of economic sabotage and encouraging corruption. This understandably caused turmoil in Britain, where race and immigration were already deeply contentious issues, and the law had been strengthened in the face of the exodus of Asians from Kenya. The British city of Leicester even went as far as advertising in the *Ugandan Argus* in mid-September 1972 to warn Asians not to attempt to settle there as the city's educational and social services were stretched to the limit. It had already experienced an influx of 3,000 Kenyan Asians in early 1968. Ealing (a London borough) and Birmingham also declared that they could not accept any more immigrants. There was also hostile reaction from sections of the press and public. But eventually the Conservative government accepted that it had responsibility for those with British passports. Plans were also laid to divide the refugees among different Commonwealth countries, the United States and Europe. Eventually around 29,000 came to the UK, 10,000 or more returned to India, Canada accepted 8,000 (mainly Ismailis), Europe about 6,000, the USA took around 3,000 and Pakistan 2,000, while Malawi, Australia and New Zealand all took small numbers. Some of these were airlifted out, while the Indian government transported its quotas in closed trains to Kenya for processing. When Amin's deadline was reached only 2,000 Asians remained in Uganda – a tragic end to a community who had made such a contribution to the evolution of the country and had often, like the Ismailis, been deeply committed to it as home.

Many of these refugees left with little or virtually nothing: although their assets were thought to be worth between £100 million and £150 million, they were only allowed to bring out £50 each. Resettlement was partly a matter of self-help, and partly the work of governments and charitable and religious organisations. In the USA the resettlement work was largely done by five voluntary agencies, such as the Tolstoy Foundation, which resettled refugees in South Carolina, where their skills were welcomed by local businesses, and their small numbers and middle class status made them welcome neighbours socially.[26] Britain set up a Uganda Resettlement Board which housed many in special centres, staffed by

[26] E. F. Strizhek, 'The Ugandan Asian expulsion: resettlement in the USA', *Journal of Refugee Studies*, Vol. 6, No. 3, 1993, pp. 260–264.

charity volunteers, when they first arrived. Although the government's policy was to disperse the refugees so that they were encouraged away from areas where there was already pressure on employment, housing and schools and social services, in practice many (probably around 60 per cent) gravitated to those areas because there were already Asian communities there and often kin who had migrated before the final crisis. The result was a high concentration of East African Asians in London and Leicester in particular. However, despite the fears of local people and their elected local authorities, and the political protests by some sections of the press and politicians, it was clear that this was a distinctive strand of migration, very different in kind from that of the unskilled Pakistanis and Bangladeshis who had arrived in the 1950s and 1960s. The East African Asian migration was familial in type, rather than being male pioneer and chain immigration. Further, those who came had significant resources either of wealth or of experience and skill. Some had managed to bring out capital before the final crisis. But all of them were comparatively well educated and had been in a range of jobs such as commerce, government service, teaching and artisanal trades. What was also striking was that the women were also well educated and used to paid work outside the home as nurses, teachers and secretaries. Of men who came to Britain 77 per cent were fluent or fairly fluent in English, as were 57 per cent of women. Over the years that followed it became clear that they had put these resources to good effect and that even if they had had to take comparative lowly jobs immediately after their arrival, many became upwardly mobile, moving into their own homes, encouraging their children to high educational standards, and becoming self-employed or professional rather than manual workers.[27]

Very soon after this forced migration from a former area of British imperial rule, another occurred in part of the former Dutch empire, Surinam, formerly Dutch Guiana. Here, too, as to so many Caribbean colonies, Indian indentured labourers had gone between 1873 and 1917. Although probably one-third returned to India when their indentures expired, there remained a sizeable South Asian population – nearly 40 per cent of the total. But as independence neared (1975) there was a mass migration of about half the population of 'Hindustanis' to the Netherlands, for fear of Creole domination. By 1987 as many as 94,000 Indians

[27] V. Marett, 'Resettlement of Ugandan Asians in Leicester', *Journal of Refugee Studies*, Vol. 6, No. 3, 1993, pp. 248–259; V. Robinson, 'Marching into the middle classes? The long-term resettlement of East African Asians in the UK', *Journal of Refugee Studies*, Vol. 6, No. 3, 1993, pp. 230–247. See also a case study of ex-East African Sikhs in Southall by P. Bhachu, *Twice Migrants. East African Sikh Settlers in Britain* (London and New York, Tavistock Publications, 1985).

are thought to have migrated to the Netherlands from Surinam.[28] Finally at the end of the century there was a further significant movement of twice-migrants from a former British colony where Indians had gone as indentured labourers – Fiji. Here again ethnic conflict as a result of colonial migrations was at the root of Indian flight. Even before independence from the British in 1970 it was clear that there was acute tension between the native Fijians and the Indian population, with the Indians just outnumbering Fijians as a percentage of the population. Because of colonial land policies Indians at independence owned very little land, and had leased land on which to grow sugar, as well as moving into other sectors of the economy. They were also poorly represented in the police and military and at the top levels of the civil administration. Although the vast majority had taken Fijian citizenship, they were fearful of their political and constitutional future. These fears were fulfilled by a military coup in 1987 and an attempted coup in 2000, both of which were accompanied by widespread violence against Indians and their property. This prompted a mass emigration of Indians from Fiji, to Australia and New Zealand and even further afield to the USA and Canada. By the end of the century about 40,000 were living in Australia alone. Like the Asians from East Africa, they tended to be fluent English speakers, and comparatively well educated and skilled; and many went into white collar work or have subsequently become self-employed. They also have been part of broad family movements, with relatives sponsoring successive waves of migrants.[29] The onward migration of so many Fijian Indians is an aspect of decolonisation, in part reflecting the movements of people in an imperial world. At the same time it has helped to fashion a new post-imperial world. Like the forced migration of East African Indians, these migration flows have contributed to new patterns of globalization. These groups of 'twice-migrants' are now part of genuinely global, transnational families, as relatives have spread across the world, binding together Europe, north America and Australasia with new kinship networks.

The lure of the Middle East

The later twentieth-century movement of South Asians into the Middle East is an aspect of yet another facet of globalisation – the development of

[28] C. J. G. van der Burg, 'The Hindu diaspora in the Netherlands: halfway between local structures and global ideologies', K. A. Jacobsen and P. P. Kumar (eds.), *South Asians in the Diaspora. Histories and Religious Traditions* (Leiden and Boston, Brill, 2004), pp. 97–115.

[29] C. Voigt-Graf, 'Indians at home in the Antipodes', chapter 7 of B. Parekh, G. Singh and S. Vertovec (eds.), *Culture and Economy in the Indian Diaspora* (London and New York, Routledge, 2003); B. V. Lal, (ed.), *Bittersweet the Indo-Fijian Experience*, (Canberra, Australian National University, Pandanus Books, 2004) chapters 18 and 19.

a world economy dependent on international flows of labour of different kinds. From the 1970s the oil-producing nations of the Middle East have experienced a major economic boom as their energy resource has been urgently needed throughout the world to fuel transport and industry and has risen dramatically in price. As a result they have become capital rich but labour scarce: their own populations are comparatively sparce, they are in general averse to lowly forms of labour, and are not technically trained in any numbers. The oil industry and the development of the infrastructure of the Gulf States and their increasingly prosperous societies demanded the import of large amounts of foreign labour. By 1975 they were finding that they could no longer recruit enough labour from their neighbouring Arab countries such as Egypt, Jordan and Yemen, which had originally plugged the gap. From then South Asians began to come in, in significant numbers, recruited by relatives and private recruiting agents, and encouraged by their own governments, particularly those of Pakistan and Bangladesh, which saw the extent to which workers' remittances could prop up fragile South Asian economies. (At this stage all three of the main South Asian countries were struggling with rising populations, low national incomes, and the juxtaposition of traditional forms of agriculture with sluggish industrialisation.) Pakistan and Bangladesh not only set up recruiting agencies to market their labour force, but also educational and training courses for workers aspiring to work in the Gulf. In 1980 the non-national workforce in the Gulf had reached 2.2 million and by 1985 5.1 million. Indians and Pakistanis dominated the movement of labour out of Asia in the 1970s but in the 1980s more were recruited from Bangladesh, Sri Lanka and the Far East. In 1975 people from India and Pakistan accounted for just over 97 per cent of the 93,100 who left for the Middle East. From 1980 these countries produced one-quarter to one-third of the growing outflow. By contrast the Far East was becoming the major supplier, with up to 57.7 per cent of the flow in 1987, while the share of Bangladesh and Sri Lanka in the supply grew steadily to produce nearly a quarter by the last decade of the century. Even the Gulf War of 1992 and the fear that migrant workers might all have to be repatriated did not stem the longer-term flow.

The early migrants from Pakistan and India tended to go into the construction industry in roles ranging from engineers, managers and accountants, to mechanics, cooks and labourers. By the 1980s 42.5 per cent of Pakistanis were unskilled labourers, 40.6 per cent were skilled labourers, and the rest were professionals or in various types of service, who had advanced themselves compared with their original employment in construction. Among Indians at the same time there were initially similar figures for the unskilled but a growing percentage of skilled workers, white collar and high skill workers, and business people: their main destinations were Saudi Arabia, The United Arab Emirates and Oman. This outflow from South Asia certainly did not constitute a 'brain drain'. Evidence from India suggests that the migrants came from many different areas of the country, but that probably between 40 per cent and 50 per cent came from Kerala, a state on the south western coast with an unusually large population of Muslims and Christians. A significant majority of Indian migrants were Muslims (as of course were Pakistanis and Bangladeshis), Christians made up as much as a quarter, while Hindus were a small minority. This was unsurprising given the dominant Muslim culture of the Middle East. Demographically this flow of South Asians was distinctive. Most were young unmarried males, and there were very few women among their number because there was little employment for women in the region, and the objective of most male migrants was to earn high wages, save as much as possible for remittance back to South Asia, and eventually to return home. Even had they wished to remain they would have found it almost impossible to gain local citizenship. So despite the consistently high numbers of South Asians in the Gulf, this was not a settled diaspora as in the UK, where family reunions led to the growth of a locally born South Asian community, but one which was constantly replenishing itself with new migrants who knew they would be temporary workers.[30]

The movement of the skilled

The final large-scale international movement of South Asians in the later part of the twentieth century occurred as countries which had once barred their doors to people of non-European descent now opened them – particularly Australia, New Zealand, Canada and the USA. This enabled the entry of many thousands from the subcontinent, particularly the skilled and well educated. The emphasis on education and skill favoured Indians rather than Pakistanis and Bangladeshis, because of the standard and availability of education in India, and within India it favoured those areas and groups with access to higher education. Of course there are still many millions in India with little or no formal education, but at the apex of the educational triangle there are universities, colleges and latterly technology training institutes which produce men and women with

[30] On the South Asian migration to the Gulf see M. I. Abella, 'Asian migrant and contract workers in the Middle East', in Cohen (ed.), *The Cambridge Survey of World Migration*, pp. 418–423; P. C. Jain, 'Culture and economy in an 'incipient' diaspora: Indians in the Persian Gulf region', chapter 5 of Parekh, Singh and Vertovec (eds.), *Culture and Economy in the Indian Diaspora*; B. Knerr, 'South Asian countries as competitors on the world labour market', chapter 8 of Clarke, Peach and Vertovec (eds.), *South Asians Overseas*.

internationally desirable qualifications. As such new doors have opened it has also enabled the onward migration of some who had originally made their homes in the UK, for example, and had now improved the skill levels of either themselves or their children and were looking for new opportunities.

New Zealand dismantled the immigration restrictions dating from the end of the previous century in 1986, and opened the way for people to make applications for entry based on skills and qualifications. In the decade before only about 8,000 Indians lived in New Zealand, but by the end of the century the number had risen to over 42,500. This was made up of people born in India, in Fiji (who had migrated for a second time), and the generation born in New Zealand itself. The nature of the Indian community greatly diversified in the process, as those coming direct from India as professionals of various kinds originated in many areas of India, compared with the pre-1970s Indian population which was heavily Gujarati.

In Australia a 'white Australia' policy dating from 1901 had shut the door to new migration from the subcontinent until the 1960s. After that immigration was regulated by skills offered, and the Indian population increased significantly, drawing migrants directly from India, and twice-migrants from Fiji, Malaysia, Singapore and other countries. Some were even three times migrants by the time they reached Australia, like one Punjabi who was born in Jullundur, original home to so many migrants, moved to Uganda in 1953 after completing higher education, and worked as a teacher until he was forced to flee to the UK. He trained as a teacher while in Britain and a year later, in 1974, moved to Australia.[31] By the start of the new millennium there were probably rather more than 200,000 Indians in Australia, just above 1 per cent of the population, very similar to the proportion of Indians in New Zealand. Of the Australian Indians just under half were born in India. Two areas in particular have provided the new flows of first-time Indian migrants into Australia – Punjab, through a network of staff and students from the Punjab Agricultural University in Ludhiana, and latterly Karnataka, the Indian state in which is located the thriving modern city of Bangalore, the training ground for some of India's brightest information technology (IT) professionals. The latter have done particularly well in Australia and many of them hope to use the country as a base from which to move to the USA or to return to a career in India. India at the end of the last century had abandoned its older socialist-inspired policies which had stifled economic growth and now encouraged private investment and entrepreneurship, leading to the

[31] Voigt-Graf, 'Indians at home in the Antipodes', in Parekh, Singh and Vertovec (eds.), *Culture and Economy in the Indian Diaspora*, p. 149.

growth of a large and vibrant professional middle class who enjoyed a lifestyle previously unheard of in India. In 1996 nearly 75 per cent of migrants from Karnataka in Australia held higher qualifications, closely followed by Punjabi migrants with a figure of just over 71 per cent. (By contrast, only 47.5 per cent of those who moved from Fiji had higher qualifications.) However, the Punjabis have not done as well as those from Karnataka and many have become train guards, taxi drivers or postal workers. Indo-Fijians by contrast have tended to be self-employed, often opening ethnic shops which cater for an Indian clientele by selling spices, Indian clothes or lending Indian videos. A final category of South Asians in Australia by the end of the century were the large numbers of Indian students – about 10,000 in 1999. Australia has worked hard to attract over a quarter of the Indian market of students wishing to study abroad. The levels of fees, living costs and visa regulations have all made Australia attractive as well as the quality of education on offer. Students are permitted to work in vacations and for a substantial number of hours in term, which helps with finances. But more significant for longer term migration is the way that a student visa can easily open the way to permanent migration, as students have been permitted since 1999 to apply to live in Australia after they have finished their studies, and if they do so within six months they arc exempt from the normal visa requirement of skilled work experience.

The other two major destinations for South Asians, as immigration policies were relaxed to admit people with much-needed skills, were Canada and the USA. Canada modified its immigration rules in the 1960s and rapidly became the globe's second largest recipient of migrants from the third world. India became by the 1990s the fourth largest sending country. By the 2001 Census the South Asian immigrant population stood at 503,895 out of a total of nearly five and a half million immigrants. (Only the UK, southern Europe, and East Asia had sent more immigrants.) Those from South Asia came mainly after 1961 compared with the European migrants, from northern and southern Europe and the UK, whose numbers tailed off after 1961. South Asian immigrants numbered just 26,600 in the decade 1961–1970, but then the numbers accelerated rapidly – 77,230 in 1971–1980; 101,110 in 1981–1990; and 295,110 in 1991–2000. The visible South Asian minority (including the Canadian born) stood at 917,075 in 2001, making them the second largest visible minority in the country after the Chinese.[32] As the new immigration rules

[32] See the 2001 Census statistics available on the official Canadian statistics website, www.statcan.ca; also G. S. Basran and B. S. Bolaria, *The Sikhs in Canada. Migration, Race, Class and Gender* (New Delhi, Oxford University Press, 2003).

placed heavy emphasis on professional qualifications as well as character, the early migrants in this new stream from South Asia were highly qualified – in 1968–1972 nearly 43 per cent of Indians entering Canada were professionals. However the level of qualification tailed off markedly as more came in later in the category of sponsored relatives; in 1983–1984 only 1.5 per cent of new immigrants from India were professionals. Some of these later, less well-qualified incomers, were older parents, as the South Asian population included by 2001 a significant group of the over 65s, including over 16,000 who were over 75. The Sikh minority among the South Asians in particular did not have high levels of education and were mainly to be found in construction and transport. All South Asians tended to cluster in Ontario and British Columbia, particularly in the cities of Toronto and Vancouver.

The USA became the Mecca for aspiring emigrants from many places in the less-developed world when it, too, revised its immigration laws in 1965, abandoning the National Origins System set up in 1924. Under the new dispensation there were quotas for the eastern and western hemispheres with 50,000 more available to the eastern hemisphere. Further, encouragement was given to family reunions as, over and above the quotas for different areas, US citizens could bring in spouses, unmarried minor children and parents, while even those who had permanent residence only and not citizenship were given preference for the importation of spouses and children. The 'Green Card' enabling permanent residence and family migration became so desirable that it began to figure prominently in marriage advertisements in Indian Sunday newspapers, where families advertise for brides and grooms and lay down not only the desirable social and physical aspects of those they seek but the attributes of their own children who are available for marriage. The points system determining access to the USA took account of much-needed skills as well as existing relatives already in the country, and this again as in Canada and Australasia favoured those with higher education and professional standing.

The rise in the Asian American population from the later 1960s was dramatic, rising from *c.* 878,000 in 1960 to nearly 1.5 million in 1970, 3.5 million in 1980 and well over 7 million in 1990. By contrast, European migration into the USA was declining and by the 1980s was just over 11 per cent of the total. In the last decade of the century Indians with a population nearing 1 million were the fourth largest Asian group in the USA, coming after the Japanese, Filipinos, and Chinese. Not surprisingly, many of those entering the USA from India (or indirectly via East Africa for example) had higher education and were professionally well qualified, and they have continued to invest heavily in good education for their children. By the 1980s nearly all Indians, men and women, aged 25–29, had high school education, and almost two-thirds of young men and just over half of young women have completed four or more years of college education. Indian men and women also earned more than their white counterparts, and the most striking contrast was between the high levels of female incomes among Indian women compared with white women. Well over half of Indian males were professionals of some kind or working at an administrative or managerial level, with particularly high concentrations in engineering and medicine. At the start of the twenty-first century there were over 38,000 physicians of Indian origin in the USA, amounting to one in every twenty doctors practising medicine. Among those who were commercial entrepreneurs there was a high concentration in two areas which could be built up with low capital outlays and hard work by family members, thus favouring Indians – the hotel and petrol trades. Here Gujaratis were predominant, and given the common Gujarati surname, Patel, led to the joke, 'Hotel, Motel, Patel'. Towards the end of the twentieth century there were significant changes in the patterns of Indian migration. The explosion of the IT industry led to the influx of thousands of young IT experts from India, particularly from the south of the country, reflecting Indian investment in technical education through a series of prestigious Indian Institutes of Technology (IITs). Many of these clustered in Silicon Valley in California and did extraordinarily well financially. Clearly the levels of education and qualifications distinguish the American Indian immigrant pattern from many others who had left the subcontinent. This in part helps to explain the wide regional span of origins of Indians now living in the USA. Whereas in the history of many other migration flows out of the subcontinent there have been clear problems in the region of origin encouraging people to leave and try to fashion new lives abroad, the American pattern has been migration from regions of prosperity and high skill levels – including Maharashtra, Delhi, Gujarat, Andhra Pradesh and Tamil Nadu.[33]

By contrast some were by the end of the twentieth century finding it harder to enter and work in the USA, in part because of the tightening of security and visa controls after the catastrophe of '9/11' in 2001, when Muslim terrorists flew planes into the World Trade Centre in New York

[33] J. Lessinger, 'Indian immigrants in the United States: the emergence of a transnational population', chapter 8 of Parekh, Singh and Vertovec (eds.), *Culture and Economy in the Indian Diaspora*; R. Daniels, 'The Indian diaspora in the United States', chapter 4 of Brown and Foot (eds.), *Migration: The Asian Experience*. An account of Indian migration into the USA which focuses simply on 'success' is A. W. and U. M. Helweg, *An Immigrant Success Story. East Indians in America* (Philadelphia, University of Pennsylvania Press, 1990).

and the Pentagon, Washington DC. This clearly affected the ability of Indian doctors to enter the USA after medical training at home, unless their spouses held Green Cards. Further barriers were the elaborate and expensive procedures necessary to prove clinical skills before admission to a residency in a university or teaching hospital, which is the precondition of practising in the USA. By contrast, entry to practice medicine was far easier in the 1970s–1980s when foreign doctors were actively recruited to help support the Medicare system for health provision.[34] There was also evidence of serious problems experienced by Indian students anxious to study abroad as visas became more difficult to obtain. Such young people are natural recruits for the next generation of permanent immigrants and before '9/11' the USA had been the most preferred foreign country in which to study among South Asians.

However, not all Indians in America achieved 'the American dream', despite the high profile of the successful. There are considerable numbers in what would be called urban working-class jobs – taxi drivers, hotel and restaurant workers, factory workers, store clerks and the like. Such people are often poorly paid and lack the security of the professions or self-employment. Often they, too, have high levels of education and little in their backgrounds distinguishes them from those who go on to be successful. They seem often to have been slightly more provincial in origin or to have attended somewhat less prestigious colleges. Their numbers may also have been swelled by the opportunities for family reunification, as was the pattern visible in Canada, enabling relatives of lower skills to migrate to join their families. Poorer Indians can sometimes be found in rural areas such as the Punjabi orchard farmers of rural California, who grow peaches and kiwi fruit. They often arrived as unskilled people and have raised their economic status by hard manual work, which has over time lifted them out of welfare and even into the ranks of home-owners.[35]

*****

This descriptive chapter has provided fundamental information about the diverse flows of people out of the South Asian subcontinent since the early nineteenth century. On this basis we can begin in subsequent chapters to examine the tasks which have to be done once migrants have arrived in their new places of residence, as they set about creating for themselves new homes; for migration is an ongoing process which lasts

[34] S. Raymer, 'Doctors help fill US health care needs', *YaleGlobal Online*, Yale Center for the Study of Globalization, 16 Feburary 2004, www:yaleglobal.yale.edu.

[35] J. Lessinger, 'Indian immigrants in the United States', chapter 8 of Parekh, Singh and Vertovec (eds.), *Culture and Economy in the Indian Diaspora*; M. A. Gibson, 'Punjabi orchard farmers: an immigrant enclave in rural California', *International Migration Review*, Vol. 22, No. 1 (Spring 1988), pp. 28–50.

well beyond the journey to a new homeland. What the evidence presented here has suggested is the development of a truly global but very diverse South Asian diaspora by the start of the twenty-first century. The diversity includes regional and later national origins, language, social status, religious background, gender and kinship patterns, and available skills and resources. The diversity reflects and has its origins in the very different strands in the migratory movements. What unifies the diaspora is not just the fact of origin in a particular part of the world, and the assumptions, social structures and cultural patterns migrants often bring with them; but also the sense of being in some way still connected with South Asia as well as belonging to their new homelands. At the same time almost all of them are conscious of being global people in a way that was impossible for indentured labourers in the nineteenth century, for example, whose horizons were curtailed by illiteracy and the lack of mass communications. Many contemporary South Asians outside the subcontinent have travelled to different places where they have encountered other South Asians in the diaspora, or have heard about them or seen them through new forms of media. Perhaps most important of all many, particularly among the more educated, now belong to what are truly transnational families, with kin spread around the globe from South Asia through Europe, Australasia and north America as a result of the processes described here. A friend of mine in New Delhi, for example, sits at her computer and talks electronically to her daughters in Europe, New Zealand and Canada. I take a taxi in Calcutta and the driver, a Sikh patriarch himself far across the subcontinent from the Sikh homelands in the Punjab, tells me of his daughter married to a doctor in Vancouver.

Like many who will read this book the evidence of the range of the diaspora is present in many areas of my domestic and professional life. My local corner shop in an Oxford suburb is run by a Gujarati who reached England by way of East Africa. Near neighbours include a Gujarati doctor and a retired Bengali Professor of History. A distinguished graduate of my college, the son of a Gujarati who had gone to Tanganyika in the 1940s but left in 1968, has become one of Britain's youngest Queen's Counsels. A colleague is an Indian from Mauritius, with forebears there and in Natal; while another international colleague, now Professor of History at the Australian National University, is the grandson of an indentured labourer who travelled to Fiji at the turn of the twentieth century. My graduate seminars have at times included South Asians born in Britain, Trinidad, America, India and Pakistan. They are just a few examples of the extent and diversity of the South Asian diaspora in a global age.

3 Creating new homes and communities

This chapter turns from charting the histories of migratory movements among South Asians to the task of trying to understand the experience of these migrants in the places which were to become home at a very deep level of perception, alongside a sense of remaining connected to South Asia. The approach is thematic rather than portraying any total picture of the many and diverse diaspora groups which have developed over the last century and a half. It looks at crucial issues facing migrants as they have sought to create new homes and communities, put down roots in new countries, and raise new generations of offspring born outside the subcontinent. Much of the rich literature on particular groups in particular places to which readers may subsequently progress should then fall into place within this issue-orientated framework, rather than overwhelming them in its detail and diversity.

Before embarking on our analysis there are several preliminary observations which are important for a proper historical understanding of the diaspora experience. Although from the perspective of the start of the twenty-first century the many strands of the South Asian diaspora seem permanent and settled, for those who journeyed from the subcontinent this was rarely seen as a permanent departure, as a fundamental uprooting. For most of the first generation of migrants there remained a powerful 'myth of return', a vision of South Asia as the place to which one would eventually return after a sojourn abroad, as one's real and final home. This was as true of bewildered and desperate men and women who chose a contract of indenture in the nineteenth century as it was, for example, of ambitious rural folk in the mid-twentieth century who saw Britain as a source of work. Only gradually did this assumption about a final return give way among first generation migrants to a gradual acceptance of permanent migration, of learning to be at home abroad. This change of perspective grew with the birth of a new generation in the diaspora, the wish to give children the best prospects in life, and eventually a powerful urge to stay in old age nearer to children and grandchildren rather than return to a village or town thousands of miles away where much would have changed in the intervening years, and where there would be decreasing numbers of contemporary friends and family members. Symbolic of this growing sense of belonging to a new homeland was the decision among many South Asians in the diaspora to take the citizenship of their new country of abode. Among Muslims in particular another powerful sign of belonging in the new homeland was the decision to be buried or to bury one's loved ones outside South Asia. Earlier it had been the custom to send bodies rapidly back to South Asia for burial, often in family burial plots in a natal village; and for this reason burial societies had been some of the earliest organisations among Muslims in the diaspora.

Although the term diaspora is a useful shorthand to denote the complex processes described in the previous chapter, it is always important to remember that these resulted in no single South Asian community overseas, nor even in any one country of destination. Politicians and journalists often refer to ethnic and/or religious 'communities' when referring to South Asians but in every country where they settled they were highly differentiated rather than belonging to a homogenous and self-conscious community. In Britain alone South Asians are divided by country of origin, regional and linguistic background, and religion, as well as socio-economic status. Their senses of who they are in turn are formed by these differences and their distinctive experiences of living in Britain.[1] Moreover it is also important to remember that the phenomenon of migration and of creating a diaspora is not a single event, not just a matter of making the journey. It is an ongoing process that continues long after stepping off a boat or plane in a new country. Migrants confront a large number of new tasks if they are to establish new homes and social networks, to arrive at a new sense of identity and to feel at ease in the diaspora; and often these tasks have to be undertaken over more than one generation. We now turn to some of these key tasks as a way into understanding the dynamics of South Asian life in the diaspora.

1 Finding a place in the host economy and creating an economic base

The first and most fundamental task facing any South Asian migrant was the search for a means of livelihood. This meant that males as individuals or as heads of family groups had to look for paid work or self-employment.

[1] See discussions of identity in G. Baumann, *Contesting Culture. Discourses of Identity in Multi-ethnic London* (Cambridge, Cambridge University Press, 1996), which draws on evidence from Sikh experience in Southall, London; and more theoretically A. Brah, *Cartographies of Diaspora. Contesting Identities* (London and New York, Routledge, 1996).

Women in South Asia had always contributed fundamentally to the family economy in many ways, but paid work outside the home or the family farm was less usual and often felt as demeaning to family honour. Increasingly in the new situation abroad women also became involved in paid work of various kinds. For most migrants a primary motivation behind migration was economic improvement for self and family, whether they were indentured labourers travelling to sugar plantations or a later generation of highly skilled information technology (IT) workers moving to America. It is important to start our analysis with the business of finding a place in the host economy, not just because economic aspiration was at the root of these particular migratory movements, but also because any successful migration, leading to investment in a stable future in a new home, depends to a considerable extent on constructing an economic base. Work and the income flowing from it were the foundation for so much else which migrants desired – the establishment of homes, purchase of houses, education of children, investment in cultural and religious practices, and the building up of individual and family prestige and honour in the eyes of other migrants and often of relatives back in South Asia.

To understand the very diverse South Asian experience of attempting to establish themselves in host economies we have to recognise two very significant variables. In the first place, the nature of the host economies to which South Asians moved over this considerable period of time were very different. The indentured worker on a Caribbean plantation faced a very different situation from the Indian trader in East Africa at a similar time, or from the Pakistani who came to industrial northern England half a century later, or the Indian professional who sought a career in the USA or Canada at the end of the twentieth century. The different strands of the diaspora were established in economic situations which can broadly be categorised as agricultural, industrial and post-industrial. But the differences do not stop there. The host economies with which South Asians engaged were rarely static, and as they changed migrants also had to adapt in order to hold their own economically and to continue investing in their new lives. Sometimes radical change occurred in the life of one generation of earners, offering new opportunities or eroding the base they had first established for themselves. More often economic change occurred over a couple of generations, requiring the younger generation to strike out into new economic activities. A further important variable was the very different skills base and socio-economic standing of different groups of migrants. There was clearly a very close correlation between initial socio-economic status and skills at the time of migration and the degrees of success in the new home. This led to very different experiences and trajectories over time. Low-skilled labourers and their descendants took much longer to establish themselves and their families and to achieve upward mobility than did those possessing at the outset more education and capital of different kinds. This variable accounts for major differences in the experience of different groups going to the same country even at the same time, such as Indians, Pakistanis and Bangladeshis in the UK in the later twentieth century, as well as groups going to different places at very different times.

Different economic trajectories

It is perhaps helpful to offer initially a basic and very broad typology of the ways South Asian migrants tried to establish themselves economically in their new homes. Three distinctive types of economic trajectory are clear from the historical evidence. Each of these was the result of a particular outflow from the subcontinent to a particular receiving economy, where the possession at the outset of a distinctive resource and skills base interacted with the opportunities and challenges of different types of host economy, whether agricultural, industrial or post-industrial. The first trajectory was that of indentured labourers and their experience when their indentures ended. The second was that of South Asians who moved to post-war industrial Britain. The third was the experience of those who moved later to northern America and Australasia into complex, post-industrial economies. Such a typology does not of course cover the experience of all migrants from the subcontinent; for example, it does not include the Indians in colonial East Africa. However, it suggests the different kinds of economic situations but similar issues all faced as they became part of a global diaspora striving not only to establish itself outside the subcontinent but to achieve upward socio-economic mobility for themselves and their descendants.

The first type of trajectory was the hard one followed by indentured and contract labourers in the nineteenth and early twentieth centuries who went to the Caribbean, Natal and South East Asia and other plantation economies, equipped only with their physical capacity for hard agricultural work. What kind of life did they face once they had completed their indentures and contracts and were free to leave the harsh conditions of the barracks and the often cruelly regulated life of the plantations? The majority stayed in the places to which they had travelled, rather than returning to an even more uncertain future in India, and tackled the business of establishing themselves as free Indians. They had arrived with few skills and resources, given their backgrounds in India; and this left them with a very restricted base from which to make a new life post-indenture, as few had been able to increase their resources and skills in the years on the plantations.

In most places Indians moved off the plantations where they had been allocated as soon as they were free to do so. Where land was available, they began to set up homes and villages as independent agriculturalists, engaging in forms of free peasant agriculture. Where no land was available for purchase they would rent plots. Many engaged in their own small-scale agriculture while still working partly for their former masters on sugar plantations, but now as free paid labour. Trinidad was a prime example of a place where Indians started to own land, because of the colonial government's policy of selling Crown lands to them from 1869, or giving them lands in lieu of the passage back to India which was available at the end of indenture, in a policy of encouraging the growth of Indian villages. They grew food crops for themselves and for local sale, and also, more commercially, produced paddy, cane and cocoa. So came into being a settled, rural Indian community which no longer thought of itself as 'migrant' and resented this description. By the beginning of the twentieth century only just over 20 per cent of Indians still lived on the sugar estates, and less than 10 per cent were still indentured. Nearly half of the Indian population were by then born in Trinidad itself.[2] Similarly in Mauritius, ex-indentured labourers began to buy land and set themselves up in peasant cane farming. By the start of the twentieth century their presence had transformed the demography of the island and the large settled Indian population was over half the total population.[3] By contrast, in Fiji, land was not available for purchase because of the official policy of retaining lands in the ownership of native Fijians. The government also discouraged racially mixed settlements, so, as in Trinidad, the ex-indentured Indian population remained largely rural and isolated. Indians rented land, often from the major sugar companies, and grew cane and later rice. By the 1940s Indians occupied, but did not own, 94 per cent of the land under cane. Their numbers as a settled, permanent population also grew as they began to catch up with the existing native Fijian population.[4] In Natal, the trajectory of ex-indentured labourers and their children was more complex. Here, too, most preferred to stay when their indentures had ended, and by the late 1880s two-thirds of

[2] See B. Brereton, *A History of Modern Trinidad 1783–1962* (Kingston, Jamaica and London, Heinemann, 1981); C. G. Clarke, *East Indians in a West Indian Town. San Fernando, Trinidad, 1930–70* (London, Allen and Unwin, 1986).

[3] K. Hazareesingh, *History of Indians in Mauritius* (London and Basingstoke, MacMillan, revised ed., 1977).

[4] A. C. Mayer, *Peasants in the Pacific. A Study of Fiji Rural Society* (London, Routledge, 1988; reprinted and augmented 1961 edition).

Figure 1. A former indentured labourer in Fiji and his wife, taken c. 1960. He was the grandfather of Professor B.V. Lal (see Chapter 5) and came from the United Provinces district of Bahraich to Fiji in 1908 on a five-year indenture to work on the sugar plantations. He died in 1962, probably aged nearly 100.

Courtesy of Professor B. V. Lal

Figure 2. Indian workers on sugar plantations in Fiji, c. 1960. Free Indians were still working on sugar plantations into the second half of the twentieth century, in the employment of the Colonial Sugar Refining company, whose overseer stands in the photograph in a clearly dominant position.

Courtesy of Professor B. V. Lal

the Indian population were free men and women. Although they were vastly outnumbered by the local black African population, they rapidly overtook the white settler population, outnumbering them by 1904. In this situation white settlers tried to control Indian numbers by the imposition of a tax on ex-indentured labourers and their offspring, but this was abandoned in 1914. This encouraged free Indians to branch out into diverse sorts of agricultural pursuits – particularly cultivation of sugar cane, maize, beans, and tobacco, rearing cattle, goats and poultry, and increasingly market gardening on rented land to supply a complex industrialising economy. In the early twentieth century Indians in Natal were still predominantly rural, but this changed rapidly in subsequent decades as Indians took advantage of the multiple work opportunities offered by a rapidly developing economy and society; and by 1971 under 5 per cent of the Indian population was still involved in agriculture.[5] Contract

[5] B. Freund, *Insiders and Outsiders. The Indian Working Class of Durban, 1910–1990* (Portsmouth, NH, Pietermaritzburg and London, Heinemann, University of Natal Press and James Curry, 1995). The problems faced by Indians trying to establish themselves as a free community in the face of whites' fears and opposition was the context for Gandhi's

labour on the rubber plantations of South East Asia was a somewhat later phenomenon than indentured labour on sugar plantations, and here the importance of rubber kept Indians as plantation workers far longer. It was not until near the end of the century that they began to move off the plantations – many decades later than Indians had moved off the sugar plantations in so many places – and began to take up urban labouring and blue collar work. But often they were still at the base of the socio-economic scale and lived in squatter communities.[6]

The histories of Indians who had been indentured or contract labourers shows the great difficulties they faced in establishing themselves as free Indians and lifting themselves out of poverty, low status and often degradation imposed on them by their earlier conditions of work. In their experience their lack of skills and capital interacted with the external economic environment to limit their options. Almost everywhere the first step in this process of socio-economic settlement and self-improvement was a rural one as peasant farmers, and even where they succeeded in this enterprise, movement into urban areas and into business of various kinds and the professions came very much later. In Trinidad, for example, the earliest urban Indians tended to be a small elite of Christian converts for whom doors were opened by the education provided them in Christian mission schools. It was only in the second half of the twentieth century other Indians began to move into towns, as the history of San Fernando indicates, as milk vendors, stall-holders, labourers and shop-keepers, and later as professionals of different kinds.[7] The quickest trajectory towards upward mobility, urbanisation and economic diversification came in Natal, where Indians were quick to seize the particular opportunities of a neo-Europe, where there was a rapidly expanding and modernising economy. Those who had diversified into market gardening, particularly in the vicinity of Durban, were able to use this as a step towards urban work of various kinds. Towards the end of the twentieth century the free Indian peasantry was fast disappearing as Indians took up work in construction, transport, and services of many kinds. They were still predominantly a working class and would remain so during the apartheid era.[8]

In an interesting contrast, the other great outflow of low and unskilled South Asian labour in response to the needs of the international economy, that of labour into the Gulf area in the later twentieth century, did not

legal work and development of direct action at the turn of the twentieth century: see his *An Autobiography. The Story of My Experiments with Truth* (London, Jonathan Cape, 1966).

6 See R. K. Jain, 'Culture and economy. Tamils on the plantation frontier in Malaysia revisited, 1998–1999', chapter 3 of B. Parekh, G. Singh and S. Vertovec (eds.), *Culture and Economy in the Indian Diaspora* (London and New York, Routledge, 2003).

7 Clarke, *East Indians in a West Indian Town*.

8 Freund, *Insiders and Outsiders*.

lead to another permanent strand in the South Asian diaspora. Here, too, South Asians were vigorously recruited for their labour as the Gulf economies modernised on the back of profits from oil. But there was no permanent place for such migrants and no chance of upward social mobility because of local social attitudes and political policies as well as the nature of these host economies. Moreoever, modern modes of transport enabled contract workers to return home to South Asia with far greater ease than their indentured counterparts in the nineteenth century; while improved communications meant that they never lost touch with their homes and relatives.

It is helpful to portray as a particularly early and rural type of socio-economic trajectory this one, in which unskilled ex-indentured and contract labourers began to make their way in host economies, where opportunities were available for free rural workers. However, this leaves out those fairly small numbers of Indians who went at the same time to places in the British Empire as imperial auxiliaries in civil government and the security professions, as well as those 'passenger Indians' who penetrated the hinterlands of East and southern Africa as traders and shop keepers. For some, this was the foundation for permanent settlement and upward mobility in the professions and business, as in Hong Kong, for example. But for the majority this potential trajectory was cut short by politics. As the previous chapter showed, in the new polities of eastern Africa that emerged from the processes of decolonisation, Indians were either made to feel unwelcome or forcibly ejected, thus eroding the prospering urban Indian communities which had established themselves by the 1960s. Such people then became twice-migrants, forced to uproot themselves yet again. They became part of the second great type of socio-economic trajectory discernible among South Asians, those who strove to make good in the industrial economy of the UK in the mid to later twentieth century.

The trajectory of those who migrated to the UK from India and the new countries of Pakistan and Bangladesh in the decades after the Second World War was very different. Here again the differences in the host economy and the skills base and resources of migrants are crucial in understanding how South Asians have fared in Britain, compared with those whose migration began with indentured labour; they are also important in understanding the differences which have opened up between different groups of South Asians in Britain as they have established themselves in the British economy and society. Migrants into Britain were all free people, who chose to move in anticipation of socio-economic improvement for themselves and their families who were with them or still resident in South Asia. They were not from the base of rural society as indentured labourers had been, but often from reasonably prosperous rural backgrounds in regions where for different reasons agricultural prospects were being curtailed. They had to pay their own fares and find work for themselves, reflecting the possession not only of some capital and credit but also a broad and dynamic world view which saw international migration as a possible option for individuals and families. Some were also professionals such as doctors who had educational and personal links with Britain. The number of those with good education, professional qualifications and other non-labouring skills was greatly enhanced by the arrival of East African Indians in the late 1960s and early 1970s, as shown in the previous chapter. South Asians arrived in a Britain which was initially hungry for industrial labour in the processes of post-war reconstruction but which gradually slid into industrial decline from the 1970s, while offering other opportunities for those with entrepreneurial and professional skills and good levels of education. How South Asians fared in this changing economic situation was a complex process.

The earliest migrants' economic strategy was single male migration, often by related kin, and it was geared to sending home remittances rather than establishing permanent homes in the UK. Single males initially took whatever work was available, often informed of opportunities by kin and friends. Young men from Pakistan, for example, often went into industrial work in northern England and the Midlands, or into the clothing industry in northern England, which they had first penetrated as peddlers and market stall holders. Indians tended to go into more diverse occupations and industries, such as the Sikhs who gravitated towards the paper mills and engineering works in Gravesend, Kent, or those who went into the rubber and food manufacturing industries of west London. Gujaratis tended to have a more business orientation and to go into different types of business and self-employment. Single male migration was a temporary phase as the politics of immigration control persuaded South Asians from the early 1960s to bring their families over while this was still possible. However, the early phase had led to a particular geographical pattern of settlement which persisted right through the twentieth century. South Asians in Britain have become urban people, regardless of their origins in South Asia; and even at the start of the twenty-first century it is rare to see an ethnically South Asian person in the countryside, either as a resident or a visitor. Indians have concentrated in the south-east and the Midlands, with a high presence in suburban rather than inner London. Pakistanis are much less concentrated in London and are to be found prominently in the west Midlands and in the northern textile towns such as Manchester, Blackburn, Bradford and Leeds. Bangladeshis, by contrast are concentrated in inner London, and at the end of the twentieth century as many as a quarter of them lived in the one borough of Tower Hamlets.

In the half century since the first post-war arrivals gained a toe-hold in the British economy an increasingly large and self-perpetuating South Asian population has established itself in Britain. But the place of different groups of South Asians in the economy has begun to diverge widely, indicating varying patterns of success in establishing, maintaining and improving their economic base. In broad terms Indians have prospered the most, including those who came directly from India and particularly those who were later twice-migrants from Africa. Pakistanis have done less well, particularly where they have become stranded in declining industrial areas; while people from Bangladesh are among the poorest. Figures for 1991 indicate that Indians had the highest proportion of men in the top three socio-economic categories (professionals and white collar workers) and fewer in the categories of skilled manual, semi-skilled and unskilled compared with the other two groups, while Bangladeshis have by far the highest proportion of semi-skilled and unskilled males. Pakistanis occupy a middle position with a sizeable group of skilled manual men. Among Pakistanis and Bangladeshis there were also high levels of unemployment, double the national average, and very low female participation in the workforce.[9] Unemployment among males in these two groups did not only affect older men made redundant by economic change, but was worryingly high among young males in the 16–24 age group: among Pakistani men of that age, who should just be entering the workforce, nearly 41per cent were unemployed in 1991.[10] South Asians are now to be found in many more types of work than when they first arrived in the UK, particularly as the British-born and educated diversify their families' economic base. (Levels of educational achievement are clearly important here and again the British-educated Indians achieve higher standards than Pakistanis or Bangladeshis – an issue which will be considered in the next chapter. Higher educational achievement of course feeds into even greater Indian socio-economic success as it does in the experience of any social or ethnic group.) But there is still evidence of a strong South Asian presence in particular ethnic economic niches or enclaves which have sustained particular groups and enabled them to accumulate capital often to break out into wider economic activity. Notable are the Indian-run corner shops which are sustained by family labour, so-called 'Indian' ethnic restaurants which are often run by Sylhetis from Bangladesh, and

[9] See fig. 4.1 in A. H. Halsey and J. Webb (eds.), *Twentieth-Century British Social Trends* (Houndmills, London and New York, MacMillan and St. Martin's Press, 2000), p. 132. See also V. Robinson, 'Boom and gloom', chapter 12 of Clarke, Peach and Vertovec (eds.), *South Asians Overseas*.

[10] See M. Anwar, *Between Cultures. Continuity and Change in the Lives of Young Asians* (London and New York, Routledge, 1998), p. 60.

Figure 3. South Asian 'corner shop': Oxford. Typical of convenience stores of this type, selling 'Indian curries', spices, pickles, chutneys, and 'Home Made Samosas' as well as British foods: note also the provision of cheap international phone cards.
Author's photograph

the Pakistani-dominated garment industry of the north-west.[11] How long such enclaves will persist is another matter, given the rising standards of education among ethnic minorities and the aspirations of a younger generation to participate in the wider economy on equal terms with their white contemporaries.

What lay behind the broadly different economic experiences of these three groups of South Asians and the marked difference in their achievement of economic security and upward mobility? Their particular origins and the skills they brought with them were certainly significant. Indians, even from rural backgrounds, tended to come from more prosperous backgrounds in well-irrigated agricultural areas and consequently to have better educational standards and other skills. There were also significant numbers of Indian professionals, and their number was greatly increased when they were joined by Indians who fled from East Africa and brought

[11] See P. Werbner, 'Renewing an industrial past: British Pakistani entrepreneurship in Manchester', chapter 5 of J. M. Brown and R. Foot (eds.), *Migration: The Asian Experience* (Houndmills and London, MacMillan, 1994).

with them experience of urban residence and employment, high levels of education and literacy in English, and professional skills. By the end of the century Indians whose origins lay in East Africa accounted for about one-third of the total UK Indian population. Social attitudes and structures also had a profound influence on the capacity of different groups to adapt to life in England and to succeed in establishing an economic base. For example, attitudes to kinship, and particularly a preference for close kin and cousin marriage among some Pakistani Muslim groups, meant that their socio-economic focus was for a considerable time the home village in South Asia, and family reunion and investment in making good in the UK came later than for many non-Muslim Indian groups; while continuing marriage ties with the Pakistani home inhibited the development of well-educated, English-knowing family groups.[12] Particularly significant have been attitudes towards women's paid employment outside the home. This has been most unwelcome to Pakistanis and Bangladeshis from Muslim societies with particularly strict conventions about appropriate female behaviour and appearance in public. Hindus and Sikhs are much more accepting of women working in a range of paid employment, as they have increasingly been in India itself; and women's incomes have consequently contributed to family capital and the capacity to invest in many of the strategies of upward mobility such as home-buying and education, as well as disposable goods. By the end of the twentieth century over half (53 per cent) of all Indian women aged 16 and over were in the formal workforce, while the figures for Pakistani women (27 per cent) and Bangladeshis (22 per cent) were far lower. East African women had a particularly strong tradition of non-manual labour, reflecting their high levels of education. But many other less educated Indian women also slotted easily into the British workforce.[13] As a result of this pattern of increasing paid employment Indian women have also on occasion found themselves at the forefront of major industrial disputes, in contrast to the popular image of South Asian women as meek and submissive. The

12 See particularly the work of Roger Ballard, who has explored the ongoing implications of differences in marriage patterns between people even from the one broad area of the Punjab, Sikhs from Jullunder (India) and Muslims from Mirpur (Pakistan). See his 'Migration and kinship: the differential effect of marriage rules on the processes of Punjabi migration to Britain', chapter 10 of Clarke, Peach and Vertovec (eds.), *South Asians Overseas*.

13 Halsey and Webb (eds.), *Twentieth-Century British Social Trends*, p. 154; P. Bhachu, 'New cultural forms and transnational South Asian women: culture, class, and consumption among British South Asian women in the diaspora', chapter 9 of P. van der Veer (ed.), *Nation and Migration. The Politics of Space in the South Asian Diaspora* (Philadelphia, University of Pennsylvania Press, 1995).

first of these was the famous Grunwick strike which lasted a whole year from August 1976 to August 1977, as workers, who were mainly Indian women from East Africa, protested against their working conditions and to win recognition for unionisation at the Grunwick photo processing laboratories in the London borough of Brent. More recently, many of the employees of a catering company, Gate Gourmet, providing airline meals for British Airways, who went on strike in protest against their treatment in 2005 were Sikh women alongside their menfolk, and it was the ties of South Asian kinship that brought out many other airport workers in protest, causing the national airline to lose millions of pounds as its planes were grounded.

Although it is possible to describe broadly different socio-economic trajectories of the three groups of different national origin among British South Asians, it is important to note that over time and the emergence of a second and third generation of those who are British-born, there has been increasing differentiation and polarisation within each group. The incidence of unemployment, particularly among Pakistanis and Bangladeshis, has pulled down some families, while others have steadily bettered their position by paid work, increasingly self-employment, and rising educational levels in the younger generations. At the most successful end of the spectrum some South Asians, particularly Indians, have done very well through participation in such professions as medicine, accountancy and law, and particularly in business. The so-called 'Asian Rich List', prepared each year by an Asian radio station in the UK, gives some insight into those South Asians who made it right to the top in financial terms. In 2004 the combined wealth of the top 300 was £14.3 billion, a figure which was £6 billion more than in the previous year. The two biggest sectors in which such wealth was generated were fashion (41) and food (33), although the really huge wealth was generated by industrialists in sectors such as steel. Of these really rich, 10 per cent had come as refugees from Amin's Uganda or Kenya. Many of those listed were comparatively young – with 53 under 40 years old and three under 30; while 25 were women, three of them in their own right and 22 as partners of family members. (Several women made their fortunes through the provision of ready-made Indian foods, such as the Patak brand, though in 2005 one new entrant had made her wealth through the travel industry.) Hindus topped the 2005 Rich List, with Lakshmi Mittal, the steel magnate, coming in top for the fifth successive year, worth £13.5 billion. He was born in Rajasthan into a steel-making family, struck out on his own in his thirties, and at the age of 54 in 2005 had become not only the richest Asian in the UK but the third richest person in the world, riding on the back of rising world prices for steel and a strategy of global acquisition of steel mills.[14]

The third broad pattern of socio-economic establishment by South Asians in the diaspora can be seen in the last decades of the twentieth century and beyond. Here again both the nature of the migrants and the type of economy they encountered was crucial. Those who migrated in this much later phase were almost all Indians directly from India or from other places where there were existing diasporic communities, such as Fiji or the UK. Immigration policies in the USA, Canada, Australia and New Zealand meant that most of these migrants were highly skilled or were family members of existing migrants, and this favoured Indians rather than people from other parts of South Asia. By contrast with Britain, where primary immigration stopped by the 1970s, in this later phase immigration continued by new individuals and families, with the result that far more were India-born, first-generation immigrants than in Britain or of course in the diaspora communities resulting from nineteenth century labour migrations. Later migrants entered complex modern economies which can be called post-industrial, where the work opportunities were more likely to be in the professions and various service industries rather than in heavy industries of the sort which had originally attracted many South Asians to Britain. Not surprisingly Indians in all these countries tend to be heavily urban in their patterns of residence – Sydney in Australia, the urban East Coast in the USA, Toronto and Vancouver in Canada. Unlike the first South Asian migrants to Britain, many of them had professional qualifications before they arrived and often went straight into the professions; where this was not the case their children did. By 1987, 78 per cent of Indian men and 53 per cent of Indian women in America held college degrees. Not surprisingly, by the last two decades of the century, Indian men were earning more than their white counterparts, as were Indian women. Over two-fifths of Indian male professionals were engineers and over a quarter doctors; while among Indian women professionals over three-fifths were in health-related occupations. As the IT industry boomed at the end of the century young men and women from South India entered the USA in large numbers, working particularly in California, forming another professional strand in the diaspora in the USA. Indians were also prominent in certain areas of business, and the number of Indian businesses escalated in the 1980s. Among them were Indian restaurants, motels and petrol stations, and stores supplying

[14] The Asian Rich Lists are available on the internet by subscription; but brief analyses of them can be found on the South Asian website, www.redhotcurry.com.

Indian goods to the diaspora population, all of which allowed migrants to draw advantage from family solidarity and labour in the same way as the corner shop had in Britain from the 1960s. It is thought that nearly 30 per cent of the country's hotels and motels are operated by Indians, and a higher percentage of petrol stations in some areas of the East Coast.[15]

Although the success of Indian migrants in the late post-industrial economies of the later twentieth century is well documented, as is the experience of those who settled earlier in Britain, there was some differentiation in the migrants' trajectories over time, and it must be remembered that some Indians never achieved professional status or the wealth which enabled social investment for the next generation. Evidence from America and Australia suggests that there is a sizeable group of less fortunate Indians who work extremely hard in more lowly service jobs and essentially form an immigrant working class, particularly in the larger towns and cities, and do not share the trajectory of growing qualifications and prosperity so publicly lauded by their more fortunate fellow immigrants. Probably many of these arrived as relatives of existing immigrants, rather than on the strength of their own qualifications: one group who fall clearly into this category are Sikh fruit farmers in rural California, who arrived without any of the skills that distinguished most of their compatriots. But even some with considerable education still find it hard to break into the professional or business world.[16] It is clear that even where a post-industrial society offers great opportunities to Indians with much-needed skills, the route of migration is never an easy one, and creating a stable economic base for oneself and one's children, on which to build a new life in the diaspora, still takes much thought, commitment and hard work.

2 Constructing social networks

While the establishment of an economic base is essential for migrants, a parallel task is the construction of a range of social networks which enable

[15] Daniels, 'The Indian diaspora in the United States', chapter 4 of Brown and Foot (eds.), *Migration. The Asian Experience*; A. W. Helweg and U. M. Helweg, *An Immigrant Success Story. East Indians in America* (Philadelphia, University of Pennsylvania Press, 1990); M. S. Khandelwal, 'Indian immigrants in Queens, New York City; patterns of spacial concentration and distribution, 1965–1990', chapter 7 of Van der Veer (ed.), *Nation and Migration*.

[16] See C. Voigt-Graf, 'Indians at home in the Antipodes' and J. Lessinger, 'Indian immigrants in the United States: the emergence of a transnational population', chapters 7 and 8 of B. Parekh, G. Singh and S. Vertovec (eds.), *Culture and Economy in the Indian Diaspora* (London and New York, Routledge, 2003). A case study of a rural working class Indian group in America is M. A. Gibson, 'Punjabi orchard farmers: an immigrant enclave in rural California', *International Migration Review*, Vol. 22, No. 1 (Spring 1988), pp. 28–50.

comfortable individual and family life. This task of social construction is vital if the new place of residence is to become home at any deep emotional level, rather than just a place of transient residence as it was for the bachelor South Asians who first came to Britain and lived in spartan boarding houses which were little more than places to sleep and eat. This was particularly important in the longer term for migrants from the subcontinent, for they came from societies which placed great importance on extended ties of family and kinship as essential to maintaining a good and honourable life. Of course this social commitment to family and kin was not peculiar to people from South Asia, although among Hindus the notion of caste reinforced kinship networks in a unique way, and the extent to which this persisted outside India will concern us later. However, this familial orientation, embedded in social experience and ideological assumptions, did mark out South Asians socially, particularly when they moved into societies where many older social networks and loyalties had been eroded among the existing population by processes of industrialisation, urbanisation and individual spatial and social mobility, and where family size had begun to drop markedly as a result of women's growing levels of education and paid work and the choices enabled by contraception.

Given these assumptions about the essential nature of family and kin ties it is not surprising that migrants invested heavily – in material and emotional terms – in rebuilding and maintaining kinship networks on arrival in the places they were to make their homes. For those who left the subcontinent under indenture or contract the problems involved in such a project were immense. Indentured labourers often left as individuals rather than as married people or family groups. On arrival life in plantation barracks was cruelly disruptive of any existing relationships between men and women, while the small numbers of women compared with men militated against stable, monogamous unions. However, as soon as they left the restrictions and abnormal social conditions of indenture Indians began to reconstruct family life, drawing as far as possible on what they remembered of family relations in India, particularly the patriarchal family where wives and daughters are carefully monitored and controlled, and senior men make crucial social and economic decisions. Over time the growth in the number of women and girls and the emergence of a more even sex ratio in the emerging free Indian populations, often only by the twentieth century, enabled the growth of stable marriages and families. In some places, such as Trinidad, the efforts of Christian missionaries reinforced this process, and they tried to train girls who came into their educational institutions to be what they conceived as good wives and mothers. By contrast immigration patterns and laws in the later twentieth century were more favourable to family reconstruction. The early chain migrations of related males into Britain in search of work strengthened kinship ties, and subsequently immigration controls quickened the pace of family reunions, leading to the rapid expansion of the female migrant population. As soon as women arrived in the UK with existing children and began bearing British-born children there was a marked change in immigrant life and the re-establishment of South Asian family norms and relationships.[17] Later still, as Indians migrated to north America and Australasia at the end of the century, family preference immigration regulations reinforced family ties in the new homeland.

There were several distinctive aspects of South Asian family life, reflecting life on the subcontinent. One was the assumption of male dominance over female family members, particularly strong where migrants were closest to more traditional village life in South Asia, and also among Muslims, but persistent even among highly educated Indians in America, for example. (More will be said about this later when we consider the strains on close social relations caused by migration.) Another was the assumption of marriage as the norm for all South Asians, and an abhorrence of divorce. The latter expectation of stable and lifelong marriage is embedded in South Asia's religious traditions, as it is in Christianity, but it also reflects the investment in socially significant marriage networks, considered later. Divorce in such situations disrupts not only individual lives but far wider circles of kin and friends, leading to personal distress, the breakdown of important social connections and the erosion of family prestige. Even where migrants have over several generations lived in societies where numbers of people in the host population remain unmarried for all or long stretches of their lives, and where marriages often end in divorce, South Asian patterns persist. At the end of the twentieth century among South Asians in the UK, for example, there is a far higher proportion of households containing married couples than among the white population; and cohabiting persons, one-parent families and single households are most uncommon among South Asians. By contrast in British society generally the number of single person households is rising sharply and has (in 2005) reached 48 per cent of the total adult population. In America the South Asian commitment to family life is clear: over 90 per cent of Indian households contain both husband and wife, and over 90 per cent of all Indian children under 18 live in two-parent families.

[17] An excellent description of this process is found in A. W. Helweg's study of Sikhs in Gravesend, *Sikhs in England. The Development of a Migrant Community* (Delhi, Oxford University Press, 1979), chapter 5.

Finally there is the question of family size – which involves both the number of people in a household and the number of children born to each couple. In South Asia family groups have tended to be far larger than in the contemporary western world. Not only have women had many more children – partly for sound economic reasons in an environment where children are security for the continuation of the family and for parents in old age, and partly because of lack of knowledge about contraception. Families have also tended not to be nuclear but to be extended to incorporate significant numbers of family members on a temporary or permanent basis. Much scholarship has been devoted to the nature of the so-called joint family in India and the various forms it has taken, but in practical terms most South Asians in the subcontinent until very recently in urban areas have not lived in nuclear family groups consisting solely of parents and children. Some of these trends persist in the diaspora, particularly in areas such as Trinidad where Indians were rural people for such a long time, and socially isolated from the rest of society.

Where South Asians have had to adapt to living in societies moulded by western norms and economic situations there are obvious changes. South Asian women have tended to have more children than their white counterparts in the UK, though the numbers per woman have dropped as educational levels have risen. This is most marked among Indian women, whereas women of Pakistani and Bangladeshi origin still tend to have more children than their white contemporaries. In America, where levels of female education and skilled employment are particularly high, Indian women have fewer children than the national average. Household size is also increased by the presence of grandparents and non-nuclear kin, either on a permanent or temporary basis. Among wealthier South Asians there is developing the phenomenon of peripatetic grandparents, who travel between their children's households in the worldwide diaspora for visits and to help out as further grandchildren are born. Where houses are small, as in the UK, family arrangements lead migrants to invest in neighbouring houses so that close kin and family members can stay physically close together. The broad pattern is that the higher the levels of education, the lower the family size and the more likely the family is to be the nuclear group. Again, to take the well-documented UK example, in the 1990s the average household size was 2.4 people, that of Indian households 3.8, while Pakistani households averaged 4.8 and Bangladeshi households 5.3.[18]

In the maintenance of preferred family structures and the establishment of more extended social networks residential patterns are also very

[18] Halsey and Webb (eds.), *Twentieth-Century British Social Trends*, p. 154.

important. Almost everywhere in the diaspora South Asians have settled near kin and others from their regions of origin, in a similar way to patterns of urbanisation on the subcontinent itself, when work opportunities and existing kinship ties led groups from the same place and social group to settle near to each other when they moved into towns. This preference in the diaspora has generated ethnic areas or enclaves, where distinctive linguistic and social groups cluster together, rather than areas which are pan-South Asian, including people of different national, linguistic and religious backgrounds.

Such clustering occurred where South Asians were primarily rural folk, coming off the plantations where they had initially worked, and taking up the opportunities of agriculture, as in Trinidad or Natal. It was equally clear where South Asians were urban people, whether in colonial East Africa, the UK, North America or Australia. In East Africa Indians in the professions and business tended to cluster residentially in urban areas, often bound together by a particular regional and linguistic connection originating in the subcontinent. Goans in Kampala, for example, clustered together, feeling distinct from other Indians, as they came from a very distinctive area of India under Portuguese control, and worked mainly in government and different kinds of services, whereas many other Indians in the region were Gujarati Hindus in businesses.[19] It is not surprising that Indians forced to leave Africa in the 1960s and 1970s headed mainly for towns and cities in the UK where they had existing social connections, even when government policy was to disperse them. First-time migrants direct from the subcontinent to the UK also chose to live in ethnic enclaves. The broad pattern of South Asian settlement in Britain has already been noted in the discussion of the impact of work opportunities on migrant settlement. But within these broad patterns, smaller sub-groups of people linked by regional background and often extended kinship have chosen to live close together, often replicating some of the features of life brought from the subcontinent. Case studies of groups of Pakistanis in Manchester and Oxford, of Sikhs in Gravesend and Southall, London, or of Gujarati Jains in Leicester, have shown the distinctive ties which bind particular small groups together in the diaspora.[20] A study

[19] See J. Kuper, 'The Goan community in Kampala', chapter 4 of M. Twaddle, *Expulsion of a Minority. Essays on Ugandan Asians* (London, Athlone Press, 1975).

[20] See, for example, A. Shaw's excellent extended study of Pakistani families in Oxford, *Kinship and Continuity. Pakistani Families in Britain* (Amsterdam, Harwood Academic Publishers, 2000). Another study shows how Christian Pakistanis in the British city of Bristol deliberately chose to settle where there were few other Pakistanis, seeing themselves as a distinctive social and religious group, and have few ties with those Muslim Pakistanis who also live in the city. P. Jeffery, *Migrants and Refugees. Muslim and Christian Families in Bristol* (Cambridge, Cambridge University Press, 1976).

Figure 4. South Asian shops in the ethnic enclave of Southall, West London.

Courtesy of Peter J. Diggle

of the district of Queens in New York City has shown how in the 1970s Indians effectively refashioned the area, making it their own urban space, for residence, business and for religious observance. As in many inner-city areas in Britain where South Asians settled in tightly-knit groups, much of the pre-existing white population moved out over time, and where some older people stayed behind they tended to feel marooned and ill at ease.[21] Some movement out of ethnic enclaves is visible where South Asians have been established long enough for second and third generations to be born outside the subcontinent. As educational levels improve and children and grandchildren become socially and economically upwardly mobile, so they often wish or need to move to homes nearer their new types of work or to areas which reflect their new status. One most obvious pattern is where the children of owners of corner shops, on reaching adulthood, no longer wish to tie themselves to long hours in a service industry with little status, but break away spatially as well as economically from the family base which sustained their immigrant parents.

[21] M. S. Khandelwal, 'Indian immigrants in Queens, New York City: patterns of spatial concentration and distribution, 1965–1990', chapter 7 of Van der Veer (ed.), *Nation and Migration*.

Although opportunities for work often pulled immigrants to live in similar areas, the social and emotional benefits of living in an ethnic enclave were also considerable. Close clustering of people with similar lifestyles and expectations sustains particular ethnic consumption patterns, reconstructing a sense of home in daily life. Ethnic areas can support businesses which import and supply all manner of desired goods, from saris and salwar kameez, jewellery, kitchen implements, South Asian spices and other cooking ingredients, to travel agents specialising in travel to South Asia. Just as there are Chinatowns in many western cities, so many towns and cities have their roads and localities which are like shopping areas and markets in South Asia. (Ethnically South Asian restaurants, by contrast, tend to be in other parts of town as they cater almost exclusively for the wider population's taste and expectations of 'Indian food'.) Ethnic residential enclaves can also support specific cultural patterns whether in the use of leisure time or in the maintenance of religious patterns of observation – most obviously in the building of temples, mosques and *gurudwaras*, as we shall see later. At a deeper emotional level living near people like oneself gives immigrants social support and security, and they have often bought homes to reinforce this. In Britain where there has been a tradition of 'council housing' provided by local authorities for families who cannot afford their own homes, it is notable that Pakistanis and Indians have preferred to avoid this type of housing and have invested in home ownership as soon as possible, becoming home owners in higher proportion to their population than the white population. (By contrast less than half of all Bangladeshis own their own homes and their living conditions are the most cramped and poor.) Often housing available for purchase by immigrants is small and run-down, as in the case of the Victorian terrace housing stock bought by many British Pakistanis. But kin groups buy houses near each other where individual properties cannot contain large extended families, thus maintaining familial connections. So kinship reinforces ethnicity, religion and regional background, creating multiple and criss-crossing connections within ethnic residential enclaves. Residents can call on neighbours for support in all kinds of situations and crises, particularly where these are kinsfolk as well as residential neighbours. This is particularly important for women in communities where women have traditionally lived secluded lives, rarely venturing out into the public space, and for women who have little command of English. The ethnic residential enclave can to an extent provide safe and semi-domestic space for such women. Moreover, the presence of neighbourly and related women means they can help each other out, accompany each other on errands which imply exposure to a wider society, and draw on the linguistic services of children who through state schooling are acquiring a fluency in English.[22]

However there has been one incidence of forced residential clustering which was deeply disruptive to the domestic lives of South Asians involved – that produced by the 1950 Group Areas Act in South Africa which controlled Indians' lives until 1991. A study of Durban, where Indian descendants of indentured labourers were becoming a substantial working class by the middle of the century, shows how this act of racial segregation by the apartheid government set up official Indian areas. This forced segregation battered older Indian social networks and family life, uprooting Indians from areas where they had established themselves and built temples. Indians were increasingly divided by class, and older extended families were broken up as new houses were designed for nuclear families only.[23]

This brief discussion of South Asian patterns of settlement in the diaspora has begun to hint at the many types of social networks generated among migrants over time. It is worth contemplating some of these networks in more detail to begin to understand the richness of South Asian life in the diaspora, and the way in which migrants have constructed homes in the broadest physical, social and emotional meanings of this term. Although I shall sketch three types of network below, it must be remembered that often these intersect, reinforcing relationships and making them muti-dimensional. A cousin or brother/sister-in-law, for example, may be a neighbour as well, and a member of a shared ethnic cultural association or a worshipper at the same temple or mosque. A local shopkeeper may be the friend of someone in the extended kinship network, while his wife may be a member of a shared devotional group. So networks of support, expectations of care and patronage, considerations of honour and repute, are built up and reinforce each other in dense sets of social relationships, creating societies which can be 'home' in the best sense of being welcoming and supportive, but which can also be claustrophobic, over watchful and for some deeply controlling.

At the simplest level there is the supportive network of the neighbourhood with its concentration of people who share much of the same background, often including language, religion and place of origin. Ties of

[22] For insights into the support systems available to women who live in ethnic enclaves see Shaw, *Kinship and Continuity*; and P. Werbner, *The Migration Process. Capital, Gifts and Offerings among British Pakistanis* (New York, Oxford and Munich, Berg, 1990). A novel portraying the experience of a new Bangladeshi bride in London is Monica Ali's *Brick Lane*, published in 2003.

[23] See chapter 5 of Freund, *Insiders and Outsiders*.

neighbourliness are often reinforced by actual kinship ties created by patterns of migration and subsequent marriages. (Marriage networks are considered below.) Studies of particular cities have shown how significant these neighbourhood social networks become. Two British urban studies of Pakistanis have shown how families build up supportive networks including kin and 'fictive kin' through elaborate processes of gift giving managed by the womenfolk. The idea of reciprocity among kin, friends and neighbours is elaborated through a complex system of gifts between connected families, and families which aspire to connection, which can often extend back to Pakistan itself. Gifts range from sweets to clothes and money on a carefully calibrated range of value. They act to enhance and maintain a particular family's prestige in the community, to cement social bonds, and to provide insurance in times of emergency when neighbourly help is needed to deal with local domestic crises or to enable an unforeseen trip back to South Asia.[24]

Among the Muslim women who invest heavily in such gift-giving networks, social ties are reinforced by religious activities such as the reading of the Koran together. For most South Asians, whether Muslims, Hindus, Sikhs, Christians, Jains or Parsis, there is an intimate connection between religion and the culture they bring with them from South Asia, and religio-cultural activities form another web of connections, creating a sense of home. As Muslim women rarely attend mosques, domestic devotional worship in the home is a common pattern of shared activity, often centering on reading the Koran to mark special events and concerns, followed by a special meal. In Hindu traditions much worship is family based, and life cycle rites in the experience of migrant families are again occasions for inviting kin and friends. People will travel great distances to share in such ceremonies as marriages and funerals, to reinforce social solidarity as well as, in the case of marriages, for the great pleasure of shared festivities as well as the opportunity to meet kin and close friends whom one might not see on a regular basis. Even in the earliest phases of the diaspora, as in Trinidad, religious celebrations in the family, the village and beyond the village, were – and still are – important expressions of neighbourliness and sociability. Formal community readings of scripture, followed by shared meals, were often sponsored by particular families and involved women's cooperation, shared religious ritual, and for the sponsors considerable prestige among neighbours. Similarly performances of the great *Ram Lila* plays staged by particular villages would attract Indians from surrounding parts of the island. As Indians in Trinidad gained in wealth

[24] See Shaw, *Kinship and Continuity*, and Werbner, *The Migration Process*.

and status there was no erosion of these religio-cultural practices but, rather, their reinforcement and elaboration.[25]

For Hindus the experience both of religion and of social life has been influenced by the institutions of caste and its ideological underpinnings. Much scholarly attention has been paid to caste as a hierarchical ordering of society, based on notions of ritual purity and pollution and associated social status, the degree to which it was immutable or flexible, and the extent to which it was the dominant form of social ordering of difference and status among Hindus in India. Increasingly, earlier ideas about a total hierarchical ordering of society have been undermined as evidence has indicated patterns of group mobility, the emergence of new 'castes', the significance of other foundations of social influence, and the likelihood that the more rigid caste society of the later nineteenth and earlier twentieth centuries in India was a very recent phenomenon connected with British colonial anxiety to settle and order Indian subjects. In India itself in the later twentieth century caste has decreased in social and public significance for a variety of reasons, including personal mobility, the development of new occupations and, of course, the pressures of urbanisation. Similar patterns are discernible in diaspora groups. Only rarely have caste groups migrated in sufficient numbers to enable them to reproduce a complex caste-based society; and of course among indentured labourers many aspects of caste were obliterated by the totally abnormal life they were forced to live on the estates. But there persist throughout the diaspora broad understandings of ritual and social status, even among Sikhs and Muslims, and particularly strong is the wish to construct marriage alliances for one's family within one's caste or at least within one of similar status. Moreover, where caste groups bring with them particular patterns of religious observance, these, as well as the kinship networks embedded within caste, are important sources of social connection and support. Gujaratis in Britain from India and via East Africa have perhaps the strongest caste networks in the modern diaspora, and among them religious observance and sociability networks reinforce each other, as does the foundation of caste associations.[26] Caste and cultural associations often bring together religion and culture and have been prominent forms of social organisation among the diaspora in virtually every part of the world where South Asians have settled.

[25] See S. Vertovec, *Hindu Trinidad. Religion, Ethnicity and Socio-Economic Change* (London and Basingstoke, MacMillan, 1992).

[26] See S. Warrier, 'Gujarati Prijapatis in London. Family roles and sociability networks', in R. Ballard (ed.), *Desh Pardesh. The South Asian Presence in Britain*, (London, Hurst, 1994), pp. 191–212.

However, by far the most important forms of social network among migrants were those constructed by the ties of marriage. As we have already noted, marriage has long been considered a fundamental and often sacred social institution among South Asians, and, as on the subcontinent, so in the diaspora, great care is taken to ensure that marriages are stable relationships between compatible individuals, and that they are so organised as to enhance and buttress a family's prestige and networks of kinship. It is still very rare to find South Asian marriages across ethnic boundaries. Even in Britain, where South Asians have lived (to the extent that residential patterns permit), worked and been educated alongside the white population for two to three generations, mixed marriages are most uncommon. For example, in 1990, among married Indian men 91 per cent of their spouses were Indians, while just over 93 per cent of female spouses of Pakistanis and Bangladeshis were from the same ethnic group. By comparison all other groups of non-white immigrants were far more likely to marry outside their own ethnic group.[27] Moreover South Asians have tended to restrict their marriage choices within religious as well as ethnic groups, so Hindus virtually never marry Muslims or Christians but sometimes Sikhs (with whom they have had kinship links in India), and Muslims marry only other Muslims. One of the only well-documented examples of South Asians marrying across ethnic and religious boundaries was in California in the first half of the twentieth century, when Indian male migrants who arrived as much-needed agricultural labour found they could not bring in Indian women and chose to marry local women, most of whom were Roman Catholic Hispanics, as California's anti-miscegenation laws prohibited Indian marriages to white women. These unions produced a unique Punjabi-Mexican community who increasingly did not see themselves as South Asian and found new arrivals from the Punjab in the later twentieth century very disturbing to their particular sense of American identity.[28] The very strong tendency elsewhere in the diaspora for intra-ethnic, intra-religious marriages has served to maintain clear boundaries between groups within the diaspora as well as stark social and ethnic division from the rest of the host society. Where inter-ethnic unions have taken place these tend to be among the very highly educated who share similar lifestyles and values and are outside the constraints of ethnic enclaves.

The ability of groups in the diaspora to maintain such firm sexual and social boundaries lies partly in the existence of ethnic enclaves as the core

[27] Halsey and Webb (eds.), *Twentieth-Century British Social Trends*, pp. 168–169, table 4.9, panel 2.

[28] K. I. Leonard, *Making Ethnic Choices. California's Punjabi Mexican Americans* (Philadelphia, Temple University Press, 1995).

of much sociability. Young South Asians of marriageable age are more likely to meet other South Asians just because of where they live and the circles in which their parents and older relatives move. The exceptions are those (increasing numbers) who leave home to go to university, and even for them there appears often to be a clear understanding that although friendships and sometimes sexual relationships between young men and women may occur across ethnic boundaries, few of these are likely to lead to marriage because of parental expectations and controls. Parental control of marriage is an even more important factor in maintaining intra-group marriages. On the subcontinent marriages were all arranged by parents at least until the later twentieth century, on the understanding that marriages were alliances between whole families and should only take place between families of similar standing, and from the same religion and region. Boys and girls were married as they reached their teens or sometimes even earlier, before the gradual raising of the marriage age from the end of the 1920s. Mahatma Gandhi was married at the age of 13, for example. This caused him considerable social embarrassment when he came to England as a student in the 1880s, and an end to child marriage was one of the key aspects of his campaign of social reform. Not surprisingly such young people had no say in the matter of their marriage, and often had not even seen their prospective spouse before the marriage ceremony. When Jawaharlal Nehru, independent India's first Prime Minister, was married in 1916 his experience was exceptional; for he was in his late 20s, and though his parents chose his bride the young couple were permitted to meet and get to know each other before their marriage. The tradition of arranged marriage persisted throughout the diaspora, for the same reasons as on the subcontinent, whether among children of indentured labourers in Trinidad, for example, or in the great industrial cities of northern England. However, changes have taken place, just as they have on the subcontinent in recent years. South Asian adolescents are of course subject to and somewhat protected by the laws relating to the age of marriage in the countries where they live, and by the age of compulsory schooling as well as increasing parental understandings of the significance of secondary education for girls as well as boys. More normal now is a form of attenuated arrangement of marriages, whereby potential brides and grooms are allowed some influence in the choice of marriage partner, and often a veto; and they are increasingly permitted to meet and socialise before marriage to get to know each other.

Studies of marriage strategies in the diaspora indicate how deeply parents care about choosing the 'right' partner for their children, for the happiness of the child as well as the long-term standing of the family and the maintenance of its status and connections. Moreover, children born and brought up in the diaspora recognise to an extent that their parents are trying to do their best for them, even if there is tension in their life experience between family norms and the wider world of sexual partnerships and chosen marriages. Parents will normally seek to arrange marriages within a broadly similar status group, and for Hindus this means consideration of caste. Increasingly there is awareness that marrying a child educated in the diaspora to a more traditional, less educated partner directly from the subcontinent is a recipe for misunderstandings and tensions. In such unions levels of education, social skills and habits, expectations of marriage and spousal behaviour, and language itself may be real sources of division. However, as the diaspora has grown by natural increase there are of course far more suitable marriage partners available in each country where there are South Asians, or, in the case of those who belong to the emerging group of transnational families, with friends and extended kin networks in diaspora communities in other countries. There is evidence that some people, even among the educated and professional, in the diaspora, find it difficult to find suitable spouses: hence the phenomenon of internet matrimonial advertisements extending the practice of newspaper advertisements in the Sunday papers in India. Caste and other markers of social standing are displayed in these as the criteria for suitable marriage partners.

An exception to this growing pattern of inter and intra-diaspora marriage are South Asian Muslim communities who practice very close kin and often cousin marriage, compared with Hindus and Sikhs who practice marriage outside the close kinship group. The search for appropriate Muslim marriages for children leads many UK Pakistani parents, for example, to consider not only kin among the Pakistani groups in the UK, but also back in Pakistani villages where siblings and cousins still feel they have prior claims in marriage and see such arrangements as a route to mobility for their children. To deny these claims is, for an immigrant family, to risk family honour and solidarity. Shaw's study of 24 marriages of children of first generation immigrants in Oxford showed that 76 per cent were with kin and 59 per cent were with cousins.[29] Even though this is the extreme end of the spectrum in marriage patterns, the matrimonial strategies of most South Asians in the diaspora confirm the strong social links within its multiple groups and their continued social distinctiveness from the host society.

However, there is one tiny religious group within the diaspora for whom marriage strategies have proved deeply problematic. These are the Parsis,

[29] Shaw, *Kinship and Continuity*; see also note 12 for the work on marriage patterns by Roger Ballard.

who are among the most westernised and successful of diaspora groups and are to be found throughout the world, generally in big cities where they have become wealthy and often well integrated into their host societies. Both the size of the group and its success mean that its very survival is in doubt. Parsi women tend to be highly educated, and as with all educated women, family sizes are smaller than those of their uneducated sisters. Moreover many Parsi men and women marry out of their community – not surprising given the small numbers of Parsis and the fact that they are just the sort of people who would wish to make their own choices according to perceived emotions and senses of compatibility, and have opportunities to do so. Conventionally in India, only children born to the marriages of two Parsis, or to a Parsi male who married a non-Parsi woman, are counted as Parsis. This has held down numbers and the group's ability to reproduce itself, and has led to great contention among Parsis worldwide as to whether offspring of mixed marriages where the Parsi partner is a woman should be accepted as full community members.[30]

Despite the apparent solidarity and strength of many South Asian diaspora communities, when viewed by onlookers from outside them, there are social stresses which stem from the experience of migration and the demands on migrants for social adaptation to the new situation. Stresses and tensions are an inevitable repercussion of rapid social change in any social group, South Asian or not, and it is not surprising that migration has generated unease, tension and conflict in many diaspora communities. South Asians bring to their new homes highly developed understandings of honour and esteem, as well as firmly established patterns of what is considered good or appropriate behaviour in most types of social interaction. These are often tested by the experience of migration over time, particularly along the fault lines of gender and generation, when older assumptions about the good man/woman or the good son/daughter are challenged and undermined. When considering these areas of stress it is important to remember that many South Asian families are not only concerned with their repute and honour within their immediate diasporic community, but often also have in mind their extended kin back in South Asia. What more conservative relatives in the old homeland might say or think is often still vitally important, particularly among migrant Pakistanis and Bangladeshis, because it affects family esteem and also the marriage prospects of the next generation. News of the actions of an

[30] J. R. Hinnells, 'The modern Zoroastrian diaspora', chapter 3 of Brown and Foot (eds.), *Migration: The Asian Experience*.

'undisciplined' wife or an 'errant' son or daughter spreads quickly when kin are in touch by phone and by frequent travel.

Issues of gender are a particularly sensitive area in South Asian social life. This is not peculiar to those who live in the diaspora. From the mid-nineteenth century on the subcontinent, there was profound and often bitter controversy in India about the role of women as society began to change, and as social reformers argued that change in the place and treatment of women was vital if India was to take its place in the modern world. Women were seen as the repositories of family honour, and changes in their behaviour were considered potentially dangerous to patriarchal society. Women's sexuality was thought to be particularly dangerous and was thus carefully controlled by early marriage and social conventions of seclusion. *Purdah*, or more extreme forms of seclusion, was primarily a Muslim practice, though it had spread to other Indian groups. But even where women were not confined to domestic space, there were widely practised customs of women covering the head and face in public and in particular among non-related and older males. Only gradually was it deemed respectable for women to come out into the public sphere, participate in public education, and eventually take their part in public life and in paid work outside the home. (For some female groups of course external work had been an economic necessity but this was considered dishonourable and was in strong contrast to the later paid work undertaken by women on the subcontinent which was increasingly considered appropriate and desirable).[31] Changes in India in social attitudes have been faster among Hindus and Sikhs, while Parsis and Christians were for different reasons much more westernised. But among rural Muslim groups from Pakistan and Bangladesh there still persist very conservative attitudes towards acceptable female behaviour, dress and social relations. These differences have been exported into the diaspora. Any consideration of gender relations in the South Asian diaspora must, therefore, take account of the timing and nature of the different migratory flows out of the subcontinent. Later migrants, particularly at the end of the twentieth century, came from homes where processes of social change had been under way for several generations in South Asia itself, while those who came from urban backgrounds were also much more likely to have negotiated many changes in family relations before they migrated. Indeed, as the history of the diaspora unfolds, and as the pace of social change on the subcontinent quickens, it may become the case that South Asians

[31] For the many complex issues relating to change in the lives of women in the subcontinent see G. Forbes, *The New Cambridge History of India IV.2. Women in Modern India* (Cambridge, Cambridge University Press 1996).

there will prove more ready to change than their diaspora relatives and counterparts, who feel the need to retain distinctive social values in the face of the wider society.

In the matter of gender relations the experience of indentured Indians was a particular case. Not only were indentured labourers among the earliest migrants, from rural backgrounds untouched by processes of social reform which were initiating change in Indian towns and cities, but they were also exposed to a life in the barracks which shattered their older social norms and relationships, and where the gross imbalance in the sex ratio exposed women to violence and sexual exploitation. Scholarship on Indian women during the period of indentured labour in many places confirms the misery of their existence, the violence they experienced from Indian and white males alike, and the breakdown of stable sexual unions.[32] However, as Indian women became free from the particular problems caused by indenture, they did not become free in any modern understanding of the term. As labourers began to establish free Indian communities once their indentures had expired, they began to reconstruct families according to norms remembered from South Asia. For women this meant tight control of their lives by senior males within patriarchal families, often accompanied by psychological, verbal and physical violence, even though – and in some ways because – the reproductive and physical labour of women was central to the processes whereby Indian men could establish themselves as free men in their new homes. The very fact that women were so valuable in the reconstruction of Indian domestic and economic life, and took on new roles outside the home, such as marketing, made men more anxious to control their labour and their reputations.

However, strict control often tipping over into forms of violence is not uncommon among the diaspora communities which have resulted from later waves of migration. In Britain and north America, where South Asians are by the end of the twentieth century more educated and have been longer exposed to ideas of gender equality, there is compelling evidence that in South Asian families wives and daughters are often subjected to treatment which the host societies would consider

[32] On Indian women in Natal see J. Beall, 'Women under indenture in colonial Natal, 1860–1911', chapter 2 of Clarke, Peach and Vertovec (eds.), *South Asians Overseas*; on indentured women in Fiji see B. V. Lal, 'Kunti's Cry', chapter 11 of his *Chalo Jahaji on a Journey Through Indenture in Fiji* (Canberra and Suva, Australian National University and Fiji Museum, 2000), and J. Harvey, 'Naraini's Story', chapter 11 in the same volume. For women's experience in Mauritius (where they were never formally indentured) see the important collection of women's 'voices' in M. Carter, *Lakshmi's Legacy. The Testimonies of Indian Women in 19th Century Mauritius* (Stanley, Rose-Hill, Mauritius, Editions de L'Ocean Indien, 1994).

unacceptable. This is particularly the case in Muslim communities from rural backgrounds; but conservative assumptions about gender roles and the right of senior males to discipline women affect many girls brought up in the diaspora, whose expectations in the matter of dress, leisure, freedom to socialise, and relationships with young men are more akin to those of their peers outside the ethnic enclaves where they live. It is impossible to quantify levels of domestic violence, but scholarly evidence makes it clear that this is a deep and disturbing demonstration of stress in diaspora families as they adapt to their new environment.[33] The proliferation of websites advising South Asian women who are subjected to violence, and pointing them in the direction of women's refuges, is further evidence of women's experiences of domestic violence. In the USA there is, for example, Maitri, founded by Indian women in 1991, or the South Asian Women's Network (Sawnet) which links users to the Office on Violence Against Women in the US Department of Justice and to various other resources including refuges, and interestingly spreads its links to British resources for women suffering violence. In Britain there are similar websites offering Asian women advice and the whereabouts of refuges. These include Ashiana in South Yorkshire and Kiran Asian Women's Aid in London. A website for women of all ethnic origins suffering violence (www.refuge.org.uk) directs South Asian women also to Karma Nirvana Refuge, intended specially for this ethnic minority, where there are people with appropriate language competence. In mid-2005 yet another refuge specially for Asian women was opened in Stoke in the northern Midlands with full backing from the Home Office. The British National Health Service has become so concerned with levels of self harm among young South Asian women that it funded research in the late 1980s into the stresses experienced by young women growing up in London. The results showed that South Asian women in the age range 15–35 are two or three times more likely to harm themselves than non-Asian women. It is clear that young women in the diaspora carry a very heavy burden as they are seen as the repositories of family and community honour, and this in turn brings them under great pressure from family, community and religion. Self harm seems to be a coping mechanism for dealing with extreme distress and pressure.[34]

[33] See the evidence of two South Asian scholars, one Hindu and one Muslim, who are deeply sympathetic to the needs and problems of diasporic South Asians: B. Parekh, *Some Reflections on the Indian Diaspora* (London, British Organisation of People of Indian Origin (BOPIO), 1993), p. 11 and H. Ansari, *'The Infidel Within'. Muslims in Britain since 1800* (London, Hurst, 2004), chapter 8.

[34] See an article based on the 1988 report funded by the NHS Ethnic Health Unit, by A. Bhardwaj, 'Growing up young, Asian and female in Britain: a report on self-harm and

However, it is clear that growing up as a South Asian girl in the diaspora is also an invitation to educational possibilities, to expanding aspirations, and to the possibilities of paid work which in turn gives some economic independence. Many families support their girls' educational aspirations, for the matrimonial and socio-economic doors it opens. (Educational standards among South Asians will receive more attention in the next chapter.) Moreover, women's paid work outside the home, which is growing in significance particularly among non-Muslim South Asians, can serve to empower women, in the workplace itself, in the context of household decision-making, or in the choice of marriage partner. Paid work is, however, not always the route to greater independence or to more equal gender relations. Men can see women's wages and salaries as a threat to patriarchal dominance, particularly if they themselves are lower paid or unemployed; and this can in turn lead to domestic violence even among younger South Asians. Despite the clear evidence that in many diaspora households women and girls are subject to strict and somtimes extreme forms of control, studies of South Asian women in Britain have shown that, whatever the tensions, many of them are actively negotiating considerable changes in gender relations and in the status of women in their families, and are drawing on their new-found resources from the wider environment in this process. Clearly the experiences of South Asian women in the diaspora, and even in one country, differ considerably according to age, location, religion and class. It would therefore be be entirely wrong to assume that there is one stereotype of a South Asian woman, oppressed and powerless in a patriarichal society.[35]

Gender often becomes a faultline in domestic relations across generational boundaries. More broadly the experiences and expectations of different generations are another source of social friction in the South Asian diaspora. This occurs acutely when parents brought up in the subcontinent find their children diverging from them as a result of their upbringing in the diaspora. Although most young South Asians grow up in locations

suicide', *Feminist Studies*, Vol. 68, No. 1 (2001), pp. 52–67. It is significant that journals read by health professionals now have numerous articles on issues such as suicide among South Asians.

35 Important literature on the changing roles and positions of South Asian women in the UK include A. Brah, 'Women of South Asian origin in Britain: issues and concerns', *South Asia Research*, Vol. 7, No. 1 (May 1987), pp. 39–54; P. Bhachu, 'New cultural forms and transnational South Asian women: culture, class, and consumption among British South Asian women in the diaspora', chapter 9 of Van der Veer (ed.), *Nation and Migration*; F. Ahmad, T. Modood and S. Lissenburgh, *South Asian Women and Employment in Britain: The Interaction of Gender and Ethnicity* (London, Policy Studies Institute, 2003). On the very slow challenge to Muslim patriarchy, even when young women are earning, see chapter 8 of Ansari, *The Infidel Within*.

where they are surrounded by their ethnic peers, they are powerfully influenced by the systems of state education in the countries where they live, and by the media which penetrate the intimate domestic lives of diaspora families. It is not surprising that there develop different attitudes towards a variety of issues including dress, leisure pursuits, religion, the use of money, careers and of course relations between young men and women, and arranged marriages. Such topics generate tension between generations within families in the host society, but they are greater in ethnic groups where parents have brought conservative assumptions and standards from a very different sort of society. At one stage social observers predicted a crisis for South Asian family life and the erosion of cultural norms because of the growth of the diaspora-born population, and portrayed young South Asians as caught between 'two cultures'. However, this is now evidently a far too simple set of assumptions. Despite tension and occasional breakdowns it is clear that many parents are adapting and modifying their views on key issues. It is still the case that parents adopt a double standard in dealing with their children, and girls tend to be more carefully controlled than sons, indicating the persistence of assumptions about the connection between gender and family honour. For their part, young people are more understanding of their parents' attitudes than might have been expected, and are often unwilling to push disagreements to the point of family rupture. Case studies of some of the most conservative Muslim communities in Britain at the end of the twentieth century have pointed to such patterns of adaptation and adjustment even among them, while acknowledging the strains between the generations within families.[36]

Some disquieting evidence does suggest that at times such strains cannot be controlled or diffused even within families and kin networks, and spill over into the wider society. In Britain, for example, there is a marked incidence of drug abuse among young Muslim males, and they represent a higher proportion of the prison population than their presence in the population at large would warrant, with one-quarter of those inside being there for drug-related offences. Between 1990 and 2005 the number of Muslim prisoners had risen sixfold, bringing the total to more than 4,000: they are mostly of Pakistani background and make up 70 per cent of prisoners from ethnic minorities. By contrast, few people from India or Bangladesh are in prison in the UK.[37] The condition of young

[36] See Ansari, *The Infidel Within*, particularly chapters 7 and 8; Shaw, *Kinship and Continuity*, particularly chapter 6; J. Jacobson, *Islam in Transition. Religion and Identity Among British Pakistani Youth* (London and New York, Routledge, 1998); also M. Anwar, *Between Cultures*.

[37] *The Times*, 30 July 2005; Ansari, *The Infidel Within*, p. 218.

Muslim men will concern us in several places later in this study, but in the context of generational strains these figures indicate a clear breakdown in shared moral standards between generations and a collapse of parental and kin control. Similarly stresses between parents and children, particularly daughters, over arranged marriage come into the wider public and legal arena where girls run away from home, where there is conflict over forced marriages which often involves taking young girls forcibly back to Pakistan, or in the most extreme and rare cases where there are so-called 'honour killings', where family members kill a female relative rather than have her enter a sexual liason or marriage with someone not deemed suitable by the family. Clearly in such cases the social networks created by migrants have collapsed under the strain of generational differences, but these are most unusual and outside the experience of the vast majority of South Asians in the diaspora.

3 Constructing religious networks and institutions

We turn finally to the task of constructing religious networks and institutions in the diaspora, a vital part of making the new place of residence home. All South Asian migrants leave their original homes with a sense of identity powerfully influenced by religion. This is not unique, and migrants from Europe before the rapid secularisation of European society in the twentieth century carried with them a profound sense that religion was a core aspect of their personal and group identity. Irish and Italian Catholics, for example, established their own religious institutions and social worlds in their diaspora experience. British people migrating within the Empire rapidly built Anglican churches and cathedrals as markers of identity, often replicating architectural designs redolent of public space in Britain, and as places of shared worship and group social reinforcement. Just as nineteenth-century European emigrants were embedded in a culture powerfully moulded by religion, so are South Asians in their modern diaspora communities.

The nature of South Asian religion in the diaspora is very significant for a number of reasons. In the first place religion is a powerful determinant of linkages and divisions within the diaspora, as has already been shown in the earlier discussion of social networks. Shared religious belief and observance can add another dimension or layer to the rich social life built up in the diaspora as it reinforces kinship and neighbourliness: but of course religious difference, in the same way, divides South Asians from each other outside the subcontinent, as on it, though not in any absolute or all-encompassing sense. South Asian societies both on the subcontinent and in the diaspora have not experienced the degree of secularisation visible in the western world, though they are not immune to the forces which have undermined religious belief and observance elsewhere. Consequently some understanding of attitudes embedded in South Asia's religions is also important in constructing a picture of the diaspora experience. But it is even more widely significant. The presence of South Asian communities in the diaspora, particularly in Europe, north America and Australasia, has created for the first time genuinely multi-religious societies. Islam, Hinduism, and Sikhism are now present and highly visible in societies which were once largely Christian by religion or at least deeply influenced by the Christian inheritance. This creates opportunities and problems, some of which will be considered in the next chapter. But the emergence and growing rootedness of South Asian religions in these societies means that no one can study them seriously without some understanding of the beliefs and dynamics of minority religions. It is impossible, for example, to understand British society without some knowledge of British Muslims, Hindus or Sikhs. It took the tragic bombings on the London transport network in July 2005, in which young British Pakistanis from northern England were involved, to wake many British people to this fact, and exposed the depth of ignorance even in government circles to the issues confronting many British South Asian citizens.

The religious experience of South Asians overseas also raises fascinating questions about the way religious traditions adapt to changing situations, and find the resources within their beliefs, practices and institutions to cope with rapid social and intellectual change, and the multiple challenges of a changing external world. This is perhaps particularly interesting in the case of what is loosely called Hinduism. This is not a tradition based on a clear creed or set of religious texts, which are by definition easily exportable; it is a cluster of traditions and practices which vary greatly and are held together by some shared assumptions and traditions, but particularly by the way of life developed on the subcontinent over centuries. It therefore seems likely that the export of Hindu practices and sensibilities may be more difficult than the practice of Islam or Sikhism, for example, which is based on belief and text, even if the actual practice of these religions is powerfully influenced by South Asian social experience over centuries. All religious traditions are at their core about the discovering of meaning in human existence, and the practice of lives which draw sustenance from that meaning and try to conform to the values implicit in it. It is therefore important to examine the extent to which South Asians in their new diaspora context feel that their traditions serve and sustain them and help them to manage the changing world in which they find themselves, and still give them powerful ideals to live by. As important are the issues of religious instruction and transmission. Have South Asians also found ways of transmitting their religious inheritance to their children and do their children feel that their traditions provide them with meaning and guidance?[38]

Before embarking on a discussion of some of these issues it is worth commenting briefly on South Asian Christianity in the diaspora. Christianity has been long established in the subcontinent, its roots in the south going back to the earliest Christian years. However, with the exception of parts of south India, such as modern Kerala, Christians were few in number until several waves of conversion occurred as a result of European missionary activity, which mainly touched those at the very base of Hindu society. However, there have been few South Asian Christians in the diaspora. Small groups of Catholic Goans, from the former Portuguese enclave in India, went to East Africa and thence to other areas in the diaspora. Tiny communities of Pakistani Christians left the new Muslim country for Britain at the same time as their Muslim counterparts. Now in the latest diaspora wave some of the South Indian IT experts arriving in America are from the old Syrian Christian community. In the diaspora itself few South Asians have become Christians. Some Indians were converted in Trinidad and Natal, for example, in the early years of the Indian presence there; and their contact with missionaries and access to education made them a significant early Indian elite. Among later migrants there have been even fewer who have become Christian, which is not surprising given the tight social networks formed in the diaspora. Anecdotal evidence suggests that South Asians who do become Christian either as individuals or in family groups face considerable social ostracism by those who remain within their traditions. Very little research has been done on South Asian Christian groups in the diaspora.[39] What there is suggests that most of the Christian South Asians in the diaspora form distinct social groups who have little to do with other South Asians, and do not intermarry with them. Although they come to countries where Christianity is the dominant religious tradition they often have their own churches where they worship in their own language, particularly in cases where they do not speak English fluently, or worship together in particular churches serving distinct localities. The fact that the Anglican church in Britain has a Bishop of Pakistani origin at the start of the twenty-first century does not reflect the status of South Asian Christians in general in Britain,

[38] A good discussion of some of these issues is the Introduction by R. B. Williams to his edited volume, *A Sacred Thread. Modern Transmission of Hindu Traditions in India and Abroad* (Chambersburg PA, Anima, 1992.)

[39] One example is Jeffery, *Migrants and Refugees*; Dr M. Frenz in Oxford is working on a study of Goans in the worldwide diaspora.

Figure 5. Methodist church, Cowley Road, Oxford, used by a Punjabi-speaking congregation. This is an example of a church shared between local people and Christian South Asian immigrants and their descendants, where the latter retain Punjabi as their language of worship for separate services.
Author's photograph

as he left his home country as an adult, already an established Christian leader. Much more work needs to be done on the adaptation of South Asian Christians to life in an increasingly secularising west, and on the possible differences between the way they live in the diaspora compared with their non-Christian South Asian counterparts.

The subsequent discussion draws on the lives of Hindus, Muslims, Sikhs and to an extent that of Parsis, because they are most heavily represented in the diaspora. But it must be underlined at the outset that this discussion cannot do justice to the great variety of religious experience in the diaspora, partly because of limited space but partly because scholars often do not have evidence on aspects of the religious life of migrants which are important but difficult to study and particularly to quantify. What is offered is an introduction to some of the big issues facing South Asia's religious traditions in the diaspora, particularly those which shed light on the way South Asians have made themselves at home in the diaspora. The themes include the re-establishment of religious traditions and practices outside the subcontinent, the way different traditions have managed change, and the way South Asians represent their religion to the wider societies in which they find themselves.

Re-establishing religious traditions in the diaspora

One of the most significant and visible aspects of South Asian life in the diaspora has been the re-establishment of religious tradition and practice. This has involved the physical construction of places of worship, the practice of domestic and personal religion, and the creation of religious leaderships. Often there have been subtle changes in the process when compared with religious practice on the subcontinent. It is appropriate to consider first the experience of indentured labourers, not only because they were the earliest Indians to migrate in large numbers, but because the battering the processes involved in indenture gave to established Indian social patterns and moral norms made the renewal of religious tradition and practice far more problematic than for later migrants. Moreover, most of them came from poor and unsophisticated backgrounds, where religious expression was mainly local and popular rather than conforming to the high theological traditions within their religions.[40] The majority of indentured labourers were Hindu and considerable work has been done on Hinduism as it was reconstructed and practised in Trinidad and Natal by indentured Indians and succeeding generations of their offspring.[41] In both places Hindus put great effort into re-establishing their religion, even though they started with grave drawbacks, including the absence of the established social world and structures which on the subcontinent provided the framework for religious observance and religious leadership through the presence of Brahmin priests and other religious functionaries.

In Natal, Hinduism as it began to develop was marked by the fact that so many indentured Indians recruited for Natal came originally from the south of India, with two-thirds of the total coming via Madras, more than

[40] Scholars of religion in South Asia often use a valuable distinction between the Great Tradition and the Little Traditions within religious experience and practice. This is particularly so within Hinduism, where local, popular religion is often only loosely linked to the world of high Hindu philosophy, theology and social theory, and the worship of deities within the all-Indian pantheon. This division between Great Traditions and popular practice also has relevance in the study of Islam and Sikhism.

[41] I am greatly endebted to the work of S. Vertovec on Trinidad and A. Diesel on Natal. See, for example, Vertovec, *Hindu Trinidad* and A. Diesel and P. Maxwell, *Hinduism in Natal. A Brief Guide* (Pietermaritzburg, University of Natal Press, 1993), and A. Diesel, 'Hinduism in KwaZulu-Natal, South Africa', chapter 2 of Parekh, Singh and Vertovec (eds.), *Culture and Economy in the Indian Diaspora*. Both scholars have shared with me their time and expertise; Al Diesel took me on a memorable tour of Hindu temples in Pietermaritzburg, and her *Hinduism in Natal* contains excellent guides to Natal temples.

double the number sailing out of Calcutta, who would have come mainly from the Gangetic plain. The earliest public manifestations of Hinduism in Natal were the building of temples and the construction of ceremonials around them. These were in the traditions of Hinduism generally practised in India in the nineteenth century, and incorporated both Brahmanical traditions and folk practices. They were physically on both the northern and southern Indian temple patterns. Among the earliest were those built on a site bought in 1883 on Umgeni Road, Durban, including a Shiva temple built in 1885. This was a wood and iron structure, but some places of worship were far humbler. Temple-building grew in pace as Indians ended their indentures and had some disposable income. Their significance to succeeding generations was clear when the 1950 Group Areas Act designated Cato Manor as a white area, even though Indians were established there as market gardeners. Eight temples were left marooned without the Indian population which had surrounded them and used them, but even so their worshippers kept them in good repair. Temple worship for Hindus has traditionally not been congregational in the sense of Muslim, Sikh or Christian worship. Temples are more the sites for individual veneration of deities. This has persisted in Natal, but has been augmented by ceremonies which are rooted in folk tradition but increasingly attracted large numbers of worshippers and onlookers. These included worship of the goddess Mariamman, originally brought by Tamil-speakers from south India, and another southern Indian import, firewalking ceremonies in honour of another goddess, Draupadi.

Some Hindus in the late nineteenth century in India became concerned about many of the practices conducted in the name of Hinduism and were increasingly determined to present it to the wider world as a serious world religion which should take its place in the modern world.[42] Numerous reformist movements developed on the subcontinent and it was not surprising that reformers turned their attention to Hindus abroad, particularly those lowly folk who as indentured labourers had taken their own versions of Hinduism with them and were practising what reformers perceived as degraded, populist forms of religion. One major movement which sent missionaries to reform Hinduism in the early diaspora was the Arya Samaj, noted in Chapter 1, a north Indian reform movement which aimed to purify Hinduism of many popular practices (such as firewalking), to encourage communal worship and to emphasise the Vedas, the earliest Hindu scriptures, as the most authoritative religious sources. They saw themselves as akin to the Protestants of the Christian

[42] See K. W. Jones, *The New Cambridge History of India III.1. Socio-religious Reform Movements in British India* (Cambridge, Cambridge University Press, 1989).

Figure 6. Preparing for fire-walking in Pietermaritzburg, Natal. The fire pit is prepared in the grounds of the Mariamman temple, and devotees are circumambulating the temple in the background. Fire-walking was a folk practice that more orthodox Hindu missionaries tried to prevent in the early twentieth century.

Courtesy of Dr A. Diesel

Reformation in the sixteenth century. Although the missionaries to Natal in the early twentieth century never rooted out what they saw as degraded practices, their version of Hinduism added another layer to Hindu practice in Natal, the building of further temples, and the elaboration of Hindu organisation with new voluntary associations for religious education and social work. The earliest of these was the Veda Dharma Sabha, founded in 1909, and an umbrella organisation for all the Arya Samaj organisations in South Africa was formed in 1925. Further reformist movements which have taken root among Natal Hindus have been grounded in the more intellectual path of neo-Vedanta, which stresses finding God in the depths of human beings, and has little time for more populist forms of worship and celebration. The Ramakrishna Movement, which follows the teachings of Swami Vivekananda, noted in chapter 1, became strong in Natal from the 1940s, and created several *ashrams*, or religious communities and centres, including one specially for women, which has done much to help women socially as well as to provide for their religious needs and

Figure 7. Devotee ready for fire-walking ceremony, Pietermaritzburg, Natal.

Courtesy of Dr A. Diesel

help them to understand the meaning of many Hindu rituals.[43] Towards the end of the century other movements loosely grounded in Hinduism such as the Hare Krishna movement have also added to the complexity of South African Hinduism. This continued flowering of Hindu activity and its development in ways which provide meaning and comfort for its followers, often in profoundly difficult external situations, is, with the continued building of new temples, a sign that the distinctive amalgam which is Natal Hinduism is not only vibrant among Indians born outside India several generations after the arrival of their indentured ancestors, but has been constantly adapting to sustain them in a rapidly changing environment.

In Trinidad, too, indentured labourers and their children very rapidly started to construct a religious environment in which they could observe what was possible and what was remembered of Hindu tradition on the subcontinent. Among the earliest manifestations were the building of shrines and temples from at least the 1860s, and the observance in the home of the domestic lifecycle rites which lie at the heart of daily religious observance for Hindus. Over time Trinidadian Hinduism became somewhat simpler than the hugely diverse traditions found on the subcontinent, observances were homogenised and standardised in a particular Caribbean form, with a particular emphasis on individual and community devotional worship. One reason for this development was the activity of reformist Hindus, among them again the Arya Samaj, and the simultaneous influence of Christian missionaries with their pattern of communal worship in church. Later, Hindu temples were even built on the pattern of churches, and designed for congregational worship. Other forms of Hindu organisation also developed in the early twentieth century, including a revived Sanatan Dharma Association, designed to teach Hinduism, to inculcate morality, temperance and social welfare, and to seek rights from the government.

Among Trinidad Hindus religion is seen as a cultural marker of their particular group. Far from being a declining force, when Trinidad experienced a temporary oil boom from 1973, Indians invested heavily in religious activity and family-based rituals such as *pujas*, and readings of the *Ramayana* proliferated, including lengthy ceremonials lasting days called *yagnas*, including *puja* and the recitation of sacred texts, which reinforced local Hindu communities and brought merit and prestige for the sponsoring family. Even when the boom ended and individuals could no longer sponsor such grand religious ceremonies, groups came together

[43] A. Diesel, 'The Ramakrishna Sarada Devi Ashram for women in South Africa', *Journal of Contemporary Religion,* Vol. 11, No. 2 (1996), pp. 169–184.

to sponsor them instead, and they have become a permanent and core activity of Trinidad Hinduism as they mark the Hindu religious calendar. Clearly religion and culture are intertwined in such developments, but they do suggest that Trinidad Hindus have found ways to perpetuate and reinvent their religious traditions which provide them with personal and group meaning.

In this context it is worth noting how important the *Ramayana* has become in the diaspora in general, and not just in Trinidad. There are many significant Hindu texts and key stories and myths, rather than one core scriptural text as in Islam and Christianity. At different times Hindus have drawn on particular parts of this inheritance to suit their present purposes and needs. Reformers, such as those in the Arya Samaj, considered the ancient Vedas to be the true source of authority for reformed Hinduism. Gandhi and others among his contemporaries relied heavily on the *Bhagavad Gita* as a guide to behaviour and to the nature of man's relationship with the divine. Hindus in the diaspora seem particularly to have drawn strength and inspiration from the story of Prince Rama. It is a text which seems to have universal appeal, rather than speaking to any specific social group, and many of its key themes touch on areas of life where migrants feel anxiety and seek guidance. It talks of exile, suffering and struggle, and of loss. It also offers moral certainties and guidance to inter-personal relations. The popularity of its public reading, from the wretched barracks of indentured and contract labourers to the wealthy homes of recent migrants to Britain or America, suggests that it is one of the ways in which Hindus have found part of their religious tradition that speaks powerfully to them in changing situations and enables them to manage the challenges of a new environment far from their original homes.[44]

Later migrants from the subcontinent have reached their new homes with their religious culture and social forms intact compared with indentured and contract labourers, and they have also had more disposable income with which to establish religious space and religious activities. They have proceeded to do this wherever they have gone outside the subcontinent. The most public demonstration of the establishment of religion in the new home has been the building of places of worship. Wherever they have gone Hindus, Sikhs, Muslims and Parsis have acquired premises for worship and where possible have built new ones, not only to provide for the needs of worshippers but also to demonstrate publicly the significance of their religion in the diaspora environment. The *gurudwara*

[44] On the *Ramayana* as a 'central text' of the Hindu diaspora, see Parekh, *Some Reflections on the Indian Diaspora*, pp. 17–20.

for Hong Kong Sikhs was dedicated as early as 1902, and Sikhs and Hindus shared the premises for worship until Hindus built their own temples after the Second World War. Early Sikh migrants to Canada similarly built *gurudwaras* such as the one opened in 1935 in Hillcrest, Vancouver Island. By the last decade of the twentieth century it was estimated that there were just over 200 *gurudwaras* in the UK, 75 in Canada, and 60 in the USA, these being the three countries where three-quarters of overseas Sikhs live.[45] Parsi communities abroad, however tiny their numbers, have also established prayer halls, but these are unlike the temples in Bombay which are the heartland, as it were, of Parsi religion, where there are full-time priests, a permanent sacred fire, and the physical provision for full Parsi rituals. Hindu temples have proliferated in the diaspora. A pan-Hindu website for British Hindus lists nearly 200 temples affiliated to it, including those in many different sectarian traditions. But the total is far higher than this. The Swaminarayan temple in north London, completed in 1995 at a cost of £12 million, is one of the latest in this creation of very public Hindu sacred space. It is the largest Hindu temple outside India, modelled on one near Ahmedabad, Gujarat, a glittering edifice in white stone, for which much of the carving was done by over a thousand craftsmen imported from India. In America, too, Hindus have built temples in many traditions, and, as in the case of the Swaminarayan temple in London, they are demonstrations both of devotion and of increasing levels of disposable income, as well as symbols that Hindus are 'at home' in their new diaspora locations. The Srivaisnava Temple in Penn Hills near Pittsburgh, USA, consecrated in 1977, recreates the sacred space of similar temples in India and serves a large number of southern Indians who are part of the surrounding professional population.[46] Muslims, too, in the diaspora, of whom the largest group are in Britain, have built mosques though often their places of worship are whatever domestic or other premises they can find, including redundant churches. In Bradford, for example, the creation of mosques began early in the modern diaspora, at the end of the 1950s, and by the end of the 1980s there were 34 in the city alone, but only two were purpose-built.[47] In the final decade

[45] For photographs of the opening ceremony of the Hillcrest *gurudwara* and of the building itself, see S. S. Jagpal, *Becoming Canadians. Pioneer Sikhs in their Own Words* (Madeira Park and Vancouver, Harbour Publishing, 1994), pp. 75 and 77. Figures for *gurudwaras* in the diaspora are in chapter 3 of D. S. Tatla, *The Sikh Diaspora. The Search for Statehood* (London, University College London Press, 1999).

[46] V. Narayanan, 'Creating the South Indian 'Hindu' experience in the United States', chapter 7 of Williams (ed.), *A Sacred Thread*.

[47] P. Lewis, 'Being Muslim and being British. The dynamics of Islamic reconstruction in Bradford', in Ballard (ed.), *Desh Pardesh*, pp. 58–87, and *Islamic Britain. Religion, Politics*

Figure 8. Building places of worship: Glen Cove Gurudwara, NY 11542. An example of a Sikh *gurudwara* built in the USA to serve the needs of the diaspora.
Courtesy of Rekha Inc.

of the century there were probably about 500 mosques in Britain as a whole.

South Asians not only brought their major religious differences with them in the contemporary diaspora. Most of the major religious traditions were also split by sectarian division, and these, too, were represented in the use of these places of worship. Not only was the shared use of buildings between the major traditions abandoned as the diaspora became established but religious buildings now are increasingly rarely for all Hindus, Sikhs or Muslims, but for distinctive sectarian traditions within them, and/or for social groups with different linguistic and regional origins. Swaminarayan temples, for example, cater primarily for Gujaratis. *Gurudwaras* function for particular social groups among Sikhs (Jats rather than Ramgharias for example). While mosques and temples increasingly operate as distinctive sectarian institutions. Even heterodox traditions can be found in the diaspora where they represent powerful local traditions in the localities from which significant groups of migrants came.[48]

and Identity among British Muslims: Bradford in the 1990s (London and New York, Tauris, 1994).

48 See the example of a heterodox tradition imported from Punjab into the UK Midlands. The folk cult of Baba Balaknath is strong in the Jullundur Doab and is now present in

Figure 9. Building places of worship: Sri Venkateswara Temple, Penn Hills, PA 15235. A new Hindu temple in the USA, built on the South Indian pattern, which has become a vibrant social and religious centre.
Courtesy of Rekha Inc

Within Hindu places of worship in Britain there have also been distinct changes in the performance of ritual, indicating how Hindus have been able to reinterpret their traditions and to adapt their patterns of worship to suit their social situations in the diaspora. Moreover, in some congregational worship is developing alongside the use of the temple for personal worship, which is the more usual pattern on the subcontinent. Evidence from America similarly shows how Hindus have modified and reinvented their patterns of worship to suit the needs of busy people who only have the weekends for public religious observances.[49] A further development in the diaspora among Hindus has been the expansion

three temples. It is popular among Sikhs and some Hindus, and draws on both Hindu and Sikh traditions: R. A. Greaves, 'The worship of Baba Balaknath', *International Journal of Punjab Studies,* Vol. 5, No. 1 (1998), pp. 75–85.

49 On the USA see Narayanan, 'Creating the South Indian 'Hindu' experience in the United States', chapter 7 of R. B. Williams (ed.), *A Sacred Thread*; I. Y Junghare, 'The Hindu religious tradition in Minnesota', in Jacobsen and Kumar (eds.), *South Asians in the Diaspora*, pp. 149–160. On a Leeds Hindu temple in the UK see K. Knott, 'Hindu temple rituals in Britain: the reinterpretation of tradition', chapter 9 of R. Burghart (ed.), *Hinduism in Great Britain. The Perpetuation of Religion in an Alien Cultural Milieu* (London and New York, Tavistock Publications, 1987). See also Vertovec, chapter 6 of his *The Hindu Diaspora,* on the changing roles of Hindu temples in London.

Figure 10. Building places of worship: new mosque, Cowley Road, Oxford. An example of the ongoing construction of new sacred spaces in the diaspora, this mosque was completed early in the new millennium. *Author's photograph*

of the role of the temple. Sikh *gurudwaras* in India are social centres as well as places of worship, but Hindu temples have rarely been such centres for community interaction. In the diaspora by contrast some temples have developed into places of worship which are the core of a wider range of social and educational activities, which further confirm ties of sociability and shared identity among adherents. This is particularly the case within the well-organised network of Swaminarayan temples in the UK which give Gujarati Hindus a distinctive form of public religious space, with special provision for the needs and activities of women and young people, and engages them with charitable work among India's underprivileged.[50]

South Asian religions are not just manifested and experienced in the context of sacred buildings. For many South Asians the heart of religious experience and observance lies in the patterns of domestic worship, and the cycle of rites to mark key changes in individual lives, such as birth, marriage and death. Many of these persist and are full of vitality in the

[50] R. Dwyer, 'The Swaminarayan movement', in Jacobsen and Kumar (eds.), *South Asians in the Diaspora*, pp. 180–199. The website of the Swaminarayan temple in London (www.swaminarayan-baps.org.uk) gives an excellent insight into its many activities.

diaspora. Muslim women in Britain have maintained and even expanded domestic Islam, as we noted earlier, as they rarely attend mosque worship or other public rituals. Domestic Hinduism is still vibrant, particularly among British Gujaratis, who are present in Britain in sufficient numbers to sustain the cycle of rites, and have elaborated them with new forms of domestic devotion such as shared singing of hymns.[51] However, in the USA there is some evidence that among such a busy professional population, which is comparatively young and has few of the grandparental generation permanently present in the household, the observance of domestic rituals is becoming more difficult.

In some ways the more modern circumstances of diaspora South Asians, particularly the ease of travel, have contributed to the establishment of religious tradition and its elaboration outside the subcontinent. Religious leaders of sectarian traditions such as the Swaminarayan movements among Hindus, and devotional cults, such as the Sufi cults which develop around *pirs*, or holy leaders, in the Muslim tradition, can visit their followers and sustain their beliefs and practices in different countries; while adherents can in turn go on pilgrimage to sacred sites and institutions back in the subcontinent. Membership of such voluntary devotional groups can give status, a network of co-devotees and meaning in a changing world. However, people who act as non-institutional religious leaders and exemplars, and are foci of particular types of religious activity, are not only generated by the Great Traditions within South Asian religions. There is also some evidence of far more local 'holy men' who heal and exorcise and are representative of a particular form of exported folk religion.[52]

Managing change

Despite the evidence that South Asians have successfully constructed religious institutions and networks in the diaspora, there remain difficult issues of the transmission of tradition to the diaspora-born, and the

[51] See M. Michaelson, 'Domestic Hinduism in a Gujarati trading caste', and M. McDonald, 'Rituals of motherhood among Gujarati women in East London', chapters 2 and 3 of Burghart (ed.), *Hinduism in Great Britain*.

[52] The emergence of localised Little Traditions in the diaspora is noted in footnote 48. Further evidence of folk religion is the study of two *Babas* or holy men among British Punjabis: S. S. Chohan, 'Punjabi religion among the South Asian diaspora in Britain: the role of the *Baba*', Jacobsen and Kumar (eds.), *South Asians in the Diaspora*, pp. 393–414. For the more routinised phenomenon of the Sufi cults in Islam, see P. Werbner, 'Murids of the saint: migration, diaspora and redemptive sociality in Sufi regional and global cults', chapter 11 of I. Talbot and S. Thandi (eds.), *People on the Move. Punjabi Colonial and Post-Colonial Migration* (Karachi: Oxford University Press, 2004).

nature of religious leadership and the authority to modify practice and reinterpret tradition for new situations. Unless South Asian religious traditions can come alive in the experience of the younger generations, the physical importation and reconstruction of the outer manifestations of religion by older migrants will be insufficient to sustain these religions in a new environment. Older people in virtually all these religious traditions are aware of this problem and worry about the significance of religion in the lives of their children and grandchildren. On the subcontinent itself there were traditionally few means of religious education for most people outside the home. Children learned their traditions and ritual practices by watching particularly older women in the household, and there was none of the formal religious education to be found in Christian traditions as the precursor to such rites as confirmation, which mark the entry into full institutional membership of the church. There are signs in the diaspora that among many South Asians there have developed new modes of transmitting tradition to younger people, and – equally important – of allowing communities of belief to discuss their practices and beliefs in quite new ways, often in order to adapt them to the new situation. The Parsis of the diaspora, often bereft of trained priests, and having no central authority to legitimise change, have engaged in pragmatic adaptation of ritual. But another development has been an elaboration in the diaspora of explanation of ritual and belief for the younger generation. In north America, for example, this has taken the form of booklets and newletters.[53] Some Hindu groups in the diaspora have also tackled seriously problems of religious education, transmission and discussion. In Britain, for example, the Swaminarayan devotional sect, which originated in Gujarat in the late seventeenth and early eighteenth centuries, not only encourages adult lay discussion and development, but has particular programmes for the young which are reminiscent of an older Christian tradition of Sunday schools for children. Its British website also suggests how it has taken hold of this new means of communicating with the educated to explore and propagate its understanding of Hinduism. In the USA the Penn Hills southern Indian temple referred to above acts for its adherents in a similar way. It is not just a centre for worship, but enables enquiry, discussion, religious publications and the education of the young. Both help Hindus in the diaspora to see their tradition as a world religion with a core philosophy, a bearer of transcendental meaning and a guide to behaviour in the modern world, and exclude from the notion of Hinduism many of the diverse traditions and rituals visible on the subcontinent as

[53] Hinnells, 'The modern Zoroastrian diaspora', chapter 3 of Brown and Foot (eds.), *Migration: The Asian Experience*.

well as the worship of many minor deities which are increasingly seen as superstitious. Sikhs, too, are increasingly engaging with issues of transmitting and reinterpreting tradition, though this often generates considerable conflict about what it means to be a Sikh. Sikh elders try to reach their young through a variety of techniques, including Sikh camps in the USA, through *gurudwaras*, and particularly a vibrant Punjabi press in the diaspora.

Muslims in the modern South Asian diaspora are predominantly to be found in Britain. Sensitive studies have found that British Muslims have particular problems when it comes to transmitting Islam to their children, and to interpreting Islam in the often problematic situations in which they find themselves. Unlike many British Hindus or Sikhs, British Muslims come mainly from rural Pakistan or Bangladesh, have little education and lack sophisticated intellectual tools for debates about religion. Children learn their religion in the home, where their mothers are rarely educated and can often not converse with their children in English, which increasingly is becoming the preferred language of younger South Asians. Boys go to the schools attached to mosques which are specifically for teaching the recitation of the Koran, but, as in rural South Asia, this is done by rote learning and recitation, and does not involve textual study or intellectual discussion. Even more problematic is the lack of Muslim leadership external to the family which could take up the task of religious education for the new environment, enabling young Muslims to study their religious tradition in an open and intellectual manner. In most of the mosques attended by South Asian Muslims the Imams who pray and preach come directly from the subcontinent, do not speak English, and lack the conceptual tools and training to engage with young enquiring minds or to help their congregations cope with the wider world. Nor, indeed, are they expected to do so by the older generation of Muslims. It is significant that Muslims in the Deobandi tradition among the small group of Indian (as opposed to Pakistani or Bangladeshi) Muslims have recognised this problem and have been trying to train young Imams who can engage with wider political and socio-economic issues, reach out to the large group of young people in their community, and take up public roles in the wider society. As a result of their particular backgrounds, and the deeply conservative manner in which Islam is presented to them, most young Muslims face a deeply confusing world. Islam is important to them, but how it might be a guide for life in a complex environment, and as they increasingly leave the sheltered world of the ethnic enclave for education and work, is deeply problematic, as they have little guidance from those who should lead them and interpret their tradition for them. This opens them to radical and often violent understandings of Islam, as we shall see in the next chapter, preached by leaders who target a bewildered younger generation. Or it leads them to abandon Islam as a guide to living, with many of the consequences referred to earlier, including the fact that the Muslim prison population is nearly three times as large as the Muslim proportion of the population as a whole.

Representing South Asian religion abroad

One final aspect of South Asian religion in the diaspora is the awareness by people of most traditions that they need to represent themselves to their host societies, in order to establish their significance in the religious spectrum, and to protect their interests. This has led to the emergence of a number of umbrella organisations which claim to speak for Hindus, Muslims or Sikhs in particular national settings. At town level these have included in the UK the Bradford Council for Mosques, set up in 1981 with a grant from the city authority to articulate Muslim interests, and also to enable local authorities to deal with Muslims who might be considered representative. At national level there have also been a number of Muslim organisations, often in rivalry with each other. These include the Union of Muslim Organisations established in 1970, and the Imams and Mosques Council and the Council of Mosques, both set up in 1984. In 1997 representatives of 250 Muslim organisations came together to form the Muslim Council of Britain, with the aim of achieving a consensus among British Muslims on significant issues, and of working on Muslim concerns in the context of the wider society. But again many British Muslims would say that this does not represent their interests or views. Hindus have also set up national organisations such as the National Council of Hindu Temples, but only about one-tenth of all temples are affiliated to it. This council in turn set up the Hindu Council of the UK in 1994, one of the aims of which was to provide a national body for UK Hindus and their organisations, which could formulate a consensus in order to deal with other religions and the laws of the British state, in order to uphold Hindu cultural values. Yet again by no means all Hindu temples or organisations are affiliated to it. The history of most of these umbrella organisations is one of conflict and faction, displaying not only personal rivalries but the huge diversity of religious identity present among South Asians. Similar patterns are visible in north America indicating the sense of a growing need to have national organisations which can deal with the state in a particular diaspora location on issues related to South Asian religious traditions, and can represent those traditions to the wider society; but also demonstrating the near impossibility of achieving a consensus even among adherents of a particular tradition in one area of the diaspora.

*****

This chapter has studied the way in which South Asians in the many strands which make up the modern diaspora have made themselves at home in their new environments. Despite the poor bases from which many of them started, most have made a considerable success of the multiple processes of migration, particularly the key tasks of establishing an economic base, fashioning dense and supportive social networks, and maintaining and handing on to their children their religious heritage. In the process they have fashioned no single South Asian identity in the diaspora. Their very diverse origins mean that in their new homes they possess a whole range of identities which mark them off from each other – those of national and regional origin, of language, religion and socio-economic status. These can be deployed to underline difference or to forge new unities as new situations require. Yet another aspect of their lived experience is the awareness for many of belonging to a transnational world, where families and kin groups may live in different parts of a global diaspora, and yet maintain close contact and sociability. This suggests a very different way of understanding oneself and one's location in one's new home and in a global perspective – when compared with the self-understanding of their ancestors on the subcontinent or the majority in the societies in which they now live. How South Asians perceive their host societies and relate to them will be the theme of the next chapter.

4 Relating to the new homeland

This chapter shifts our discussion of the South Asian diaspora from the complex processes of putting down roots and establishing new homes and communities, to the way South Asians relate to the state and society in the places where they have made their homes outside the subcontinent. As this new relationship with a new homeland is forged over time, both one-time immigrants and the host societies acknowledge that South Asians are permanent residents and citizens in their new homes, particularly as their children and grandchildren grow up in the diaspora, knowing no other homeland. The approach is again thematic, as I highlight central issues rather than attempting any total history of the many elements in the diaspora. What becomes clear is that there is still much research to be done on the detail of how many of these issues are worked out in the very diverse strands of the diaspora. In general there is less evidence on the older South Asian communities overseas and more relating to those areas where South Asians have more recently migrated to modern states with developed economies and a much larger commitment to greater knowledge of their citizens, and provision of state services for them. Reflecting this understanding of the appropriate relationship of state and society it is striking, in relation to Britain for example, how scholars and researchers from so many different disciplines, as well as from government agencies, have felt a need to understand the dynamics and problems of South Asian groups in contemporary society: they include historians, political scientists, sociologists, geographers, health professionals and people interested in remedying profound inequalities. The result has been an abundance of evidence on the diaspora experience in Britain compared with many other areas. I focus here on some key problems and also contributions in relation to their new homes in the South Asian diasporic experience: but the previous chapter has of course touched on other themes in this evolving relationship, particularly the economic role of South Asians in the diaspora, their demographic impact on the places where they go, and the changes they bring to the public manifestation of religion.

1 Ethnicity and national identity

One of the most important themes in this broad area is the relationship between national identity and ethnicity. Some knowledge of this underlines just how difficult it has often been for South Asians to establish home 'abroad', not just in an economic sense, but in terms of reactions in the host society to the South Asian presence. Migrants and their descendants have experienced a whole spectrum of negative reactions, ranging from verbal comments and acts of petty discrimination to overt hostility, and even wholesale eviction. The ambiguities of their position are also demonstrated where immigration controls prevented their arrival in some places for lengthy periods, as we saw earlier, or, as in the UK, after an initial period of easy entry, curtailed immigration drastically often as a result of hostility in the host society. However, these problems also have to be set against the fact that understandings of the nation and of national identity are neither static nor objective. They are senses of belonging, created in the hearts and minds of both insiders and outsiders, by shared experiences and inheritances. They are also deeply contextual, and can vary greatly over time according to lived experience. Consequently, South Asians overseas can find themselves included or excluded from host understandings of national identity at different times; while their own senses of belonging can also alter.

It is important at the outset to remember two major variables which had a considerable impact on the degree to which South Asians were made to feel welcome and part of a national community and polity. Firstly, the societies where they have made their homes in the diaspora vary greatly. In particular they vary in their degree of homogeneity. We need to know whether a receiving society was diverse and open, accepting that migration was a necessary and positive way of building up the nation, as in the case of the USA in the later twentieth century. Alternatively, was the receiving society more homogenous, where ethnicity, language, religion and shared history reinforced a distinctive and restrictive view of national identity? Britain for much of the twentieth century probably falls into this category, despite the long history of migrations which have gone to make up modern Britain, because many of those earlier waves of migrants came from Europe where there were fewer differences of ethnicity and religion to mark them out as in-comers. (It should be remembered that Irish and Jewish migrants, for example, have faced real problems of acceptance and even overt hostility at different times in recent British history.) The variable of homogeneity has had a considerable impact on whether South Asians are seen as a welcome part of the developing national community or are viewed as threatening or diluting a particular vision of national identity.

The second major variable was the difference between South Asian migration into a free, democratic polity, and movement into areas under colonial control which then struggled to become independent nation states in the mid-twentieth century in the decades when the European empires were dismantled. In such colonial and post-colonial polities ethnic pluralism often became extremely problematic. As local colonial nationalisms developed in Africa and Asia, ethnic minorities, particularly those seen as having been imported, encouraged or protected by imperial rulers, were often despised or feared. They were seen to be separate from ethnic majorities with their developing senses of national identity, where ethnicity and shared culture and religion were proclaimed as the markers of belonging to an emergent nation which claimed its own national polity. The prospect of an independent nation state offered not only ideological fulfilment but more material prospects for people newly liberated from imperial control. The leaders of such states often publicised an exclusive rather than inclusive notion of the nation as a way of bonding their followers, while exclusion from key jobs of ethnic outsiders (even if they had lived in the area for several generations) opened up positions and incomes for followers and supporters, cementing political parties and attracting voters. In such situations South Asians who had been secure under colonial control, often finding jobs or economic positions which sustained colonial rule, were now dangerously vulnerable.

Several different patterns developed as South Asians overseas related to the societies and polities in which they established themselves and confronted issues of ethnicity and national identity. One prominent pattern was the experience of South Asians who migrated into colonial areas, with the encouragement of colonial authorities, and often initially took their place as very lowly labourers at the base of the local socio-economic hierarchy. Often they lived apart from local indigenous people and were disliked or feared by them. As they established themselves as free men and women, reared the next generations in their new home, and as articulate elite groups emerged among them, they engaged in a series of struggles with the colonial authorities to better their conditions in many areas of life and to claim membership of the colonial polity with clear rights as British subjects. One area of contention was the recognition of non-Christian marriages. In many places in the British empire Hindu, Muslim and Sikh marriages were not initially recognised outside the subcontinent, and this placed Indian women in the category of concubines, and rendered any children illegitimate: understandably this was considered a great slur on Indian respectability, particularly where the status and behaviour of women was seen as fundamental to the honour of men and of the family and kin group. Gandhi, for example, made the status of Indian marriages one of the planks of his final campaign in South Africa in 1913–1914. Indians in Trinidad had petitioned for the recognition of Hindu and Muslim marriages since the 1880s, and as some raised their socio-economic status and began to organise themselves they began lobbying the colonial legislature at the same time as Gandhi was campaigning on the issue half a world away. But internal divisions among them slowed down change and Muslim marriages were only recognised in 1936 and Hindu marriages in 1945. Yet another issue was that of voting rights, as colonial authorities began to liberalise the political arrangements in most colonies in the early twentieth century. Just as Indians at home were campaigning through the Indian National Congress for changes in the colonial political system, for more consultation with Indians, and for an expansion of the franchise whereby Indians were elected into local and all-Indian legislatures, so were Indians overseas, in many colonial areas where they had settled. The outcomes varied from area to area, as colonial authorities juggled the pressures from Indians, white settlers and indigenous populations. In many areas Indians were separated out and given special seats in colonial legislatures, rather than being admitted to a common electoral role which would have been symbolic of their status as British subjects with white settlers. Indians in Trinidad, one of the most constitutionally advanced areas of the British Empire, apart from the self-governing Dominions, gained universal suffrage in 1946, alongside the rest of the population, after campaigning against a proposed barrier to enfranchisement of those who, like many of them, did not speak English. Indians on the subcontinent did not gain the universal right to vote until after independence, in the general election of 1952, the first under the new constitution for the Republic of India.[1] Another area of experience where Indians increasingly became aware of their poor conditions and lack of equality was the world of work. In many colonies they began to campaign for better working conditions, particularly during the 1930s under the impact of depression, whether as tenant farmers of the Colonial Sugar Refining Company in Fiji, as estate labourers in Mauritius, or in Natal as they organised to protect their jobs from African encroachment.[2]

[1] A detailed discussion of Indian campaigns for political rights is H. Tinker, *Separate and Unequal. India and the Indians in the British Commonwealth 1920–1950* (London, C. Hurst and Co., 1976). On Fiji, and growing Indian awareness of their political inequality there, see chapter 7 of K. Gillion, *The Fiji Indians. Challenge to European Dominance 1920–1946* (Canberra, Australian National University Press, 1977).

[2] For Indian labour organisation and protest in various areas see Gillion, *The Fiji Indians*, chapter 8 on labour issues in Fiji in the 1930s; K. Hazareesingh, *History of Indians in Mauritius* (London and Basingstoke, MacMillan, revised edition, 1977) on labour unrest leading to a Commission of Enquiry in 1937; B. Freund, *Insiders and Outsiders. The*

However, as the component parts of the British Empire achieved independence, following the example of India in 1947, the position of Indians became even more ambiguous. No longer could they claim rights as British subjects and seek to influence British colonial authorities. Instead they had to deal with governments of newly-independent states, which were in turn wrestling with major social and economic problems as they tried to set their countries on new paths of development, and create new and cohesive polities. The 1948 British Nationality Act gave many Indians and Pakistanis in the diaspora citizenship of Britain and the Commonwealth, and the right to enter Britain. Britain had campaigned for the concept of Commonwealth citizenship which would recognise shared rights without denying citizenship of the component countries of the Commonwealth. Independent India for its part constituted its own citizenship, but did not extend this to Indians overseas and encouraged Indians in the diaspora to take the citizenship of the countries where they lived. But as different colonies attained independence it became clear that in many places Indians would suffer from more restrictive views of national identity and belonging. In Burma and Ceylon many Indians were effectively denied local citizenship because of strict regulations requiring lengthy prior residence in the country. Even where Indian migrants and their descendants applied for local citizenship, as many did, this was no lasting protection as so many East African Indians discovered at the end of the 1960s. As we saw in Chapter 2, many thousands fell victim to a vision of nationhood in Africa which had no place for ethnic South Asian minorities, particularly when they were thought to be – or could be presented as – taking jobs from indigenous Africans, and were forced to leave and look for yet another country which they could make their home.

Even though physical expulsion was rare and at the most violent and coercive end of the spectrum of treatment received by South Asians in the context of decolonisation, in many newly independent countries long established South Asian communities fell foul of ethnic nationalisms which worked to discriminate against visible ethnic minorities. This was the case in Malaysia, as the new government pushed for Malays to take over the civil service, which had been a prime channel of upward mobility for middle class Indians. In Guyana after Forbes Burnham seized power in 1968, Creoles came to dominate the government and the state's repressive apparatus at the expense of Indians, even though they made up about half the population. In Fiji at independence in 1970, Indians were just

Indian Working Class of Durban, 1910–1990 (Portsmouth, N.H., Pietermaritsburg and London, Heinemann, University of Natal Press and James Curry, 1995) chapter 4 on labour segmentation and militancy in Natal.

under half the population and outnumbered ethnic Fijians, though their percentage of the population was dropping. For nearly two decades it had seemed that the complex arrangements of the independence constitution had contained ethnic conflict, though Indians were aware of profound anti-Indian sentiment among Fijians, particularly when the Fijian Nationalist Party founded in 1974 called for the expulsion of all Indians from the country. Fijians dominated the government apparatus, the armed forces and the police. That the Indian position was grievously threatened, despite their numbers, was clear in 1987 when two coups overturned a newly elected coalition government led by a Fijian but dominated by Indians, who had 19 out of the 20 positions in it. This and a further attempted coup in 2000 were accompanied by widespread anti-Indian violence. It was no wonder that so many Fijians decided to leave the country to become 'twice-migrants' (see Chapter 2), joining a flow of Indians who chose to leave the places to which their parents and grandparents had come, for fear of what might yet happen to them as a visible ethnic minority in the context of strident ethnic majority nationalism. This flow included 'voluntary' migrants from East Africa, Surinam, Guyana, and a Sri Lanka engulfed by civil war between Tamils and indigenous Sri Lankans from the 1980s.

One long-established Indian diaspora community, which originated mainly in indentured labour, experienced a very distinctive relationship between ethnicity and national identity. This was the South African Indian community in the years of apartheid. Natal was joined with the other three areas of white settlement in South Africa to form the Union of South Africa in 1910, as a self-governing dominion within the British Empire. As we saw earlier, Indians faced discrimination by the white population and hostility from the black population. Their position as inferior citizens was dramatically displayed and solidified with the implementation of a system of apartheid in the early 1950s, whereby the Nationalist Party, which had come to power in 1948, began to implement a vision of white national identity which involved white dominance of the state structures and the political system, and draconian control of the non-white peoples of South Africa, including spatial segregation and separate social facilities. Among the provisions which hurt Indians the most was the 1950 Group Areas Act which forcibly redrew the social geography of Durban, the Indian heartland, as by then over three-quarters of the Indian population were urban rather than the rural labourers they had been at the start of the century. However, their position was deeply ambiguous. They were indeed inferior citizens, excluded from the vision of a white national identity, but increasingly the apartheid regime offered them incentives for cooperation with and co-optation into the apartheid state which recognised their permanent position in the country and enhanced their socio-economic and political opportunities. Politically they were given their own Council in 1969 and then their own Chamber in the tricameral Constitution of 1983. In 1977 an Indian Industrial Development Corporation was set up; and further opportunities for Indians to enhance their skill base were provided with the introduction of compulsory education for Indians in 1973 and the foundation of a separate Indian university, Durban-Westville, which was to focus on practical subjects such as engineering. It was not surprising that Indian political responses were fragmented. Some chose to ally with black resistance while others felt that cooperation and compromise with the regime was the best option in a profoundly difficult situation. Although Indians undoubtedly welcomed the end of apartheid in the final decade of the century, their relationship with the emerging sense of national identity is still far from clear. Despite Nelson Mandela's initial insistence on the importance of building what he called a 'rainbow nation', in which all ethnic groups could feel secure and equal, it remains to be seen whether pressure from black voters, frustrated at the lack of material change in the lives of so many of them, rebounds on Indians in similar ways to the impact of emerging ethnic nationalisms in the earlier period of decolonisation.[3]

The experiences of South Asians who have migrated to well-established democratic societies in the western world have been very different from those of migrants into the British Empire and its successor states. However, even here there are divergences in the way their distinctive ethnic backgrounds have interacted with pre-existing senses of national identity. In the United States, South Asians only began to arrive in significant numbers after the change in immigration law which was itself a spin-off from the civil rights movement. In effect they arrived after America had fought its own deepest battle over equality and national belonging in relation to its own black communities, and at a juncture when national identity was seen as emerging from a 'melting pot' in which people of all ethnic backgrounds could participate and fashion a new shared identity which still recognised distinctive cultures of origin. A common national identity beyond ethnicity and rooted in shared political values was powerfully reinforced in schools through the teaching of civics and the constitution. Moreover, South Asians who were admitted to America were just those who shared many of the same qualities and aspirations as did white Americans: they were mainly urban and middle class in background, well educated, and cosmopolitan in outlook. They came from places in the

[3] See Freund, *Insiders and Outsiders*, chapter 6; A. Lemon, 'The political position of Indians in South Africa', chapter 6 of C. Clarke, C. Peach and S. Vertovec (eds.), *South Asians Overseas. Migration and Ethnicity*. (Cambridge, Cambridge University Press, 1990).

subcontinent where rapid socio-economic change was already occurring, and were adaptable and upwardly-mobile in aspiration – just the sort of people who could buy into 'the American dream'. This is not to say that South Asians in America do not suffer discrimination. Professionals feel that there are glass ceilings which they cannot penetrate. Ignorance and fear have led to anti-Indian violence, as in the case of Sikhs who were attacked after the 2001 bombings in New York, just because they wore beards and turbans and bore some resemblance to the Muslim advocates of holy war against the USA who were prominently visible on television. Pakistanis particularly have felt that since '9/11' they have born the brunt of suspicion and increased vigilance by officials in the visa and home security parts of the administration. But in broad terms South Asians have taken their place in American society alongside Chinese, Japanese, black Americans and very diverse groups of people of European ancestry with relative ease; and their ethnicity is not seen by other Americans as a threat to American national identity or as a source of inferior status.

By contrast South Asians in Britain have a far more ambiguous relationship with the host society and the dominant ideas of British identity. Original migrants from the subcontinent in the 1950s and 1960s came at a time when British identity was still powerfully moulded by attitudes which had underpinned the British Empire, including ideas of racial superiority and inferiority. Being British was still associated with being ethnically Caucasian, having roots in one of the regions of the country (and local loyalties persisted right through the century generating deep atavistic senses of belonging, of being an insider or an outsider), sharing a Christian, and mainly Protestant, culture even if individuals were not personally believers, and bearing a proud political heritage symbolised by the monarchy. The Second World War had, if anything, deepened some of these views, reinforcing myths of a distinctive British character and superiority. Such a vision was manifested in a great variety of ways, ranging from the suspicion of American soldiers based in Britain during the war ('over-paid, over-sexed and over here', as the saying went), to the celebrations of the Coronation of Queen Elizabeth II in 1953 and talk of a new 'Elizabethan era', or the profound reluctance of many to consider Britain to be part of Europe. Even the emergence of the idea of a new Commonwealth in place of the old Empire fed on this idea of Britain as distinct from the other countries of Europe, destined still to be a world power and a senior partner in a new multi-national community. Into this situation came South Asians, preceded by an earlier wave of migrants from the Caribbean colonies, whose arrival had already generated ethnic anxiety and hostility, even though their labour was badly needed. Moreover, South Asians, unlike West Indians, were not Christian, nor did they often speak English fluently. They dressed differently from the local population, their women folk adopted patterns of modesty quite alien to that of most English women, and their cuisine was different and pungent. Senses of cultural difference reinforced visible ethnic difference, and these were in turn deepened as South Asians settled in large numbers precisely in areas where they lived and worked alongside a white working class who increasingly felt that the incomers constituted a threat to their culture and livelihoods. Racial tension, outbreaks of anti-black violence and voters' concerns about a coloured 'influx' soon penetrated the world of the politicians, leading eventually to the immigration controls noted in Chapter 2. Although much of the extensive public debate about immigration was couched in terms of the social 'problems' caused by migrants, underlying this was a concern among many that non-white immigration was threatening British national identity and the British way of life. National identity and ethnicity were thus bound together in a highly emotive discourse.[4]

If ethnicity was so profoundly implicated in ideas of British national identity widely espoused in the host society, how did South Asians, who hurried to Britain in even greater numbers as immigration controls became imminent, fare on a daily basis, and did prevailing notions of national identity expand to include them and their British-born descendants? In formal terms Britain espoused a policy of multiculturalism, permitting distinctive groups to retain their own cultural forms and ways of life (except in very specific cases as we shall see in the next section), extending citizenship to those permanently established in Britain. Immigration control went hand in hand with state attempts to manage relations between ethnic groups in Britain in order to prevent the sort of race violence which had been visible in the USA. The 1960s saw the emergence of legislation banning discrimination on grounds of race, and the development of policies designed to integrate minorities into mainstream British life in areas such as housing, education, social services and employment. By the mid-1970s it was clear that little fundamental change had occurred and that ethnic minorities continued to suffer considerable

[4] There is a large literature on the many interlocking issues which contributed to racial intolerance in Britain, and to the way ethnic minorities have been dealt with. A helpful basic introduction is J. Solomos, *Race and Racism in Contemporary Britain* (Houndmills and London, MacMillan, 1989). An account of citizenship and immigration built on detailed archival research which takes issue with Solomos on the degree of racism among politicians and civil servants is R. Hansen, *Citizenship and Immigration in Post-war Britain. The Institutional Origins of a Multicultural Nation* (Oxford, Oxford University Press, 2000). R. Karatani, *Defining British Citizenship. Empire, Commonwealth and Modern Britain* (London and Portland, Or., Frank Cass, 2003) focuses on the evolution of ideas of citizenship rather than on perceived identities, but is an important contribution to the understanding of the development of legal understandings of national belonging.

discrimination on a daily basis and persistent disadvantage. The problem was spelt out in a White Paper of 1975, entitled bluntly, *Racial Discrimination*. A year later a Race Relations Act sought solutions, by broadening the definition of discrimination to include both direct and indirect discrimination, and setting up a Commission for Racial Equality, which was to work to eliminate discrimination, to promote equal opportunities and good relations between ethnic groups, and to keep under review the working of the Act. At the start of the new century it is still the most powerful administrative weapon in the battle for equality among British citizens, having power to investigate organisations, help individuals with their complaints, and issue codes of practice designed to eliminate discrimination. As its mission statement proclaims; 'We work for a just and integrated society, where diversity is valued. We use both persuasion and our powers under the law to give everyone an equal change to live free from fear, discrimination, prejudice and racism.'[5] Despite a firmly established culture of ethnic monitoring in recruitment and employment, particularly in institutions which are publicly funded, there is still evidence of persistent discrimination on grounds of ethnicity and of institutionalised racism in a number of areas in British life, and even where this is ebbing it discourages ethnic minorities from trying to take up new roles. The police service is one example, and the small numbers of South Asian police has in turn considerable effects on how young South Asian men in particular view policing and its impact on them.

Government policy and public rhetoric is extremely important in defining the place of ethnic minorities in state and society. However they do not provide the whole picture. It is clear that despite the passage of four decades since the earliest legislation promoting ethnic harmony in Britain, the reality of lived experience is very different in the experience of some South Asians and other minority groups. There is still a vocal strand on the far right of the political spectrum which is overtly 'white nationalist'. Its earliest manifestation was the British National Front, founded in 1976, which brought together the League of Empire Loyalists, the British National Party and the Racial Preservation Society: the names of its component parts alone indicate the flavour of its agenda. It opposed British entry into the European Economic Community and argued for the compulsory repatriation of immigrants from the New Commonwealth, that is, those of non-European ethnicity. It organised noisy demonstrations, but its political base was tiny, probably never more than about 20,000, who came from among the self-employed and blue-collar workers who

[5] See the Commission for Racial Equality website which gives an excellent insight into its range of work: www.cre.gov.uk.

resented immigrant competition in the labour market. Its place at the far right of the political spectrum was taken in the 1980s by the British National Party (BNP), founded by a former member of the National Front. Among its policies are the repatriation of all illegal immigrants, the introduction of a system of voluntary repatriation of existing legally settled immigrants, and the repeal of all equalities legislation. It is openly racist and only admits as members those of 'British or closely kindred native European stock'. Its hostility to ethnically mixed marriages – as destroying a white family line – echo South Africa's apartheid legislation and Nazi concern for Aryan racial purity. The former leader of the British Conservative Party, Michael Howard, once claimed that the BNP was 'a bunch of thugs dressed up as a political party', and it is true that some members of the party's leadership have records of violence. However, its electoral success is very limited. It has no MPs and in the 2005 general election put up 119 candidates who between them polled just under 200,000 votes or 0.7 per cent of the total. Its success is mainly in local council elections, and in late 2003 it had 17 local councillors in the whole of England. Despite the condemnation heaped on it by all mainstream political parties it reflects a persistent element in British life and popular discourse, and its members and supporters are implicated in sporadic outbreaks of anti-minority violence.

More significant for the lives of South Asian citizens in Britain is the daily and personal experience of harassment and discrimination. The dimensions of this are impossible to quantify and it clearly differs both by socio-economic status and by region within Britain. Early migrants suffered considerably as they went about their daily business, attempted to get jobs and to find housing, as a recent study of the experiences of first-generation migrants to the Manchester area has indicated. This could range from verbal abuse to harassment at work or damage to property. When asked why it had taken South Asians so long to become a more integral part of British society they cited several factors such as poor English, the fact that they had not been through the British school system (unlike their children), problems of unemployment as local textile mills closed, thus closing off workplace friendships across ethnic boundaries, the closed lives and primarily domestic roles of most women, and the lack of private transport. Interestingly, even these problems did not prevent many of these first-generation diaspora South Asians from feeling strongly that Britain was home.[6] Among younger South Asians, born and educated in Britain, there is still experience of prejudice and a sense of

[6] A. Thompson and R. Begum, *Asian 'Britishness'. A Study of First Generation Asian Migrants in Greater Manchester* (London, Institute for Public Policy Research, 2005).

being excluded by many from an understanding in the host society of what it means to be British. For them it is the more painful because they have no other home and do not see themselves as immigrants, for the simple reason that they are not. It is particularly marked in the experience of young Muslims as a result of the rise of Islamophobia in the western world towards the end of the twentieth century. This was initially as a result of the reporting of Muslim politics in the Middle East and Afghanistan, but latterly because of '9/11' in the USA, and the 2005 attacks on London's transport system by groups of South Asian and African Muslims who had been resident in the UK after being admitted as asylum-seekers or had been born here to long-settled Muslim families.[7]

However, understandings of national identity change over time, and it is also true that as young South Asians progress through the British educational system, mix with their young white British peers, speak the same language, enjoy the same leisure pursuits, and watch the same television, there develop shared identities and experiences which go far to bridge the stark ethnic gulfs of their parents' generation. Symbolic is the young Amir Khan, aged 17 in 2004, who won a silver medal for boxing for Britain in the Athens Olympic Games. His family live in Bolton in north-west England, having come from Pakistan in 1970, but he proudly stood wrapped in the Union Jack and declared that he felt 'English through and through' and hoped he would be a role model for young Asians in British sport.[8] Boxing has been his route into mainstream British society. However some sports in the UK are also sites of exclusion as experienced by South Asians. Football is one example. Although many young South Asians keenly follow football and play in local or ethnic teams, they do not seem to play in those where talent scouts seek young recruits to the professional game.[9] For many other young South Asians the route towards affective British identity and acceptance in the wider society comes through education and professional employment. Differential educational achievement between different South Asian groups is significant, however, and this will

[7] For Young Muslims' experiences see chapter 4 of J. Jacobson, *Islam in Transition. Religion and Identity among British Pakistani Youth* (London and New York, Routledge, 1998). Further evidence of cross-generation South Asian experiences of prejudice is in chapter 6 of M. Stopes-Roe and R. Cochrane, *Citizens of this Country: The Asian British* (Clevedon and Philadelphia, Multilingual Matters Ltd., 1990) which draws on research in the Birmingham conurbation. Anti-Muslim prejudice in particular, rooted in a growing Islamophobia in the later twentieth century, is discussed in a paper published by the Runnymede Trust, *Islamophobia: A Challenge for Us All* (London, 1997). The Trust was established in 1968 to promote a multi-ethnic Britain: see its website which also lists its range of useful publications on ethnic issues, www.runnymedetrust.org.

[8] *The Times*, 26 August 2004.

[9] J. Baines and S. Johal, *Corner Flags and Corner Shops. The Asian Football Experience* (London, Victor Gollancz, 1998).

be considered in the next section. It remains true that discrimination and varieties of exclusion occur mainly where ethnic difference, region and class reinforce each other. So the bright South Asian university student, lawyer, doctor or IT professional is far less likely to move in a social and work milieu where he or she experiences overt discrimination than a school leaver with no professional qualifications or likelihood of employment, who lives in a northern city where job opportunities are scarce, and where class, ethnicity and long-standing senses of regional belonging reinforce majority senses of who belongs to Britain and who does not.

2 Citizenship and participation

We now turn from a consideration of the varied experiences of diasporic South Asians in the interface between ethnicity and national identity in their new homelands, to their experiences in the public arenas of the countries where they came to live. We look at what could be called the realities of citizenship, both in active public participation in the polity and in sometimes ambiguous relations with public provisions and expectations.

Patterns of South Asian political participation in their new homes have evolved somewhat differently, reflecting the timing and nature of particular strands in the diaspora. In former colonial territories South Asians have tended to engage in specifically ethnic politics, organising as ethnic groups, rather than round ideologies or socio-economic interests. This tendency stemmed from an earlier history of the poor position of many of the earliest migrants, the nature of imperial rule, imperial understandings of distinctive groups within local societies, and often provisions in the emerging constitutions which encouraged ethnic groups to act as political unities. It was also for many South Asians a defensive mechanism for dealing with emergent majority nationalisms and pressure on ethnic minorities. Although this is broadly true, it is also evident that almost everywhere South Asians never acted politically as one homogeneous party, but were often splintered, reflecting the fact that they were never single communities, but divided by language, religion and increasingly class. In Malaysia, for example, the emergence of an overtly Malay nationalism and the changing nature of the regime increasingly marginalised Indians in politics, and weakened the trade unions which had once been an Indian political base. Indian politicians also lost their earlier influence via multi-ethnic opposition parties and the Malay Indian Congress became their major voice and vehicle. However, religious differences split the South Asian political endeavour as Indian Muslims began to organise separately. In Fiji Indians had organised their own party, the

Federation Party (later the National Federation Party, or NFP) before independence, while ethnic Fijians similarly organised themselves in a predominantly Fijian party. At independence politics were racialised still further by the provision of communal, i.e. ethnic, representation, despite the NFP's wish for a common electoral role. The coups of 1987 indicated that even when the Indian political party came lawfully to power in a multi-ethnic coalition, this could be overturned by force on the part of the ethnic majority. It was not surprising that so many Indians decided to leave, convinced that democracy was a poor system for their protection, despite their numerical strength as voters. In Trinidad appeals to ethnicity developed with the advent of universal suffrage in 1946, and since independence politics have continued to be organised on ethnic lines, with the dominant People's National Movement, founded in 1955, identified as a 'black' party representing the interests of Afro-Trinidadians. However, clear ethnic divisions in post-colonial polities have not always led to ethnic political conflict. In Mauritius Hindus are just a majority in the population and had a slightly larger percentage of the seats in the legislature in the late 1990s. But politicians know that in order to retain their positions they have to attract the support of many kinds of people, and cannot just rely on support from one ethnic group. Moreover, each ethnic group is split – in the Hindu case between Tamils, Telugus, Marathas and North Indians – further confirming the need for multi-ethnic alliances.[10]

By contrast later migrants from the subcontinent settled in well-established democracies in which existing political parties were organised on ideological issues, and drew support from many different regional, religious and socio-economic groups. South Asians did not settle in sufficient numbers to overturn this pattern, nor did they feel the need to do so. In Britain, the western democracy with the largest number of South Asian residents, all three main parties had realised towards the end of the twentieth century the potential of the South Asian ethnic vote, particularly in those constituencies where they were sizeable or critical local minorities, and began to take their views seriously and attempt to incorporate them into party activity. Because of the particular clustered pattern of South Asian settlement, South Asian voters could form minorities of between 10 and 20 per cent in certain parliamentary constituencies, and were

[10] On Mauritius see A. Nave, 'Nested identities: ethnicity, community and the nature of group conflict in Mauritius' in chapter 3 of C. Bates (ed.), *Community, Empire and Migration. South Asians in Diaspora* (Basingstoke, Palgrave, 2001). In contrast, the political experience of Indians in Malaysia is examined in C. Muzaffar, 'Political marginalization in Malaysia', and R. A. Brown, 'The Indian political elite in Malaysia', chapters 8 and 9 of K. S. Sandhu and A. Mani (eds.), *Indian Communities in Southeast Asia* (Singapore, Times Academic Press, 1993).

actual majorities in some wards in local elections in urban areas such as London, Birmingham and Leicester. However, the actual participation of South Asian citizens in the political process has been slow, despite their numbers.

South Asians living in Britain have always been able to vote in British elections. This is so even when they do not take British citizenship, as all citizens of Commonwealth countries can vote alongside those who have British citizenship – a provision which harks back to the vision of a British and Commonwealth citizenship of the 1950s. However, South Asian voters were initially often not registered, and even at the end of the century they are still under-registered compared with the white population. In 1990 15 per cent of Asians were not registered, compared with only 6 per cent of the white voting population. Asian turnout, however, is higher than that of white and other voters. Even in the 1979 general election, which was early in the diaspora experience and well before any British-born South Asians could have voted, one study of three key constituencies in the north-west where Pakistanis were heavily clustered and formed 42 per cent of the electorate, showed that Asian turnout was 73.1 per cent while non-Asian turnout was 56.5 per cent.[11] South Asians do not, however, turn out uniformly at election time. In the 1997 general election over 80 per cent of Indians voted alongside 79 per cent of white voters. In comparison only 76 per cent of Pakistanis voters and 74 per cent of Bangladeshi voters turned out.[12] (In India in the run of elections since independence voter turn-out has steadily increased and is high compared with western democracies where voting is not compulsory.) Broadly speaking Asian voters have tended to vote for the Labour Party in greater numbers, in part because so many belong to the urban and less privileged working groups which have traditionally voted Labour. However, the Conservative Party has begun to make a pitch for Asian (and particularly Indian) voters on the lines of shared family values, conservative moral standards and the position of the self-employed. It is also a significant development that, although Asians do not vote as an ethnic bloc, the Muslim Council of Britain during the 2005 general election distributed to British Muslims (of whom nearly 70 per cent are South Asian) a voter card with ten questions to ask of all candidates. These included queries

[11] M. Anwar, 'The participation of Asians in the British political system', chapter 13 of Clarke, Peach and Vertovec (eds.), *South Asians Overseas*; M. Anwar, *Between Cultures. Continuity and Change in the Lives of Young Asians* (London and New York, Routledge, 1998), pp. 164, 165; M. Anwar, 'Ethnic minorities' representation. Voting and electoral politics in Britain, and the role of leaders', chapter 1 of P. Werbner and M. Anwar (eds.), *Black and Ethnic Leadership in Britain. The Cultural Dimensions of Political Action* (London and New York, Routledge, 1991).

[12] H. Ansari, *'The Infidel Within'. Muslims in Britain since 1800* (London, Hurst, 2004), chapter 8.

about support for various pieces of legislation designed to protect Islam in Britain, about a just foreign policy (in part reflecting the contemporary situation in Iraq after the Iraq war in which Britain had been the major partner of the USA), support for the withdrawal of British troops from Iraq, state funding for Muslim schools, and allowing religious views on such issues as abortion and euthanasia to be fully heard. Other umbrella Muslim organisations such as the Muslim Association of Britain and the Imams and Mosques Council (UK) also urged the duty of exercising the vote on Muslims.[13] Although South Asians are an increasing force in national political life through the exercise of the franchise, very few reach Parliament. In 2005 after the election there were eight South Asian MPs, all of them Labour. There were also 16 South Asian Peers, nominated to the House of Lords, mainly Labour or sitting on the cross-benches. The Peers, being senior in their particular professions and occupations, were mainly born in South Asia, but those who reach the Commons are increasingly likely to have been born and educated in Britain.[14]

In local politics South Asians are also becoming increasingly participant as voters. From among them are also emerging aspirant leaders and spokesmen of various kinds, using the opportunities provided by the political system and by the needs of local authorities of various kinds to find community workers and spokesmen for ethnic minorities whom they believe to be in some way representative, and with whom they can deal in the increasingly complex world of minority rights and provisions. This has opened the way for younger political activists who can work the political system, in contrast to more traditional leaders or business people of an older generation of migrants. But despite a political rhetoric of ethnicity, local ethnic groups are almost always so internally divided that even at the local level they do not speak with one ethnic voice or support one ethnic candidate.[15] From the perspective of the early twenty-first century, fifty years after the start of considerable South Asian migration into Britain, it becomes clear that former immigrants and their children have increasingly learnt the ways of politics in Britain, have become part

[13] *The Times*, 20 April 2005.

[14] See the lists of MPs and Peers and their biographies on the Parliamentary website, www.parliament.uk.

[15] See J. Eade, 'Bangladeshi community organization and leadership in Tower Hamlets, East London,' chapter 14 of Clarke, Peach and Vertovec (eds.), *South Asians Overseas*; J. Eade, *The Politics of Community. The Bangladeshi Community in East London* (Aldershot, Avebury, 1989); J. Eade, 'The political construction of class and community. Bangladeshi political leadership in Tower Hamlets, East London', chapter 3 of Werbner and Anwar (eds.), *Black and Ethnic Leadership in Britain*; P. Werbner, 'The fiction of unity in ethnic politics. Aspects of representation and the state among British Pakistanis', chapter 4 of the same volume. On struggles to become 'ethnic leaders' among Pakistanis in Oxford, see A. Shaw, *Kinship and Continuity. Pakistani Families in Britain* (Amsterdam, Harwood Academic Publishers, 2000), chapter 9.

of the broader political community, and are increasingly adept at working it to their advantage in a growing culture of official concern for provision for minorities.

Evidence from the USA also indicates that South Asians there, coming mainly from India at a time when the post-independence constitution and the practice of democracy had become firmly embedded in public life, and being fluent in English from the point of arrival, have also been adept at learning the particular ways of the polity where they have become citizens. None have reached the level in the national political system which South Asians have in the UK, but they are a significant force in some areas in local politics and have learned the art of lobbying and mobilising money and numbers to pursue issues significant to them. Like their UK counterparts they have also learned that it pays to set up umbrella organisations to enable different, and often rival, groups to seize on and exploit ethnicity as a political resource, and to claim to represent a significant ethnic minority, in an environment when it is politically correct to nurture ethnic diversity.[16] One sign of the clout Indians are hoping and beginning to wield in political life was the creation of a Congressional Caucus on India and Indian Americans in 1993, with the aim of being 'a vehicle to effectuate change through the lens of the Indian-American community'. In 2005 it comprised 105 Democrats and 68 Republicans. In 2004 a similar caucus was created in the Senate, the 'Friends of India'. In Canada an overt policy of multiculturalism has also helped to legitimise ethnic organisation and assertion, and claims for protection of cultural and religious difference. There, too, South Asians are learning the ways of local and national politics. In British Columbia the younger generation of Sikhs in particular is becoming more prominent in the public and professional life of the province, and is producing new politicians who work within the framework of established political parties.

The issue of public provision for ethnic minorities leads to the broader question of whether South Asians in the diaspora can take advantage of their status as citizens in a broader sense than just voting, and actually take hold of provisions and benefits available to citizens of a modern state predicated on the idea of care for citizens in return for fulfilment of citizens' obligations, including the payment of taxes. Or do migrants and their children remain disadvantaged in key areas, unable to make citizenship a reality in material terms? There is a very wide spectrum of experience throughout the diaspora. At one end would be that of South Asians in the USA who are of a socio-economic status to know what is available to them and to be able to pay for provision where the state does not provide

[16] See P. Kurien, 'Religion, ethnicity and politics: Hindu and Muslim Indian immigrants in the United States', *Ethnic and Racial Studies*, Vol. 24, No. 2 (March 2001), pp. 263–293.

adequate facilities, as in the case of health care. At the other end would be those in parts of South East Asia where they are often still inhabitants of squatter camps on the edges of towns, with little access to state provision of housing, health or education. As in the case of political organisation and electoral practice there is much evidence from the UK, partly because of the size of the South Asian population in the country, but also because of the practice of monitoring public provision consequent upon legislation prohibiting discrimination on grounds of ethnicity. The UK is also a good case in which to test out this issue because, unlike the diaspora in the USA, so many South Asians were initially deeply disadvantaged groups at the base of society. The areas of health care and education are particularly significant as indicators of well-being in the broadest sense and mobility in the new homeland. There is comprehensive provision of health care and education to the age of 18, free at the point of delivery, for all citizens. So here, if anywhere, it might be expected that South Asians would have experienced considerable improvement over time in their health and education.

The evidence suggests that British South Asians have considerable health problems. These include diabetes, which is six times more common among South Asians than the general population, and heart disease where the incidence is 46 per cent higher for men and 51 per cent higher for women of South Asian origin than for the general population. They also have a higher incidence of TB, which had been virtually wiped out among the white population with the provision of vaccination for school children; while Pakistani women have particular problems associated with childbirth. Some of these problems reflect genetic tendencies, and/or diet and attitudes to exercise. TB is a particular problem for people who regularly visit areas such as South Asia where it is still endemic, so South Asians who make regular visits to kin, often in rural areas, are at risk compared with holiday-makers or businessmen who are protected by their standards of travel and hotel accommodation. It also reflects poor housing and crowding, just as it did among the white population before the rise in living standards and health care after the Second World War. In general poverty and poor health are intimately linked, whatever the variations in ethnicity among the population. So it is hardly surprising that many poorer South Asians suffer ill-health in greater proportion than the white population. We have already seen that for various cultural and economic reasons Pakistanis and Indians have preferred to own their houses rather than wait for 'council housing', and in some places this has meant living in very poor housing, particularly for Pakistanis in northern cities. Those with the worst living standards are Bangladeshis, who have the poorest housing, the largest families and the most crowded conditions of all South Asians.

A further dimension of the problems associated with health care for South Asians is that of communication. Where older adults and often still some young women do not speak fluent English it may be very difficult for health professionals in primary care practices and in hospitals to communicate with their patients and clients, to explain the nature of their problem, the choices of treatment, and the ways they can help themselves. Gender issues are also a potential barrier to clear communication as Muslim women are often reluctant to consult male professionals. Moreover, poor knowledge of biology also prevents some from understanding their problems, particularly in areas relating to reproduction. Muslim girls do not get good information on their own bodies from older women, and often do not attend sex education classes in school, as we see below. I myself witnessed a situation where a recently-married Pakistani woman who had not been in England for a year, and was expecting her first child in a major university hospital, could find no one to explain what was happening to her in Urdu until the Indian wife of a doctor arrived to have her own baby and was able to communicate to her in the basic Hindustani which both Urdu and Hindi-speakers can understand. In kin groups which practise close cousin marriage there is also the danger of congenital abnormalities, which is again a problem of the utmost delicacy and cultural sensitivity. The death of family members in hospital can also cause great cultural misunderstandings and leave South Asian families deeply unhappy as their conventions and needs are not understood. Perhaps even more demanding is the issue of mental health and the provision of care for those of South Asian background who suffer in this way. Here again there are great barriers for less educated South Asians in understanding mental health in the same terms as those who might diagnose and treat them, and cultural gaps between patient and professional in an area where empathy and good communication is perhaps even more vital than in the case of physical illness. The National Health Service is well aware of many of the particular health problems of South Asians, of cultural and linguistic issues in communication, and of real problems in delivering health care to many ethnic minority citizens, but it struggles to address these when it is already under great pressure.[17]

Education is another area in Britain where there is free provision for all children up to the age of 18, when examinations are taken which are the

[17] It is significant that among health professionals and in their journals there is much discussion about the delivery of health care to minorities. An internet search on various aspects of health among South Asians in the UK demonstrates both the range of concern and research and the self-help initiatives within the diaspora. Some scholars are making a study of particular problems experienced by South Asians in relation to health and health care: for example, Dr Alison Shaw on the consequences of close cousin marriage among Pakistanis, and Dr Shirley Firth on issues relating to death.

entry point for university. There is also a small private sector, but only a few of the wealthiest Indian professionals can afford the fees for their children, and in general South Asians are high users of the public system because of their socio-economic levels and their comparatively large families. There are two main areas of concern in judging whether South Asians are using the system in a way which enhances the life chances of the younger generations, and whether they feel they are treated as citizens in relation to it. The first issue is that specifically relating to Muslims and their expectations from the educational system, because as early as the 1970s Muslims began to feel that the state system was failing their children in many ways.[18] In broad terms Muslims have campaigned for schooling which reflects their idea of appropriate behaviour for and treatment of girls. They prefer single-sex schooling after puberty but often this is impossible as comprehensive schools which deliver secondary education are virtually all co-educational. They have asked for and mostly received special provision for single-sex physical education, for girls to wear trousers/*salwar kameez* rather than skirts, and there have been no major conflicts over the wearing of the Muslim headscarf in school as this is deemed acceptable in Britain compared with France, where it has become a major issue and the headscarf has been banned as undermining France's public secularism. (Wearing trousers does not now mark out Muslim girls at British schools as more and more girls in the wider population are opting for trousers in line with wider changes in daily women's wear: according to one major supplier, in 2005 the sale of school trousers overtook skirts for the first time.) More generally issues relating to religious education in state schools became less acute in the UK as public provision of education became more overtly multi-cultural from the later 1970s, compared with an earlier period when daily and specifically Christian assembly was observed and where Religious Studies was Christian in emphasis and orientation. Muslim pupils can also be withdrawn from sex education lessons, have time off for festivals or Friday prayers, and are given *halal* meat. However, in recent decades Muslims have organised not just on issues within state schools but to provide independent Muslim schools and to demand state aid for them in the same way that many church and Jewish schools are what is known as 'voluntary-aided'. By 2002 there were 77 independent Muslim schools in the UK, and four with voluntary-aided status after the new Labour government cautiously accepted the idea after it came to power in 1997. Debate over Muslim schools has often been heated, and many in the wider society feel that they go against the ethos of British public life, or that they are

[18] See chapter 10 on British Muslims and education in Ansari, *The Infidel Within.*

divisive rather than encouraging the integration of young people from different backgrounds. Here the experience of the divisive impact of Protestant and Catholic schools in Northern Ireland has made many wary of encouraging further development of religious schools on the mainland.

More generally it is clear that among South Asians some groups of students are performing poorly compared with others and with the wider white society. Pupils who do not go on to take the higher level examinations can leave school at 16 and the public examination at that stage is the General Certificate of Secondary Education. Figures for 2003 indicate the discrepancies in performance between different ethnic groups. The national average of pupils in the state sector achieving five satisfactory passes (i.e. from A* to C) is 46 per cent for boys and 56 per cent for girls. The white students' performance was almost identical with the national average. Indian students performed far better, with 60 per cent of Indian boys and 70 per cent of Indian girls achieving this level. Pakistanis and Bangladeshis were both considerably behind, and in both groups girls did much better than boys. For Pakistanis the figures were 36 per cent for boys and 48 per cent for girls, and among Bangladeshis the figures were 39 per cent for boys and 53 per cent for girls. There is much discussion about why this lower performance for Pakistanis and Bangladeshis should be so. Clearly parental levels of education play a significant part, as they do in any ethnic community; so does the language spoken at home and the degree to which children integrate socially with their peer group in the wider society and learn to be at ease in public institutions and public space. Teacher expectations and role models are also significant. But a key factor (as in health) is social deprivation. Of Pakistani and Bangladeshi households, 65 per cent are classified as 'low income' compared with 18 per cent of white households. Further evidence is that 44 per cent of Bangladeshi children in primary school and 33 per cent of Pakistani children are eligible for free school meals, compared with 16 per cent of white children and only 12 per cent of Indian children at the same stage.[19] It is not surprising that among the different ethnic groups, according to figures for 1991, more Indians go on to achieve higher qualifications (15 per cent) than white young people (13.4 per cent), while just over 7 per cent of Pakistanis and 5 per cent of Bangladeshis do. At the level of elite education the differentials are very clear. Oxford University's 2005 entry statistics showed that of just over

[19] *Ethnicity and Education: The Evidence on Minority Ethnic Pupils* (report of January 2005 published by the Department for Education and Skills, and to be found on their website, www.dfes.org.uk). The Runnymede Trust (London) published in 1997 a paper, *Black and Ethnic Minority Young People and Educational Disadvantage*.

10,000 home applicants (i.e. from the UK) 3.5 per cent were Indian, 1.2 per cent were Pakistani and only 0.4 per cent were Bangladeshi. The success rates among the last two groups were 10.5 per cent and 14.6 per cent respectively; while 21.6 per cent of Indian applicants succeeded, nearer to the 29.7 per cent success rate of those classified as 'white'. The barrier occurs principally at school level rather than at the point of university entrance.[20] Clearly despite improvements in educational levels of South Asians over the decades, and in contrast to the actual levels of achievement many migrants brought with them, 'being British' still has not enabled many whose families originate in Pakistan and Bangladesh to overcome this initial handicap. A comparatively low level of educational achievement in relation to the wider society and in relation to Indians still remains. This also has immense implications for the life opportunities for young people (and males in particular) whose families came from these two countries, as they face an adult future in the diaspora where employment and all the 'goods' that flow from a regular income are dependent on the possession of educational qualifications and skills. The fact that they are also Muslim and are the largest group of British Muslims also has significant implications for Britain as a country coming to terms with religious pluralism.[21]

It is also important to note the issue of South Asian immigrants and the law. In most places law has evolved through a mixture of legislation and cases to reflect the norms, assumptions and aspirations of the local society. Laws can change of course, and reflect changing aspirations or ideas, for example, in Britain in relation to such emotive issues as the death penalty and abortion, or in the case of minorities to the prohibition of discrimination. But they do in general reflect dominant cultural norms. What happens when people migrate and bring with them rather different cultural patterns and assumptions about what is right and wrong, and find themselves living under laws which have evolved in very different societies and cultures? This is a significant issue and very little research has been done on the South Asian experience in different strands of the diaspora. Earlier discussion here has touched on one aspect of the broader question, the campaigns in some places to achieve proper legal recognition for South Asian marriages which were not celebrated according to

[20] See *Undergraduate Admissions Statistics 2005 Entry* (Oxford, Oxford University, 2005); also M. Anwar, *British Pakistanis: Demographic, Social and Economic Position* (Centre for Research in Ethnic Relations, University of Warwick, 1996).

[21] Of Muslim males in the UK, 31 per cent have no educational qualifications at all compared with an average of 16 per cent, and 14 per cent of Muslims are unemployed compared with 5 per cent among the wider population. These figures relate to all British Muslims, however, not just those from the subcontinent; *The Times*, 20 April 2005.

Christian rites.[22] South Asians come from a background where people have lived under personal law applicable to the religious group to which they belong – a feature of law on the subcontinent which emerged as British imperial rulers in the nineteenth century were reluctant to trample on what they saw as indigenous customs and laws. So such issues as marriage, divorce, inheritance and adoption were all subject to 'Hindu law', 'Muslim law', and 'Christian law', for example. In India today there is still not a common personal law and this is a cause of concern for many feminists, for example, and others who feel that there should be one secular law for all who live in the country. In terms of criminal law, however, there was one penal code for all people under British rule. Where South Asians have become citizens of modern societies they find themselves living where there is not only a common criminal law but also a law common to all citizens, which can be seen as intrusive on personal behaviour in a way which is culturally unacceptable, particularly if it is at variance with deeply held religious beliefs and cultural ideals. There are many issues where there is a potential for conflict – for example, the age of marriage, the treatment of women and girls within the domestic environment, wearing of clothes which are cultural and religious signifiers, or the way animals are slaughtered for food.

Britain had some experience of legal issues arising out of religious pluralism before the arrival of significant numbers of South Asians, particularly in the requirements of the Jewish population. But the arrival of South Asian Hindus, Sikhs and Muslims led to a considerable amount of adjustment both in the law and in administrative regulation to accommodate the sensitivities and needs of new ethnic minorities. In general legal protections have been given and exceptions made in relation to social practices which are both cultural and religious, where these are seen as not undermining core values and norms of British society, and where adaptation is conducive to peaceful pluralism. So the butchering of meat in the *halal* manner is permitted, as it had been in the case of *kosher* meat for Jews, despite complaints from animal welfare and rights campaigners. As already noted, Muslim women and girls may wear the *hijab* in the work place or at school. Sikhs fought battles with bus companies in England in the 1960s for the right of Sikh men to wear their turbans in place of bus conductors' caps; and in 1982 the House of

[22] There is also an interesting discussion of how Hindus in Britain have managed to bring together their own cultural needs in relation to the celebration of a marriage and the state's legal requirements for registration; W. Menski, 'Legal pluralism in the Hindu marriage' chapter 10 of R. Burghart (ed.), *Hinduism in Great Britain. The Perpetuation of Religion in an Alien Cultural Millieu* (London and New York, Tavistock Publications, 1987).

Lords ruled that Sikhs were an ethnic minority, and therefore effectively enabled to wear turbans at all times. Some Muslims have in fact suggested that British Muslims should have a separate system of family law, but this has received little support either among Muslims or the wider society.

However, it is in the area of family relations, the treatment of women and marriage, that there has been a clash between the law of the British state and some of the more conservative norms of South Asians in the diaspora. As we noted in the previous chapter, some South Asians now in Britain, particularly Muslims from Pakistan and Bangladesh, came from conservative rural sections of their own societies and had not been exposed to forces of social change as had those who came from urban backgrounds or had already moved outside the subcontinent. They brought with them clear understandings about the place of women in the patriarchal family and the way women's behaviour sustains or undermines family honour, and also conventions of arranged marriages often with close kin. Where these cultural norms clash with the expectations of young women brought up in the diaspora there is the potential for intra-family conflict and violence against daughters and sisters, and contravention of state law and support for human rights. The issue which has caused the most concern for the British authorities has been forced marriage. This must not be confused with arranged marriage, which, as we have seen, is still common throughout the diaspora but has been undergoing subtle modifications, as it has on the subcontinent itself. More often than not, young South Asians have been able to negotiate with their parents new ways in which they can make their feelings known in the business of finding an appropriate spouse, and often have the right of veto. Forced marriage occurs when young women (and sometimes young men) are pressurised into an arranged marriage to which they have not given their consent. The most common way this is achieved is by taking a young woman apparently for a holiday to Pakistan, for example, and while in a rural environment where she is often a stranger and unsupported by her peer group, she will be effectively imprisoned, and her British passport removed, until she gives her 'consent'. This practice came to light as a second generation of South Asians in Britain came to physical maturity. Often the first sign was an adolescent Muslim girl being removed from school and staying away for a long time. At other times the girls themselves or their friends in the UK have approached the UK police or the British diplomatic authorities abroad and alerted them to the fact that a young British citizen is being socially manipulated and even physically threatened into an unwanted marriage. After considerable reluctance to be drawn into sensitive domestic issues relating to diaspora groups (and thereby risk accusations of discrimination or cultural imperialism) the British government launched an extensive consultation, the upshot of which was a 2000 report by a working group on the issue entitled 'A Choice by Right', and ultimately the launch of a Forced Marriage Unit in January 2005 jointly between the Home Office and the Foreign and Commonwealth Office. Its role is to consider policy in this area, to launch projects and give practical advice to young people at risk. It draws a clear distinction between arranged and forced marriage and declares that the latter is one where one or both people are coerced into a marriage against their will. 'Duress includes both physical and emotional pressure. Forced marriage is an abuse of human rights and cannot be justified on any religious or cultural basis . . . Government takes forced marriage very seriously. It is a form of domestic violence and an abuse of the human rights. Victims can suffer many forms of physical and emotional damage including being held unlawfully captive, assaulted and repeatedly raped.' The Home Office website gives clear guidance and phone and e-mail contacts for people who fear that they themselves or someone they know is in danger and assures readers that they will even go to the lengths of launching a rescue mission overseas in conjunction with the local authorities. The new Unit runs a very user-friendly website for young people (www.missdorothy.com) and issues guidelines for the police, the education services and social services. Immigration for marriage is also now controlled with an eye to possible forced marriage and is only permitted where the incoming intended spouse is 18 or over rather than 16, and this is an attempt to give young people time to mature and resist family pressure. The fact that an extra immigration office is envisaged at Islamabad indicates that the problem lies mainly, but not only, in Pakistan.[23] There have been instances when girls have indeed been 'rescued' while abroad. But clearly the authorities prefer that the dangers of forced marriage should be tackled by education and persuasion rather than by bringing older family members to court. The police are also being educated in the culture in which forced marriages might take place; and in 2005 three British police officers of Indian origin visited Punjab, Haryana and Delhi to investigate this question. In this case they were particularly concerned with the problem of local Indian girls who might be tricked into marriage with unscrupulous Indian men from Britain who had their eyes on a handsome dowry, but had no intention of remaining married to their wives, who would then be left stranded – and probably un-marriageable.[24]

[23] See the link to 'forced marriage' on the Home Office website, www.homeoffice.gov.uk.
[24] *The Times of India*, 1 April 2005.

The British courts are, however, prepared to treat under criminal law abuses against young people relating to forced marriage. In April 2005, for example, a Sikh woman in London who preyed on young South Asian women in trouble (mostly through drug addiction and student debt) with the offer of modelling bridal wear in India, was discovered to be forcing them into sham marriages with men who wanted entry into the UK as spouses, then abandoned their 'brides'. Often this trickery was reinforced by rape if the girls attempted to refuse to agree to marriage. She was caught when she began 'arranging' marriages in the UK itself to illegal South Asian immigrants and was jailed for ten years. Police believed she had made nearly £1 million through this sham marriage factory run from a private home in Hillingdon, north London.[25] A further but rare problem when minority cultural norms clash with state law is that known as 'honour killing'. This is where family members go to the length of killing a daughter/sister/cousin if she has entered into a marriage, or more often an extra-marital sexual relationship, with a man of whom her family disapproves, and where this constitutes a perceived threat to family honour. It is a problem on the South Asian subcontinent itself and its importation into the UK reflects some of the most conservative norms still prevailing there. For decades the British police were ignorant of the phenomenon and the culture surrounding it, and it was only early in the new millennium that they began to recognise its existence and to look at a range of earlier deaths to discover whether these, too, could be murders in the name of honour. It should be emphasised that this is very rare indeed. Even in conservative families parents are becoming far more aware of their daughters' aspirations and rights, and murder in the name of honour is a sign that there has been a total breakdown in a family's capacity to talk and negotiate. But of course the publicity involved in such cases can influence majority attitudes to all South Asians in the UK, confirming a pre-existing mixture of ignorance and prejudice in the wider society.

3 Religious pluralism

A further theme of considerable significance in the evolving relationship of South Asians in the diaspora to their new homelands is that of religious pluralism. To many observers in the mid-twentieth century it seemed that in many societies throughout the world the prevailing trend was towards increasing secularisation of public life and the relegation of religion to private choice and observance. In this situation diasporic communities

[25] This case was reported in *The Times*, 26 April 2005.

would easily be able to fit into very different host societies, as their religious traditions became part of a mosaic of private observance. Indeed this did seem to be the case. Where South Asians had migrated in the later nineteenth century in any numbers they settled in societies which were undergoing considerable change and where there was often existing religious pluralism. In few places was there opposition to the incomers on grounds of their religion, or hostility between religious groups. In the mid-twentieth century South Asians took their religious traditions to the increasingly secular societies of the western world, and were able to create sacred space with comparative ease, acquiring or building places for worship, reconstituting domestic observances and creating umbrella religious organisations to represent their interests, as we saw in the previous chapter.

However in the later twentieth and early twenty-first centuries it has become clear that this pattern of accommodation leading to the creation of new religious pluralisms is being threatened by a variety of forces. Among them has been the resurgence of radical and often fundamentalist strands within many religious traditions, including Christianity, Islam and Hinduism. This in itself militates against easy co-existence as each tradition produces vocal and active adherents who preach their own vision of their tradition as the only way to salvation, or the only authentic religious truth. In places this has produced unlikely alliances as the proponents of different fundamentalisms join forces to push for conservative and anti-secular social policies. (We noted earlier British Muslim calls at election time in 2005 for aspiring candidates to heed religious and moral opposition to such things as abortion and euthanasia, a view which would be shared by many Roman Catholics and Evangelical Protestant Christians.) The development of the mass media has played an important role as news of such radicalism and opposition to other traditions is widely reported, from the slaughter of Muslims in Gujarat, India, in 2002, to the murder of Christians in Pakistan, or the prolonged Serbian attack on Bosnian Muslims. Worldwide news, now in graphic television pictures as much as in print, brings people increasingly into a global community of perception and misconception. But most particularly religion and politics have become deeply entangled in parts of the Middle East, and Muslims worldwide have become convinced that their religion is under threat. They are particularly incensed by the problems faced by Palestinians and their inability to achieve statehood against the might of American-backed Israel. Here at least three radical/fundamentalist versions of great world monotheisms are involved – Islam, Judaism in its Zionist manifestation, and American Protestantism of the far right. The repercussions of these developments on the relationship of South Asian Muslims to their host societies have been particularly apparent in Britain, not least because Muslims constitute a far larger proportion of the diaspora there than in north America, Australia or New Zealand, and because Britain is evidently a close ally of the USA.

If we turn to the British case we can see a number of trends which are replicated to some degree in other parts of the world where South Asians have settled, but which are most obvious in Britain because of the size of the diaspora and its religious composition. At one level there has been the continuing trend of overt religious pluralism, as Hindu, Muslim, Sikh, and Parsi religious sites and institutions have become established in increasing numbers to service the growing diasporic population. The state has responded to this with official protection for minority religions and a conscious commitment to pluralism, for example in the way religion has been taught in schools since the 1970s. Christianity now takes its place as one of a number of world religions in 'religious studies' curricula, and it is expected that all school children will receive some instruction in the beliefs and observances of religious traditions other than Christianity. This raises very interesting questions about how South Asian religious traditions, for example, are presented to school children and to the wider society. Normally this is done through the presentation of a package of core beliefs and practices, including public festivals, thus simplifying the traditions often beyond recognition to insiders who can be quite bemused at what their own children tell them about what is taught in school about their own tradition. Hinduism is thus presented as 'a religion', though as we noted in the previous chapter Hinduism is an umbrella term given to a vast range of traditions and beliefs, and there is certainly no single Hindu faith or pattern of observance in South Asia or in the diaspora. Islam, too is presented as a homogeneous monotheism with little understanding of the sectarian differences within it, or the internal struggles among Muslims in many places as they seek to understand how to be good Muslims in a rapidly changing world. However, despite its inevitably crude over-simplifications, the teaching of religious studies has opened the eyes of younger British people to the religious diversity around them in an accepting way, which is very different from prevailing attitudes even fifty years ago.

The Christian churches in Britain and elsewhere have also responded to the new religious pluralism at home by gradually embarking on processes of conversation which enable adherents of different traditions to gain some understanding of each other's beliefs and practices. This Christian response to pluralism can be seen at several levels. At the level of theology there has been a serious consideration of the nature of revelation and of religious truth, and a recognition that these can be found outside the

Christian fold. This has caused immense controversy inside Christianity and considerable heart-searching. But in general the dismissive and often condemnatory attitudes towards other traditions generally prevalent until the middle of the century have been modified, except among those who adhere to a very strict interpretation of scripture. Most theologians now take very seriously the religious insights of other religious traditions. At the level of institutional religion there has been a mushrooming of official mechanisms for inter-religious 'dialogue', as it is often called.[26] It is also significant that at important national occasions, traditionally celebrated in one of the great Anglican London churches, the representatives of non-Christian traditions are invited to be present and participant. Such representatives are also present officially at that peculiarly British and highly emotive annual remembrance of those who died in war for the nation at the Cenotaph in London on the Sunday nearest 11 November, the day the First World War ended. Implicitly and visually South Asians are seen to be part of the nation, in its imperial past and its plural present.

Despite such manifestations of inter-religious dialogue and the official acceptance of a religious pluralism as an evident aspect of British life, there have also been occasions which can only be described as explosive, which indicate that at times some elements among Britain's religious minorities have felt that their tradition is endangered in British public space. This has in turn produced an incredulous and condemnatory response from secular and liberal members of the wider society who are as shocked at these manifestations in contemporary Britain as are the protestors horrified at what they see as insults to their beliefs condoned in the public space of their homeland. One such was the notorious 'Rushdie Affair' in 1989, when many British Muslims complained bitterly about Salman Rushdie's recent book, *The Satanic Verses*, which they claimed was insulting to the Koran and to the founder of Islam himself. (Rushdie himself vigorously denied that this was in any way his intention.) Street demonstrations were held, the book itself was publicly burnt in Bradford, and many British South Asian Muslims supported the *fatwa* issued by the Ayatolla Khomeni in Iran sentencing Rushdie to death for apostasy. Public campaigns persisted for some time, and Muslims lobbied MPs and the government in an attempt to get the book withdrawn from circulation. They did not succeed, though the author had to go into hiding for his own safety. The whole issue was highly emotive and hurtful for many young Muslims, even though most of them probably never

[26] An interesting indicator of the changes within Christian circles by the later twentieth century is R. Hooker and J. Sargant (eds.), *Belonging to Britain: Christian Perspectives on Religion and Identity in a Plural Society* (London, Council of Churches for Britain and Ireland (CCBI) Publications, c. 1991).

read the novel; but it was symbolic of their fear for Islam in the diaspora and their sense of being a minority excluded from the mainstream of British life. Rather similar though much shorter lived was the outcry over a play entitled *Behzti* (dishonour) late in 2004. Written by a Sikh woman author, it included scenes of sexual abuse and murder in a *gurudwara*. It was due to be performed in Birmingham, where there is a sizeable Sikh population, but public demonstrations by some hundreds made it impossible to hold performances and the play was eventually cancelled on grounds of safety. Many local Sikhs professed themselves satisfied at the outcome, though there was considerable condemnation in the wider society that a minority could by violent demonstration effectively cause artistic censorship. But one thoughtful Sikh academic and author argued courageously that Sikhs themselves were the losers in reverting to a militant stance which focussed on narrow communal interests. In so doing they were undermining the position they had built up in British society, and also failing to give serious leadership on the real concerns of young Sikhs growing up in Britain. He also noted how official multiculturalism encouraged people who stood forward to 'represent' Sikhs and Sikhism in the public sphere, thus collaborating with officials and their needs; but this overlooked the serious contest going on within minority groups on crucial issues, including the often violent treatment of women.[27]

The same themes of increasing public militancy in response to perceived affronts and attacks on religion, of profound internal contestations about the meaning of religious tradition, and the failure of a leadership to connect with younger British-born and educated in the diaspora, are also present in the relationship of British Muslims to each other and to the wider society. This was made dramatically and painfully clear in July 2005, when the first wave of bomb attacks on the London transport system was carried out mainly by young, reasonably educated Pakistanis from Leeds, a large northern British city.[28] (Subsequent attacks were by non-South Asian Muslims, mostly young men born in eastern Africa but long-settled in the UK as part of asylum-seeking families. This indicates that many of the problems experienced by young Muslims are not confined to those of South Asian origin.) The predominant reaction in the UK among the wider population was horror combined with

[27] Comment by Professor Gurharpal Singh of Birmingham University in *The Guardian*, 24 December 2004.

[28] Of the four bombers who died in their own explosions on the London transport system three were South Asians from Leeds. They were aged 18, 22 and 30, and all were reasonably educated. The youngest had left school in 2003 with seven GCSEs, the next had been a sports science student, and the oldest was a teaching assistant in a primary school. The fourth bomber was a Jamaican born convert to Islam, aged 19, who had spent his childhood in Huddersfield, not far from Leeds.

incredulity. How could people born and educated in Britain attack their own homeland? Even the attacks of '9/11' in the USA had been the work of outsiders. However, July 2005 showed only too clearly how the rise of radical Islamism had the potential for unleashing religiously motivated violence in the heart of a western, plural and secular society. Clearly this phenomenon had its roots in complex international situations, from the murderous civil strife which followed the break-up of Yugoslavia in the Balkans, to the unresolved Palestinian conflict with the Israeli state, and the American-led attempts to end particular Muslim regimes in Afghanistan and Iraq. Many British Muslims, along with Muslims in many other countries, interpreted this as a concerted latter-day crusade against Islam; and the British state was seen as particularly complicit in this. The possible connections with this international phenomenon and Britain's own society and politics were being discerned by scholars and writers of fiction long before 2005. Hanif Kureishi published a short story in 1993, later to become a film, *My Son The Fanatic*, which described the gulf which opened up between a British Pakistani taxi-driving father and his far better educated son who turns to radical Islam and a vision of *jihad* against western society. Monica Ali's 2003 novel, *Brick Lane*, also described the controversy between two London Bangladeshi men about the rectitude of suicide bombing in defence of Islam: it was the Londoner who supported *jihad* as the result of living in Britain's plural and secular society, rather than the first-generation migrant who was anxious to lay hold on what London could offer him in work and upward social mobility.[29]

However, in the wake of the 7 July bombings in London it has become clearer why Britain, despite its attempts to accommodate its own Muslim population and consciously to assist the emergence of a religiously plural society, should have become the target of violence by insiders. Of all the western societies where South Asian Muslims have settled permanently Britain has by far the largest population. Moreover, their origins on the subcontinent were among social groups which had been little touched by the sophisticated discussions within South Asian Islam, that had developed since the mid-nineteenth century on such issues as the nature of religious authority and the interpretation of scripture, the grounds for social reform (particularly in relation to the treatment of women), or the ways in which Muslims should relate to modern secular state structures and authorities. Further, as South Asian Muslims settled in Britain and

[29] One of the most profound accounts of South Asian Islam in Britain, which portrayed the often anguished world of young Muslims, was published in 1994; P. Lewis, *Islamic Britain. Religion, Politics and Identity among British Muslims: Bradford in the 1990s* (London and New York, Tauris, 1994).

established mosques for worship and other patterns of Islamic observance, they had no leadership which could give them serious religious guidance on how to live in a very different society, or which could relate to younger British-born Muslims and engage with them on urgent political and social matters. Many Imams who served the Pakistani and Bangladeshi communities in particular were trained in South Asia, spoke little or no English, could not understand the dilemmas of younger Muslims, and were not independent of conservative elders, but beholden to the mosque committees which employed them. It was not until some months before the 2005 attacks that the government took steps to control the immigration of ill-educated Imams, by insisting that they must have some command of English. Nor was there a coherent lay leadership to guide the thinking of young Muslims; and the umbrella organisations which attempted to represent South Asian Islam were deeply divided among themselves and spoke with contrary voices.

It is hardly surprising that young Muslim men in particular should have become deeply confused about how to live their lives as Muslims in the modern, secular world, as they were left rudderless and unable to communicate at any deep level with their parents' generation at home or with their supposed religious guides. This was compounded by the pressures of unemployment and a sense of exclusion from British society, as well as the frustrations and hurts generated by international news. Some have despaired of finding meaning to their lives; and it is these young men who have found their way into drugs, crime and prison. Others, often the most educated and thoughtful, have listened to the preaching of radical Islamist Imams and other propagandists, and have pondered in front of their computers the meaning of a range of Islamist websites. It is understandable why radical Islam should be so appealing in a diaspora context. It makes far more sense and is more fulfilling than adhering to the Pakistan-orientated Islam of their parents' generation, which is not only parochial in outlook but accessible only through such languages as Urdu with which British born South Asians do not feel comfortable. By contrast radical Islam is accessible in English and is couched in global terms. Some of those attracted by this vision of Islam have decided to visit Islamist *Madrassahs* in Pakistan to learn more about Islam and often violent ways of defending it in South Asia and in the wider world. Many more receive their 'education' in a radical and violent version of Islam at home in Britain, contacted by groups who target vulnerable and confused young men in prisons and colleges.

It has also to be said that the very openness of British society has permitted the operation of preachers and organisations who overtly argue for a violent response to the problems of Muslims in the contemporary world; and political leaders from countries in the Middle East and South Asia which have faced Islamist terror on their own soil have long complained that Britain is a haven for those who preach hatred and violence. The British authorities are in an unhappy predicament, as the aftermath of 7 July showed. They need to control by imprisonment or deportation those who preach religious hatred, and in the process they risk confrontation with groups who champion civil liberties and human rights. Yet they also have to work hard to convince British Muslims that they are not a specifically targeted group in society when it comes to immigration control and anti-terror policing. One of the core problems in the relationship of South Asian Muslims with the wider society and the state, clearly manifest in the wake of 7 July, is the considerable ignorance on the part of most Britons and their political leaders about the inner dynamics and problems of the various British Muslim communities, and the failure of liberal multiculturalism to enable both meaningful discussion between groups and the emergence of minority leaders who can really 'speak for' the great diversity of British Islam. Again, the low socio-economic status of so many Muslims, and their encapsulation within their own minority social worlds, has worked to create profound barriers of misunderstanding between them and society at large.

4 Cultural interactions and contributions

If the new millennium has laid bare some of the deepest tensions felt by some South Asians in their new homelands, it has also seen a wide range of cultural interactions which have influenced not only migrants and subsequent generations of South Asians in the diaspora but the societies where they have settled. Previous chapters have indicated how South Asians in the diaspora have taken up new economic roles which have transformed their socio-economic status as well as contributing to aspects of the economies of their new homelands, how gender roles have begun to change as a result of women's education and paid employment outside the home, how religious observations have been modified, and how those born and educated outside the subcontinent have learned to share in the tastes and recreations of their peer groups in the wider society, whether in sport, food, music or clothes. This has often occurred alongside a continuing sense of South Asian cultural inheritance, kept alive by the influence of the family, and the ability to keep in touch with the culture of the subcontinent in many ways, as we shall see in the next chapter. For every young South Asian who contemplates violence and rejects the society into which he or she has been born in the diaspora, there are thousands who grow up in vibrant social worlds where they move between ethnic enclaves, home environments and the worlds of school, college and work, and manage in a highly sophisticated manner a whole range of opportunities and identities now open to them. However, it would be impossible to conclude this part of our discussion on the experience of those living in the diaspora without briefly indicating some of the ways that their presence in their host societies has in turn enriched and diversified the culture of those societies. This is as significant a theme in the diaspora's relationship with their new homeland as are those which are more ambiguous and problematic.

Discussions of religious issues have already indicated how the rooting of South Asian religious traditions has changed the religious landscape of many societies where South Asians have settled. Particularly in western societies where the prevailing culture has been Christian or post-Christian, this new religious pluralism has opened up new worlds for Christian believers and theologians, and also for young people being educated alongside Hindus, Sikhs and Muslims for the first time. For example even half a century ago in Britain the only people of different faith traditions a school child was likely to encounter were Jews, and then only in very particular parts of Britain, such as London or Manchester, where there were Jewish settlements of long standing.

In far more material ways South Asians are making their cultural mark. The most obvious is in the area of cuisine. South Asian cooking has of course been part of the domestic culture of diasporic communities worldwide, although in different areas it could take on a local flavour depending on the nature of local ingredients before the easy importation of South Asian spices and other ingredients. However, where South Asians have settled in economies which have generated considerable disposable income in the wider society, and with it the incentive to eat out for recreation and to save domestic time, so particular groups in the diaspora have seized the opportunity to open up public culinary space. The 'Indian' restaurant and 'take-away curry' are now almost worldwide phenomena; though, as we have already observed, what is served in such places is often adapted to the local palate and is not at all the same as the domestic cuisine of diaspora groups. Moreover, until very recently it also offered monochrome food described as 'Indian' which did not reflect the immense diversity of cuisines on the subcontinent, drawing on the different ingredients available in different regions, and on the cultural traditions of different parts of the subcontinent. From the Indian restaurant as an initial base, versions of South Asian ethnic food have spread into the provision of ingredients for ethnic food in specialist ethnic shops and eventually into ordinary supermarkets, and then into ready-made South Asian food either mass-produced, or cooked as a home-industry by the women of households which run corner or ethnic shops. A South Asian-run mini-market in my home shopping parade advertises 'home-made samosas', for example. It is also noteworthy that western cookery books now often include recipes for varieties of 'curry' and other South Asian dishes, alongside other ethnic dishes which reflect the growing pattern of foreign travel and holidays to many places with distinctive regional cuisines. In earlier generations almost the only British people to cook 'Indian' food would have been women who returned from living on the subcontinent in the days of the Empire, who would have replicated Indo-British dishes, such as curry and rice or kedgeree, cooked for European consumption in the days of the raj.

Dress is another area in which the influence of South Asia has had an impact on the wider society. Sometimes this comes directly from South Asia at the hands of South Asian entrepreneurs and exporters; but often there is a diasporic contribution both in the design and in the economics of cultural diffusion in this area of material consumption. Fabrics are often imported from the subcontinent, particularly cotton and silk, with easily recognisable South Asian designs, perpetuating a long tradition of cultural export and influence emanating from the subcontinent. However, the actual clothes worn by Indians were in the past a distinctive cultural marker, both on the subcontinent and in the diaspora, and they carried profound political significance for their wearers. Indian nationalists followed the example of Gandhi in casting off western style clothing as a sign of aspiring to national independence; while Europeans in India maintained their own attire even when it was most unsuitable for the climate, as a signifier of racial difference and assumed superiority. In the diaspora communities South Asian dress has been perpetuated, particularly among women, as a marker of modesty and respectability, in contrast to 'western' clothes often thought to be immodest and revealing, although among many young Asian women jeans and tops are now common as informal wear. Half a century after independence there is considerable fashion-creep, as South Asian styles of clothing are either adopted abroad or influence the way other ethnic groups wear or modify their own clothing. For men the so-called Nehru jacket, which in fact draws on a long established north Indian style of masculine dress, is one example, as is the collarless shirt. For women the wearing of a tunic over trousers echoes the comfort and modesty of the *salwar kameez* worn by Punjabi women and girls; while the *pashmina* shawl or the long silk scarf is a more direct importation and is worn in various ways which often reflect how South Asian women have worn shawls and scarves for warmth and for modesty over centuries. Similarly the influence of South Asian styles of jewellery is widespread, either in motifs adopted in the creation of expensive jewellery, or at the popular end of the market as South Asian stall-holders sell cheap imported earrings, bracelets, anklets and rings, which appeal particularly to younger members of the wider host society from many different ethnic backgrounds.

There is also a growing South Asian influence in the worlds of music and film in countries where there is a considerable diaspora. The growing awareness of the richness of the high South Asian musical tradition may well owe as much to a more general globalisation of cultural sensitivity and knowledge as to the presence of musically knowledgable South Asians in the diaspora, just as an appreciation of the work of some of the most talented Asian film-makers such as Satyajit Ray would probably have developed outside the subcontinent, regardless of the modern diaspora. However, at a more popular level diasporic influence is clear. The BBC in Britain, for example, catering for all those who pay the British licence fee, has in mind the South Asian diaspora when it puts on 'Bollywood' films or indeed when it has coverage of such a major Indian religious festival such as the Kumbh Mela in 2001 in Allahabad, celebrating a Hindu creation story, to which many British Hindus went or watched from afar through television. In 1991–1993 it also showed in 94 episodes the acclaimed version of the great Hindu scripture, the *Mahabharat*, which attracted audiences of several million. Entertainment programme series on television are also the means by which the diaspora becomes part of mainstream popular culture: examples include the comedy series, *Goodness Gracious Me* and *The Kumars at No 42*. These are only possible on prime time national television because of the size of the diaspora in Britain, and the fact that the characters and their situations are recognisable and funny to the wider society as well as to the ethnic minority. Films about the South Asian diaspora shown in the cinemas and then often at a later date on television are as much social commentary for attentive viewers as they are entertainment. To take just two examples which became hugely popular, *Bhaji on the Beach* (1993) about a group of South Asian women on a day trip to the Blackpool seaside, reveals much about Asian women's dilemmas and hopes in Britain; while *Bend it like Beckham* (2002) which follows a young Punjabi girl from Hounslow, London, desperate to play football despite her parents' horror at such an 'inappropriate' sporting activity for a girl, is socially realistic and deeply touching. It shows not only inter-generational misunderstandings and conflict, and suspicion of white society, but also the way different generations in the diaspora negotiate difference successfully. A one-off Channel 4 drama screened in January 2005 offered insight into a darker side of the diaspora experience. *Yasmin* was the story of a young British South Asian Muslim woman, forced into a marriage with her goatherd cousin from Pakistan to help him migrate to

Britain, who found her world transformed by the aftermath of the attacks of '9/11'. Outside the formal world of cinema and television the diaspora influence in the world of popular culture is evident in music and dance, for example in the spread of the Punjabi folk tradition of *bhangra*, which originated in Punjabi celebrations of harvest.

*****

This chapter has discussed four key themes in the interaction of South Asians in the many strands in the diaspora with the societies where they have become 'at home', focussing particularly on their experiences in public space. We have examined the interaction of ethnicity and national identity, the realities of being a South Asian citizen in the diaspora, the implications of religious pluralism, and cultural interactions, in an attempt to discern how comfortable South Asians are in their new homelands, and how they have been seen by their fellow non-South Asian citizens. What has become clear is that living in the diaspora is an experience shot through with ambiguity and tension, as well as being a status that is freely sought and accepted on a permanent basis. However, that experience is not static. The changing worlds of international and national politics can profoundly change the experience of living in the disaspora, as can the internal dynamics of diaspora communities. What is also clear is that the accommodations achieved by one generation may well not serve the next generation. So those who are born outside the subcontinent (as the majority now are except for those who live in areas such as north America where large-scale inward migration was comparatively late) have to address questions which their parents answered for their generation, but which now seem very different for those who have no remembered home on the subcontinent, whose perspective is determined by experiences in the only homeland they know, and whose aspirations are fashioned in and by that homeland and its society. However, even for South Asians born in the diaspora, the subcontinent remains a point of reference, and often a part of their affective world. We turn in the final chapter to this piece of the mosaic which constitutes living in the diaspora.

5 Relating to the old homeland

This chapter investigates some of the main ways in which many South Asians in the diaspora relate to the subcontinent. The title, 'Relating to the old homeland', is perhaps a misnomer, because for so many living outside the countries of the subcontinent by the end of the twentieth century it was not in a real or affective sense a homeland because they had been born and brought up far away. On visiting South Asia such people are obviously 'foreign' to those locally born, despite their shared enthnicity: they are distinguished by dress and body language, sometimes hardly able to speak or understand a South Asian language, and at times confused by what they find. Moreover, few who have left the subcontinent have ever returned permanently to it as their final home. It was explicable that indentured labourers rarely wished or were able to return; and decades later when it was possible, few did, even when, like many East African Asians, they were evicted from the places they had made their new homes. An added dimension to the ambiguity of the idea of a former homeland is the fact that South Asia is itself changing, in many places very rapidly. So there is no 'going home' even for older people born on the subcontinent.

Our first consideration must be the experience of those who left in profoundly disadvantaged circumstances in the earliest of the modern diasporic flows, and quickly formed permanent Indian populations abroad once they were freed from the bonds of indenture or other forms of contract. They were effectively cut off from the subcontinent for several generations by poverty and poor communications. They reconstituted family and community life from their own demographic resources, their language diverged considerably from that spoken by their kin at home and their descendants, and their social organisation and religious observance reflected what was possible outside India with only memory to guide them. Occasionally there would be contact with India, as when Arya Samaj missionaries arrived in Trinidad and Natal with the intention of rescuing Hindus overseas from what they saw as degraded practices. Even so, India remained a point of reference for them, a place of familial, cultural and religious origin which marked them out as different from other people in the societies where they settled. In a sense 'India' became a myth of origin rather than a lived reality. Most descendants of indentured labourers had no reason to return there in the twentieth century, even when they could have done so, having lost contact with family members, and often not knowing where their ancestors came from, except in the most general terms.

Some descendants of indentured labourers did make this journey to India, often with misgivings and anxiety. V. S. Naipaul was one example. Born in 1932 to Trinidadian Indian parents, descended from indentured labourers, he studied at Oxford and was already known as a writer when he visited India for the first time in 1962. His subsequent account, *An Area of Darkness* (1964) was marked by anger and fear: the cocktail of profound and mixed emotion made him write that it was a journey he should not have made. Nearly two decades later a Fijian Indian, a professional historian descended from an indentured Indian grandfather, did make the journey and has given us a deeply moving account of it.[1] Brij Lal's grandfather went to Fiji in 1908 and died in 1962 at an age he thought was nearly 100. He came from Bahraich, an impoverished district in the United Provinces in northern India, and had continued to correspond with his relatives there until the 1950s, expecting one day to return. He never did because he was always in financial difficulty, had his own family to bring up, and because his marriage to a woman from another caste would have brought dishonour to him and his family back 'home'. Brij Lal went instead in 1978 as he embarked on academic study of indentured labourers, making the journey, as he wrote, for his grandfather's sake as well as his own. The visit to his ancestral village was deeply draining, emotionally and physically, but he felt profoundly moved at seeing where his grandfather had come from, and meeting his great-uncle's son and grandson: the older of the two relatives sobbed uncontrollably as he embraced him. However, he recognised that, despite his own emotion, there would be no 'going home', for India was an alien country to him. Yet the visit had solved many puzzles of his childhood and reopened the doors to that vanished world in Fiji where older folk had still spoken a local United Provinces dialect and had danced and sung in ways remembered from India.

By contrast, those who live in countries which are home to later strands in the South Asian diaspora have a very different experience of relating to a subcontinent which is a living reality, where they have multiple

[1] B. V. Lal, 'Return to Bahraich', chapter 2 of his edited volume *Chalo Jahaji on a Journey through Indenture in Fiji* (Canberra and Suva, Australian National University and Fiji Museum, 2000). See the photograph of Brij Lal's grandparents taken c. 1960, Fig. 1.

connections with the country of family origin. Many of these have been made possible very recently by technological developments in communications and travel. For example, South Asian culture at various levels of sophistication can be kept alive and reinvented right in the diaspora domestic space through audio and video cassettes and, latterly, via DVDs. One study of Punjabi homes in Southall, London, at the end of the twentieth century, discovered that most had very large video collections, often between 50 and 100. Of these nearly 70 per cent were Indian films, representing the pure entertainment end of the spectrum. Others enabled experience of religious tradition, such as those of the television version of the *Mahabharat*, seen earlier in India and Britain. When viewed in Punjabi homes these were often used as a mode of worship, accompanied by incense and *puja*, and people refrained from eating while they were being shown. Such resources supplement what is available in diaspora public space, particularly in Hindu temples or in the gatherings addressed by visiting religious leaders and holy persons. This is an important contrast with the cultural and religious isolation of earlier diaspora strands, and is particularly important for women who speak little English, and for families who watch such resources together and renew their sense of cultural distinctiveness. However, young people often feel that Hindi films, for example, lock the older generation in a fossilised version of 'India' rather than the India which is changing rapidly; and when they view by themselves rather than as families they tend to choose programmes made in England or the USA.[2]

South Asians abroad have often developed their own print media outlets to serve local diaspora communities and keep them in touch with their regions of origin on the subcontinent. Some of these are in English and therefore 'pan-diaspora' in outreach within each country of diaspora residence, such as *Eastern Eye* in the UK or *India West* and *India Abroad* in the USA. Others are in vernaculars, as in the case of the flourishing Punjabi press in north America and the UK. They also use local Asian radio stations, such as Sunrise Radio in London, to keep them in touch with news from the subcontinent as well as news about the diaspora in the UK, and again the older generation like these particularly for their cultural provision. But for young people, particularly the better educated and fluent in English, diaspora internet sites are a new and vibrant way of keeping in touch with their particular interests as South Asians

[2] M. Gillespie, *Television, Ethnicity and Cultural Change* (London and New York, Routledge, 1995). Another important case study of the way South Asian culture is kept alive in the diaspora is E. Nesbitt, 'Celebrating and learning in community: the perpetuation of values and practices among Hindu Punjabi children in Coventry, UK', *Indo-British Review. A Journal of History*, Vol. 21, No. 1 (not dated), pp. 119–131.

outside the subcontinent, and with news of the subcontinent itself. They cover a huge range of topics, from news in the country of the diaspora and the subcontinent, to business issues, 'Bollywood' films, leisure, food, property, plants and gardens, and horoscopes. They also carry advertisements for travel to the subcontinent, for DVDs, and for Asian jewellery and clothes. There are also numerous specialised sites for matrimonial advertisements and online dating. Here the newest technology is taking on a pattern established with the technology of newsprint: instead of the matrimonial pages of the Sunday papers in India, for example, people in the diaspora now reach out via the web and e-mail to search for brides and grooms around the world. One long-standing Asian marriage bureau established in Southall, London, in 1972, has also gone online to expand its range of clientele. As is common, all provide for aspirants or enquirers to define themselves by region, caste, religion and language, as well as offering more personal details. One specially for Sikhs and other Punjabis, '1st Place Punjabi Matrimonials', based in London, gives statistics for its clients, who numbered almost 3,000 in mid-2005. The number of men on its books was more than double the number of women, and most of both sexes were very well educated, having qualifications of a BA/BSc or higher. Most were Sikhs or Hindus, with Sikhs just outnumbering Hindus. Most were under 30 and had never married; but 29 who had been widowed were seeking to re-marry, and there were 82 clients who were 41 or over. It is significant that the largest single age cohort was that between 26 and 30, just the age when families would be becoming concerned if they had failed to see their children successfully married through the usual social networks.[3] Further research in this area would be very revealing, to understand why the people who use these sites do so rather than use the more normal familial networks, and also to assess the longer-term success of marriages arranged in this way.

E-mail is of course another way in which educated South Asians keep in touch within the diaspora and with family and friends in the subcontinent. But even the less well-off will use the telephone on a regular basis, reflecting the development of the communications infrastructure on the subcontinent as well as the desire of kin to stay in touch. (As one scholar in the USA discovered, international phone calls produce bills which working class South Asians can find their most problematic.[4]) Video recorders have also more recently become popular means of sharing major family events across the boundaries of time and space. However, the single

[3] www.punjabi-marriage.com.

[4] J. Lessinger, 'Indian immigrants in the United States: the emergence of a transnational population', chapter 8 of B. Parekh, G. Singh and S. Vertovec (eds.) *Culture and Economy in the Indian Diaspora* (London and New York, Rontledge, 2003).

greatest change in communications over the past half century to have an impact on the continued connections between the diaspora and the subcontinent has been the development of rapid and much cheaper air travel. Most flights from the UK to Pakistan or the western part of India are now non-stop and take around eight hours, shaving several hours off the time taken in the 1960s and 1970s; connecting flights from the USA through Europe are also quicker. The cost of tickets on major national carriers has dropped in proportion to personal income levels, and the opening of flight slots to private and low-cost carriers at the start of this century has further brought down the price while increasing the number of flights. Moreover flights are now possible from provincial cities where there are critical numbers of South Asians, increasingly to airports in the regions of the subcontinent from which diaspora families originated. In the UK, for example, it is possible to fly direct from Manchester to Islamabad, thus saving Pakistanis in northern Britain the journey to London airports; while Sikhs and other Punjabis are well served by a new direct service between Birmingham, in the Midlands, and Amritsar in the Punjab. The results of these improved connections are very clear. South Asians in the diaspora visit their families on a regular basis, to nurture kinship links, to attend weddings and to arrange new marriages. Children are encouraged to visit the homes remembered by an older generation, and to make connections with cousins and other kin. Moreover, new kinds of visits are also made possible. Many South Asians now combine family visits with tourism and pilgrimage. The tourist industry within India particularly is developing rapidly, serving a growing internal market as well as foreign visitors. Indians from overseas used these facilities to attend the Kumbh Mela, a great and infrequent festival in Allahabad, in 2001. They also visit, and take the younger generation to visit, the holy sites in the Himalayas and in the south of the subcontinent, thereby refreshing both the cultural and religious roots of diaspora families.

When South Asians visit families still living in South Asia they unfailingly take with them a considerable quantity of presents, as signs of affection but also among some as part of a culture of gift-giving to establish status and significant social connections, as was clear in Chapter 3. These gifts are often much-prized goods which are harder to buy in the poorer parts of the subcontinent, and bring status to the giver and also to the recipient in the eyes of local society. They can range from electronic goods and household appliances to clothes, particularly for babies and children. Such gifts are part of a far larger pattern of economic returns to the subcontinent and a key element in the web of connections which ties the diaspora to the countries from which their families came. It is very difficult to quantify the amount of money flowing into South Asia from the diaspora to the countries on the subcontinent, because of the very different public and private flows involved, and the fact that much of the money never surfaces in public records. They range from personal and familial transfers of money, to formal bank deposits and foreign direct investment. Whatever doubt there is about precise figures, these remittances are highly significant for individuals, families and the locations where they spend their foreign money, and also for the national economies of the three countries of the subcontinent from which members of the diaspora have come.

In the fifty years since independence much of the subcontinent has remained agricultural, and economic development has been held back by lack of investment and technological change and by the absence of an educated workforce. Simultaneously a rapidly rising population of unprecedented dimensions has put immense strain on all economic and social resources. Here there has been no parallel to the East Asian 'miracle' which produced the vibrant 'tiger economies' of that area. The forces of nature have often worked against development, as monsoons – so vital to much agriculture – fail, and, in low-lying Bangladesh, cyclones produce severe inundations with consequent loss of life, livestock, property and crops. India had the most developed economy in 1947, and later the highest degree of urbanisation and industrialisation, and considerable agricultural modernisation which despite a swiftly rising population enabled the country to feed itself. But state policies of strict control of key industries and of patterns of investment held back industrial and infrastructure development until the 1990s, when near international bankruptcy in 1991 drove the government down the path of liberalisation.

In such conditions remittances from migrants settled outside the subcontinent have been crucial to the three national economies. In the early 1980s, for example, remittances from overseas workers to Bangladesh rose to between $421 million and $628 million. This represented between 42 per cent and 79 per cent of national export earnings, and effectively paid for between 14 per cent and 41 per cent of imports (varying annually). By 1992/3 the inward flow was officially estimated at $800 million, and played a very large role in the macro-economic viability of the country, particularly in bridging the savings/investment and balance of payments gaps which undermined economic growth.[5] In Pakistan, inward remittances were thought to be running at over $2,500 million in the

[5] On the importance of remittances to Bangladesh see B. Knerr, 'South Asian countries as competitors on the world labour market, chapter 8 of C. Clarke, C. Peach and S. Vertovec (eds.), *South Asians Overseas. Migration and Ethnicity* (Cambridge, Cambridge University Press, 1990). M. Islam, 'Bangladeshi migration: an impact study', in R. Cohen (ed.), *The Cambridge Survey of World Migration* (Cambridge, Cambridge University Press, 1995) pp. 360–366.

early 1980s, this being in some years more than all the money earned from merchandise exports, and paying for between 40 per cent and 50 per cent of exports. It helped the country begin to liberalise trade policy and build a more competitive industrial structure. For both Pakistan and India the remittances sent home by labourers in the Gulf were particularly significant in the early years of South Asian migration to that area before their numbers were overtaken by people recruited from Bangladesh, Sri Lanka and further east.[6] From the mid-1980s remittances to India from the USA overtook those from the Middle East. The Indian economy depended less on remittances in the 1980s than did those of other South Asian countries. Volumes were roughly the same as those coming into Pakistan, but they were only equivalent to a quarter of earnings from exports and paid for under 29 per cent of imports. After the fiscal crisis of 1991 and the subsequent shift in industrial policy which began to dismantle the economic controls first set up under Prime Minister Nehru, the Indian government, and individual state governments, made significant attempts to attract more deposits and direct foreign investments from those who became known as NRIs – Non-Resident Indians, with some success. This strategy was not surprising, given that it is thought that NRIs worldwide may have from $130 to $200 billion to invest. But the official comparison with the Chinese diaspora was misplaced, as Indians overseas are far fewer in number than overseas Chinese, and have a far lower total income. Special NRI accounts were created, earning interest rates 2–3 per cent above those offered to domestic savers, and it is thought that via these and other special schemes overseas Indians contributions to India quadrupled, yielding $14.3 billion in 1999–2000, for example; though there were fluctuations in inflows rather than a steady rise. During the 1990s as a whole net NRI inflows represented under 10 per cent of all direct foreign investment, leading one scholar to note that India's relationship with its diaspora was a 'missed opportunity'. There have been special schemes for NRI direct investment, and it seems that Indians in the diaspora have been particularly attracted to investment in food processing, textiles and services, including health services. However, they have often been alienated by the fears of Indian business of potential expatriate competition and local suspicion of their possible agenda in India, and remain wary of being too entangled in the continuing bureaucracy and webs of corruption which bedevil all investment in India.[7]

6 On remittances to Pakistan see Knerr, 'South Asian countries'; M. I. Abella, 'Asian migrant and contract workers in the Middle East' in Cohen (ed.) *The Cambridge Survey* pp. 418–423.

7 On India see Knerr, 'South Asian Countries'; S. Thandi, '*Vilayati Paisa*: some reflections on the potential of diaspora finance in the socio-economic development of Indian Punjab', chapter 11 of I. Talbot and S. Thandi (eds.), *People on the Move. Punjabi Colonial and*

Although it is possible to get some broad idea of the dimensions of inward monetary flows of different kinds, and their macro-economic significance to the economies of South Asia, we know comparatively little about the impact of diaspora money when it is spent directly by individuals and families in the regions of the subcontinent where their families originated. More research needs to be done in South Asia to assess the impact of immediate diasporic connections to complement the few case studies there are. More investigation has been done on the Bangladeshi experience than elsewhere.[8] Here distinct regions such as Sylhet and Chittagong have been heavily involved in outward migration and much of the impact is localised and clear. Diaspora money seems to be spent most of all on the purchase of land, which has traditionally been the source of local power and status, and as security for the future, and also on the building of big, new houses, again marks of status. A smaller proportion is spent on making fixed deposits, repaying loans and investing in business; while the rest goes, in descending order, on paying for weddings, buying equipment, vehicles and consumer durables, getting medical treatment, making gifts to relatives, and educating children. A similar pattern of spending is evident in the 'home village' of many Jat Sikh families who migrated from India to Gravesend, Kent, in the UK. There also are to be found expensive, new multi-storey houses with all modern conveniences, though these are often not inhabited for much of the time. A considerable number of new tractors were bought with foreign money; and people so wished to buy land that if they could not buy it in the village they would buy in neighbouring areas or even outside Punjab in United Provinces or Rajasthan.[9] Such diaspora spending patterns in the old homeland have considerable long-term, socio-economic consequences there. One of the clearest is inflation of the price of land, driving it out of the reach of those without migrant connections, and thus disadvantaging them and downgrading their local status. Simultaneously families with migrant wealth and land often personally abandon agriculture and take to trade and services, thus increasing their status even more, while agricultural labour is done by migrant workers from outside the locality. Another area of inflation, as seen in Bangladesh, is that of

Post-Colonial Migration (Karachi, Oxford University Press, 2004); a much more complex economic analysis is D. Nayyar, *Migration, Remittances and Capital Flows. The Indian Experience* (Delhi, Oxford University Press, 1994). See also M. C. Lall, *India's Missed Opportunity. India's Relationship with the Non Resident Indians* (Aldershot, Ashgate, 2001).

8 See the general study by M. Islam, 'Bangladeshi migration' in Cohen (ed.) The *Cambridge Survey*: an excellent case study of a Sylheti village is K. Gardner, *Global Migrants, Local Lives. Travel and Transformation in Rural Bangladesh* (Oxford, Clarendon Press, 1995).

9 A. W. Helweg, *Sikhs in England. The Development of a Migrant Community* (Delhi, Oxford University Press, 1979) pp. 88–93.

marriage costs, as weddings become more elaborate and dowry becomes more prevalent. Migrant males become desirable grooms for individual brides as well as for the connection such males bring to the bride's family. Ironically here foreign wealth leads to the reinvention of tradition, and investment in traditional markers of status. There are also visible changes for the better in people's lives, including better infrastructure, provision for education above primary level and better educational levels among girls as well as boys, better health care and a reduction in infant mortality. The impact on women is not uniform. Although they benefit from better education and health, there is some evidence that the female age at marriage is dropping while the male age at marriage is rising, in Bangladeshi migrant areas, while among men there is some increase in polygamy. Moreover, older traditions of modesty, shame and honour persist, and there has been no radical change in women's status as a result of diasporic connections.

Investment in the old homeland is not just a question of putting foreign wealth into resources which raise personal and familial status. There is also a very broad range of what could be called charitable investment, often done out of sincere religious conviction, but also aimed at fostering a particular vision of a desirable society and polity in the country of familial origin. Sikhs in the diaspora regularly engage in various forms of service, or *seva*, in India, either by sending money or giving their own labour. For example, diaspora Sikhs helped Sikhs, particularly widows, orphans and the elderly, in Delhi, Haryana and Punjab after the violence aimed at them in 1984 after the assassination of Indira Gandhi. Others go personally to help with the refurbishment of religious sites, in programmes organised by a big *gurudwara* in Delhi; and often such work is the first time young Sikhs visit India. Diaspora Sikhs also contribute to welfare societies in their ancestral villages and give money to Punjabi educational and medical charities.[10] Hindu organisations such as the Gujarati Swaminarayan sect in the UK and Muslim and Hindu umbrella organisations in the USA send charitable donations to projects for the disadvantaged and underprivileged, targeting those groups they wish to uplift in order to incorporate them into their vision of India. The Swaminarayan programme is one of the most developed, having taken its modern form in the early twentieth century. Its leadership now publicly proclaims that spirituality and social service are intertwined, and the organisation is involved in a complex network of social programmes in India, particularly in Gujarat and

[10] A. Murphy, 'Mobilizing *seva* ('service'): modes of Sikh diaspora action' in K. A. Jacobsen and P. P. Kumar (eds.), *South Asians in the Diaspora. Histories and Religious Traditions* (Leiden and Boston, Brill, 2004) pp. 337–372; D. S. Tatla, *The Sikh Diaspora. The Search for Statehood* (London, University College London Press, 1999) chapter 3.

Bombay. These include medical projects, among them eight charitable hospitals, clinics and dispensaries, donations to hospitals for the purchase of modern medical equipment, anti-addiction campaigns, and mobile medical vans in tribal areas of Gujarat. Educational programmes include schools, research centres, provision of student hostels, and financial aid to schools and colleges. Work particularly among women includes health programmes and anti-dowry campaigns, including the holding of mass marriages contracted without dowry. In December 1995, for example, 85 couples were married in this way in Bombay. (It should be noted that dowry is illegal in India but seems to be increasingly prevalent as disposable incomes rise. It has long been a target for Hindu social reformers who consider it wasteful, ostentatious, and deeply damaging for the position of women.) Swaminarayan organisations have also offered relief in India at times of natural disasters such as floods and earthquakes. They particularly target the tribal population of Gujarat, which is about 14 per cent of the state's total. Among their work for what they call 'upliftment' of tribals is medical care, education, literacy, the provision of cultural and moral centres, and campaigns against addiction to drugs, tobacco and alcohol. They aim to free these disadvantaged people from 'addictions, superstitions and poverty', according to their website. The agenda is, of course, in the name of Hindu spirituality, to incorporate tribal people into mainstream Hindu society, as participants in a Hindu polity, out of a conviction that India is essentially Hindu in nature and is endangered by secularism and pluralism, as well as by the disadvantage of generations of poverty among tribal and low-caste people, which opens them to potential conversion to other religions and to growing hostility to a state and society which has long benefited those of higher social standing. By contrast, the outpouring of help from British Pakistanis to victims of the 2005 earthquake centred in Pakistan-controlled Kashmir was largely prompted by ties of kinship, as so many British Pakistanis had relatives in the devastated areas.

Investment in the old homeland, understood in broad social and economic terms, has generated a particular type of concern about the right political connections between people in the diaspora and the nation states of the subcontinent, particularly in relation to India. This is concern about the issue of citizenship: should ethnic Indians who have taken or possess other citizenships be able to claim Indian citizenship as well as that of the countries where they have settled? It is understandable why this should be a peculiarly Indian concern. Indians in the later strands of the diaspora have been comparatively wealthy, educated and articulate. They are also likely to keep lively connections with the subcontinent, and of course are aware that their money and investment potential is eyed with particular interest by a government anxious for new foreign investment. They rapidly take citizenship of the countries where they settle, for their own sake and the way this enables them to bring in family members, as in the USA. But not having Indian citizenship can be inconvenient: they need expensive visas for each visit to the subcontinent and they face bureaucratic complications in relation to investment.

The Indian government had, since independence, been wary of any discussion of joint citizenship, and it took the line that Indians who settled abroad should embrace their new homelands and have their primary political loyalties there. This alienated many in East Africa when they were under acute pressure and threat of eviction in the late 1960s and early 1970s.[11] However, economic compulsions forced later Indian governments to recognise the financial significance of Indians abroad and the political claims which might come with financial contributions to the old homeland. The category of NRI came to be used officially from the late 1970s and referred to those of Indian ethnicity and citizenship living abroad, although it has been used conversationally to denote any Indian in the diaspora. At the end of the century the privileges extended to such people were also given to those who were of Indian origin but had taken local citizenships. They were also offered what was known as the PIO Card – for a Person of Indian Origin, and 'origin' could go back to a great-grandparent who was an Indian citizen. This was not only an economic enticement for the wealthy (and the card itself was not cheap to acquire, at $1,000 for 20 years) but a significant step on the road to dual citizenship. Soon after, in 2000, a High Level Committee on the Indian Diaspora was set up under the chairmanship of L. M. Singhvi, a former High Commissioner in London who had first-hand experience of the mood of Indians in the UK. It was clear that the Indian government was actively wooing Indians overseas, and it also inaugurated annual celebratory and information-providing Diaspora Days in India from 2003 on the anniversary of Gandhi's return from South Africa in 1915 after two decades abroad. These were organised by the Ministry for Overseas Indian Affairs and the Federation of Indian Chambers of Commerce and Industry. This trend culminated in the decision in 2004 to grant overseas Indians Indian citizenship. At the time of writing the details of this still have to be worked out. It is, however, a very significant step for Indians in the diaspora, as it will undoubtedly ease a whole range of their continuing connections with India itself, and will be a new affective as well as material link binding the diaspora to their old homeland. It is also a

11 A. Gupta, 'India and the Asians in East Africa', chapter 9 of M. Twaddle (ed.), *Expulsion of a Minority. Essays on Ugandan Asians* (London, Athlone Press, 1975).

development which is not free from ambiguity and potential stress in the relationship between India and its diaspora, as there are powerful political and economic interests on the subcontinent who would not relish the intervention of wealthy outsiders who may have very different interests and priorities.[12]

The involvement of the diaspora in the public and political life of the subcontinent is not just in the area of investment in the local and national economies, and in charitable projects. It is also significant in some of the profound conflicts which have emerged in South Asia. This is not surprising, given that so many migrants come from just those areas which have been engulfed in turmoil and violence, and still have kin in those places. As we saw in Chapter 2, a significant number of Pakistanis who settled in Britain came from Mirpur, a district in what is known as Azad Kashmir. It is thought that possibly two-thirds of British Pakistanis are Kashmiri in origin, with most coming from Mirpur or Kotli which are both in Azad Kashmir. About 250,000 left these two districts alone, thus reducing the local populations significantly but also creating very strong links with the UK. They tended to cluster in inner city, urban areas in the UK, such as Luton, where housing was relatively cheap and accessible and where there was low-skilled work. Unlike some other migrant groups, they have not tended to move out to the suburbs but have consolidated their settlements in inner urban areas, where residential proximity reinforces the very close ties of kinship which they bring from Kashmir and which still link them with Kashmir.[13]

It is therefore entirely explicable that they should have exported their own concerns, and that of their wider kin, about the conflict over Kashmir which has bedevilled relations between India and Pakistan for nearly sixty years since independence. The origins of the conflict lay in the partition of the subcontinent at independence because of the inability of nationalist politicians to agree on the nature of a unitary state to take over power when the British announced their intention of rapid withdrawal after the Second World War. When it became clear that there would be two successor states, a secular India with a Hindu majority, and a Muslim Pakistan, the princes with their semi-independent states were pressed to join one or other of these two. The Maharajah of Kashmir was a Hindu, ruling a predominantly Muslim population, and he acceded to India when he was

[12] See Lessinger, 'Indian immigrants in the United States', chapter 8 of Parekh, Singh and Vertovec (eds.) *Culture and Economy in the Indian Diaspora*, particularly pp. 174–178.

[13] On Kashmiris in the UK and their politics see P. Ellis and Z. Khan, 'Political allegiances and social integration: the British Kashmiris' in S. Weil (ed.), *Roots and Routes. Ethnicity and Migration in Global Perspective* (Jerusalem, Magnes Press, 1999), pp. 119–134.

threatened by a tribal incursion into his territory from Pakistan, backed by the new Pakistani state. Indian troops flew in to protect him and the resulting conflict between India and Pakistan led to the *de facto* partition of Kashmir along a ceasefire line, which remains to this day. Each country had a particular interest in Kashmir which militated against any longer-term peaceful resolution of the conflict. For Pakistan it was a Muslim majority area which should rightfully have become part of Pakistan at Partition. For India (and for Nehru who had Kashmiri origins himself) it was the symbol that India was not only for Hindus but was a secular state and a composite nation in which different religious groups would find their home. The continuing division of the area and Indo-Pakistan conflict arising from it, and the degree of violence and abuse of human rights by Indian security forces in Indian Kashmir in the last two decades in response to Kashmiri militancy, has deeply incensed Kashmiris in the diaspora. They feel they have a rightful role in the politics of Kashmir, not just because of kinship ties, but because the Azad Kashmir legislature has a representative of overseas Kashmiris, of whom those in Britain are the largest group.

Kashmiris in Britain are closely involved in the regular civil politics of Azad Kashmir, keeping close personal and financial links with politicians there and organising parties in Britain which are an extension of political parties in the region, including pan-Pakistan parties such as the Muslim League or Kashmir-specific parties such as the Muslim Conference and the Liberation League. They also involve themselves in politics specifically to achieve a united and independent Kashmir. This often takes the form of membership of the Jammu and Kashmir Liberation Front, founded in Birmingham in 1977, and one of the many parties involved in Kashmir's internal politics and armed struggle. It is an organisation with a tortured history of internal splits, hostility to Pakistan (which views Kashmir as an integral part of itself rather than autonomous) and terrorist activities. Kashmiris in the UK also work to raise awareness of issues relating to the position of Kashmir among Kashmiris in the UK as well as lobbying within the wider polity to influence the British Parliament, the European Parliament and even the US government. Some also personally participate in liberation politics on the subcontinent. It is significant that support for a united and autonomous Kashmir is not just to be found among older British Kashmiris who remember their area of origin, but also younger members of the diasporic community who are moved particularly by the record of human rights abuses there.

The other internal South Asian conflict which has brought those in the diaspora into new forms of organisational activity abroad, and also into anti-government activities within South Asia, is that involving the Sikhs in the Indian state of Punjab. Like Kashmir, Punjab has also been a major source of out-migration. Moreover, just as Kashmiris are deeply conscious of having a distinctive ethnicity and way of life, *Kashmiriyat*, so Sikhs have a very distinctive religious and social identity with overt public marks of belonging, particularly for men the unshaven hair and the wearing of turbans, and a religious language, Gurmukhi, with a script of its own. They also have a longstanding homeland area within India, the Punjab, though this was shared with Muslims and Hindus before Partition and with Hindus afterwards, with whom they had a shared daily language, Punjabi, which is akin to Hindi. Sikh politics on the subcontinent are deeply fractured and one of the issues at stake is the extent to which Sikhs feel the need for an autonomous state (Khalistan) in Punjab to enable them to flourish as a distinctive people. A sense of being both a religious community and an ethnic group with a territorial base only developed strongly after the partition of India, which involved the partition of Punjab, and particularly during the 1980s when there were long periods of virtual civil war in the Punjab and the imposition of military rule by the central Indian government in an attempt to control a movement for an autonomous Sikh state. All Sikhs, both at home in the Punjab and at home abroad, were deeply shocked and hurt when, in 1984, the Indian army attacked the most holy shrine of Sikhism, the Golden Temple in Amritsar, to flush out armed opponents of the central government. Not all Sikhs support the idea of their own state, and some of lower caste origins find the idea threatening as it is primarily the vision of higher caste Jat Sikhs. In the diaspora, for example, many ex-East African Sikhs were Ramgarhias rather than Jats, and as well as being of lower status they had, as twice-migrants, fewer affective ties with Punjab. Khalistan was not for them an attractive cause. However, the increasingly violent politics of Punjab could not help but draw in the concerns and often the active participation of many Sikhs abroad. Sikh sensibilities and a sense of difference from other Indians were inevitably heightened by the appalling violence against their co-religionists in Delhi after the assassination of Indira Gandhi by her two Sikh bodyguards in the aftermath of the government assault on the Golden Temple. As we saw in Chapter 2, Sikhs form a very substantial Indian minority within the worldwide Indian diaspora. By the later twentieth century about three-quarters of overseas Sikhs lived in Britain, the USA and Canada. Their location overseas, in polities where increasingly rights have been accorded to recognised ethnic minorities in attempts to promote equal opportunities in increasingly plural societies, has also encouraged migrant Sikhs to present themselves as a distinct ethnic minority, and this again reinforces the linkages to the Punjab and increases concerns about internal Indian politics.[14]

Sikhs campaigning for a separate state in South Asia have been very active in the USA, Canada and Britain and have also forged links between these three diasporic locations on the issue. Not only have they created organisations to pursue their campaigns, such as the World Sikh Organization (1984) and the International Sikh Youth Federation (1984) in the USA, thereby separating themselves from Indian Hindus in the diaspora, but they have also organised meetings in *gurudwaras*. This has meant that these holy places have sometimes become the sites of power struggles between those who do and do not wish for this sort of involvement with the politics of the subcontinent. They also use the media, organise rallies, and use the political systems of the countries where they are located, in an attempt to put pressure on the Indian government by mobilising lobbies on human rights and the Punjab. The Indian government was convinced that Sikh secessionists were operating abroad and drawing financial and other support from the diaspora. It stepped up surveillance of Sikh groups abroad, tightly controlled visas for Sikh visitors to India, and pressurised governments in north America and Britain whom it blamed for being soft on supporters of terrorism. Despite the concerns of some politicians about human rights, the British and Canadian government did agree to cooperate more fully with the Indian authorities in such matters as extradition and the tracing of terrorist funds. Although Punjab politics became far more peaceful by the end of the century, and the demand for Khalistan ebbed, this acute phase of Sikh conflict with the Delhi government had a lasting effect on Sikhs' self-identification in the diaspora as well as in India, and demonstrated the potential within the diaspora for significant interventions in Indian politics.

South Asians in the diaspora have in many places constructed images of themselves and their places of origin, not least for consumption by the polities in the host societies where they settle. The Sikh claim to distinct ethnicity is only one example. The various parliamentary groups and caucuses created by diasporas in western democratic politics are also vehicles for producing images of the 'old homelands' as well as orchestrating specific issues in relation to them. But in very recent times there has been

14 The best description of Sikhs in the diaspora, their linkages with Punjab and the demand for statehood is Tatla, *The Sikh Diaspora*. Other illuminating discussions of the ambiguities of the idea of Sikh statehood and the diversity of Sikh attitudes include R. B. Williams, *Religions of Migrants from India and Pakistan. New Threads in the American Tapestry* (Cambridge, Cambridge University Press, 1988), pp. 69–84; V. A. Dusenbery, 'A Sikh diaspora? Contested identities and constructed realities', chapter 1 of P. van der Veer (ed.), *Nation and Migration. The Politics of Space in the South Asian Diaspora* (Philadelphia, University of Pennsylvania Press, 1995).

a novel and very clear attempt at reconstructing the image of the Indian nation specifically, both in South Asia itself and among Indians in the diaspora. What is at stake is the understanding of 'Indianness' in cultural and political terms. This has led to a profound sea-change in political discourse and activity in India itself, and also involves many in the most recent strands of the Indian diaspora.

Independent India came into being in 1947 as a secular state because for decades the main vehicle of Indian nationalism, the Indian National Congress, under the leadership of Gandhi, had claimed to represent a nation which included all religious minorities and all sections of society. This claim became the more urgent as a distinctive Muslim nationalism emerged and attained partial fruition in Pakistan in the context of the particular circumstances of Britain's imperial policies on the subcontinent during and after the Second World War. Nehru, who became India's first Prime Minister in 1947, was himself a secular person, but he recognised also that many of his compatriots were not, and were likely to participate politically in terms of religious community and caste identity. However, he argued passionately that India was a composite nation and that the nation state, as well as the Congress party, must nurture a national identity which would include India's remaining Muslim, Christian, Sikh and other minorities. This ideal lay behind the new constitution with its provision for fundamental rights including rights to equality and freedom of religion.[15] However, a strand of overtly Hindu nationalism persisted in public life, although for many years it was dampened by memories of the assassination of Gandhi in 1948 by a Hindu nationalist, and then by the political dominance of the Congress party and members of Nehru's family. It resurfaced and began to gain considerable ideological and electoral support towards the end of the twentieth century, and its primary political vehicle, the BJP (Bharatiya Janata Party) was returned to power in several states as well as in Delhi in the 1990s. The changes in the ethos of public and political life were clearly visible – both in the rhetoric of national identity and in the lived experience of religious minorities.[16] The core idea behind the ideology of Hindu nationalism is *Hindutva*, 'Hinduness', which was expounded and elaborated between the two world wars as an alternative to the Gandhian nationalist rhetoric of inclusiveness. It was overtly majoritarian and subscribed to an ethnic vision which saw

[15] For Nehru's vision of India and also his continuing struggles with those who disputed the idea of a composite nation, see Judith M. Brown, *Nehru. A Political Life* (New Haven and London, Yale University Press, 2003).

[16] There is now a large literature on this phenomenon. A subtle analysis is T. B. Hansen, *The Saffron Wave. Democracy and Hindu Nationalism in Modern India* (Princeton, Princeton University Press, 1999).

Hinduness as far more than just being a Hindu in terms of religious identification. *Hindutva* was an ethnic identity defined by links of race and blood; it was also defined by love of a holy motherland, India, and possession of a Hindu cultural inheritance and essence. *Hindutva* demanded in the modern age a nation state encompassing a specific territory, where ethnic identity, cultural essence and a sacred land would all be protected from defilement and would enable its members to flourish in their own specific way. In this vision of India, minorities such as Muslims and Christians were deemed alien and threatening (although they had no other homeland and their ancestors had lived in India for many generations). Moreover, the disadvantaged in society who were also likely to feel alienated from this essentially high caste vision of India would need to be reformed and uplifted to be included in *Hindutva*. A whole family of organisations, both cultural and political, have pursued this objective from the 1970s, and prominent among them is the Vishwa Hindu Parishad (VHP), founded in 1964, which aims at consolidating Hindu society, spreading Hindu values, and linking all Hindus outside India as well as within it, while also hoping to re-incorporate those who might have left the Hindu fold. It is noteworthy that the 'Hinduism' pursued by this and similar organisations does not reflect the great diversity of lived Hindu religious experience on the subcontinent over centuries. It projects a standardised and homogenised version of 'Hinduism' which it argues is a world religion just as are the great monotheistic traditions. It is hardly surprising that India's religious minorities have become deeply anxious about their position in an India where political parties which subscribe to this vision have attained power quite legitimately through the ballot box and have used that power to nurture the vision of *Hindutva*. Even though at a national level successful political parties have to forge multiple alliances and to modify stridently sectarian rhetoric in order to retain national power, at the local level state governments and their allies among cadres of Hindu activists have in some places made life difficult and dangerous for non-Hindus. The destruction by Hindu activists of a mosque built on what was said to be the birthplace of the Hindu god, Ram, in 1992 was a dramatic example, and it sparked serious violence throughout much of the country. A decade later, in 2002, there was a virtual pogrom against Muslims in the state of Gujarat. Even though Congress returned to power in 2005 as the dominant party in a coalition, the strand of Hindu nationalist politics retains a powerful appeal in India.

In any understanding of the linkages between diaspora South Asians and the subcontinent this ideological and political development in India is very significant because it has attracted the support of many Indians outside the subcontinent, particularly in the West. The proponents of this vision of India in India itself have targeted the diaspora, both in terms of religion (as the VHP's aims make clear) and financially in the context of globalisation. It was a BJP government in Delhi that seized the chance of binding Non-Resident Indians and Persons of Indian Origin into the project of rebuilding a strong Hindu India, although the successor regime has built on that foundation for sound economic reasons. Many Indians in the West have found the vision of a Hindu India deeply attractive for a number of reasons. The newer strands in the Indian diaspora have included many people who have become successful in the professions and in business, and they are the same sort of middle class people who have supported the VHP and BJP in India, in the hope of creating a strong modern society and polity where they can achieve success for themselves and their families. In India, as outside, the opportunities offered by globalisation to people like them are very enticing, and in the Hindu nationalist project they sense an environment which will help them lay hold of these opportunities, in contrast to earlier decades of government regulation in the name of state socialism, and a history of persistent national poverty and low rates of growth. Few of them are in any sense intellectuals who would have any profound understanding of Indian history or of Hindu tradition, and the vision of India offered is straightforward, attractive and without the uncomfortable ambiguities historical understanding requires. Moreover, in the specific context of the diaspora a package of clear teaching about Indian identity, culture and 'Hinduism' is a sustaining resource. It can help them deal with anxieties about the impact of western culture on their children, as well as with their own experiences of alienation from mainstream society and of discrimination. Further, in western polities that increasingly engage in the rhetoric and politics of equal rights for minorities, a clear Indian identity is an important resource in dealing with the host society.[17] Despite the popularity of this particular version of Indian identity there are some groups who are hostile to it and fear its influence in the diaspora. Among them are Indians whose lifestyles and gender attitudes do not conform to the moral ideals preached by this homogenised version of 'Hinduism'. Lesbians and gays, for example, in the USA and elsewhere have formed their own associations for mutual support, and use internet sites to develop specifically South Asian networks, in part reflecting the social condemnation or misunderstanding

[17] There is some good evidence on the relationship between Hindu nationalism and the diaspora. See C. Bhatt and P. Mukta (eds.), special issue of *Ethnic and Racial Studies*, Vol. 23, No. 3 (May 2000), which has considerable discussion of the phenomenon in the UK and USA. On Canada see J. Lele, 'Indian diaspora's long-distance nationalism: the rise and proliferation of 'Hindutva' in Canada', chapter 3 of S. J. Varma and R. Seshan (eds.), *Fractured Identity. The Indian Diaspora in Canada* (Jaipur and New Delhi, Rawat Publications, 2003).

they encounter in the wider diaspora. Moreover, Indians from minority religions can also feel profoundly threatened in the diaspora by this Hindu construction of their old homeland, as well as the attempt to define Indian as Hindu in the diaspora. In the USA Sikhs are increasingly separating themselves out from a pan-Indian identity, and Indian Muslims are organising, as in the American Federation of Muslims from India, both to project India in more plural terms and to send money back to India for their own charitable and political projects.[18] There are also, of course, many Indians in the USA and elsewhere who are not concerned with such issues and concentrate on living successfully in the diaspora, and taking the economic and social opportunities it offers them and their children.

Support in the diaspora for a specifically Hindu nationalism and definition of Indian identity takes various forms. One of the clearest is the spread of institutions closely linked with those supporting *Hindutva* in India itself. The VHP has appeared quite dramatically overseas. By the end of the 1990s there were 12 branches in the UK, 25 in the USA and two in Canada. In the UK there were also about 60 branches of the RSS (Rashtriya Swayemsevak Sangh), a militant activist arm of Hindu nationalism in India. The core body to which these branches (and other Hindu nationalist organisations) report in the UK is the HSS UK (Hindu Swayamsevak Sangh UK) founded in 1966 and registered as a charity in 1974: its headquarters are in Leicester. This location is significant because it is the home of so many Indians of Gujarati and East African origin, among whom this vision of India has long been of importance. In the USA a powerful umbrella body is the Federation of Hindu Associations which seeks to coordinate Hindu public action in the name of Hindu nationalism. These diasporic arms of the *Hindutva* movement's organisations have a wide span of work in the diaspora itself, organising local groups of activists and giving them ideological and physical training, including annual training camps, putting on large nationwide gatherings in the countries where they operate, such as the 1989 Virat Hindu Sammelan in the UK to celebrate the birth centenary of one of the founding ideologues of *Hindutva*, publishing journals such as *Sangh Sandesh* in the UK, and inviting preachers from India to visit the diaspora and talk about Hinduism. They also make contact with and organise Indian students in universities. In the UK, for example, the National Hindu Students Forum has branches in about 30 Universities and is an affiliate of the *Hindutva* movement. Much of this is very similar to the work

[18] P. Kurien, 'Religion, ethnicity and politics: Hindu and Muslim Indian immigrants in the United States', *Ethnic and Racial Studies*, Vol. 24, No. 2 (March 2001), pp. 263–293.

done in India itself. Many of the organisations supporting the broader movement also make active and substantial contributions to work which supports the *Hindutva* cause. I have already noted the particular regional and social thrust of the charitable work of the Swaminarayan movement. In the USA sizeable funds, possibly running into millions of dollars, are collected for heritage, development and relief causes, many of which are clearly related to the promotion of *Hindutva*.

One further way in which the connections between the diaspora and India forged in support of *Hindutva* manifest themselves is in the growing tendency to intervene in the way 'Hinduism' is portrayed in the wider society. Where school curricula offer a broad religious studies programme, as in the UK, it is hardly surprising that locally resident Hindus will want to offer guidance about the way their tradition should be portrayed. The UK branch of the VHP prepared a guide for teachers, entitled, *Explaining Hindu Dharma* (1996) which is offered as authoritative and comprehensive, so that British schools can teach Hinduism correctly. Similarly, a range of Hindu organisations in the diaspora through their websites offer definitions and descriptions of Hinduism, so claiming the space opened up by the politics of multiculturalism. However, interventions designed to promote and protect the image of Hinduism have on occasion been far more confrontational. Serious scholars who work on Hindu texts and myths have found themselves the object of a barrage of criticism emanating from anti-intellectual diaspora sources, and at times they and their students have been physically threatened and even assaulted. Wendy Doniger, a senior and respected scholar in the field of Hindu mythology, was the target of a whole series of denunciations and even physical attack, much of it orchestrated by an American-based website aimed to link Indians worldwide. The protest also led to the removal of her article on Hinduism for *Encarta*, the Microsoft encyclopedia. Behind the protests lay a xenophobic belief that 'foreigners' should not try to interpret Hinduism; and also a vision of Hinduism as an austere world religion suitable for modern times, in which the overt sexuality of many Hindu myths has no place.[19] Another serious scholar, a Professor of Religion at an American university, was hounded by people he described as 'cyber vigilantes', again via an American website widely read by Indians, in reaction to a book he had written about the Hindu god, Ganesha. A hostile internet petition collected 4,500 signatories, demanding that the book be banned. Other opponents wanted his book to be withdrawn from student access, demanded that he should

[19] *New York Times*, 31 January 2005: the website where criticisms were posted was www.sulekha.com.

cease teaching in the area of Hinduism, and that his university should make him apologise. Some even threatened his life. His university protected him and the web petition was withdrawn; but his Indian publisher removed the book from its catalogue.[20] Diaspora Indians' attempts at academic and literary censorship have also extended into the institutional world of academia, particularly where local diaspora groups have put up funds for the establishment of posts in aspects of Indian studies, and wish to control who is appointed and how they teach their subject. There have even been attempts at intervention in appointments even where there have been no financial strings to pull. The prestigious Library of Congress in Washington D.C. has a scholarly centre where eminent academics are invited to hold visiting appointments to enable them to do creative work and research. In 2003 a renowned scholar of ancient India, Professor Romila Thapar, was elected to one of these appointments and again some Indians in America orchestrated a campaign of global criticism and an attempt to get the Library to withdraw its invitation. They did not succeed, and a powerful international academic community rallied in her support. Her 'crime' was her subtle historical analysis of the various cultural traditions which made up India's past, instead of subscribing to a vision of a monolithic Hindu version of Indian history, and her courageous critique of contemporary trends in Hinduism.[21] Such attacks on scholars and their modes of textual and scholarly analysis demonstrate some of the profound anxieties about the image of India and of Hinduism prevalent among Hindus in the modern diaspora, as well as a puritanical simplicity in some preferred diaspora visions of the old homeland. They also indicate how the internet in particular has enabled another strand in the complex web of connections through which the diaspora relates to the subcontinent.

*****

An explosion in modern technologies of communication has transformed the experience of South Asians living in the diaspora in the later twentieth century, compared with the isolation of older diaspora communities from the subcontinent. This has led to the development of multiple linkages between the global diaspora and the old homeland, ranging from

20 See Professor P. B. Courtright's article in the British weekly for academics, *The Times Higher*, 28 November 2003: his book which so enraged some Hindu critics was published in 1985, *Ganesha: Lord of Obstacles, Lord of Beginnings* (New York, Oxford University Press).

21 See R. Thapar, 'Imagined religious communities? Ancient history and the modern search for a Hindu identity', *Modern Asian Studies* Vol. 23, Part 2 (May 1989), pp. 209–231; also her 'A historical perspective on the story of Rama' in S. Gopal (ed.), *Anatomy of a Confrontation. The Babri Masjid-Ramjanmabhumi Issue* (New Delhi, Penguin Books India, 1991) pp. 141–163.

the family telephone call and visit, through a multiplicity of material and cultural investments in the place of familial origin, to campaigns, particularly among diaspora Indians, for political status in India and incorporation into a new vision of a strong Hindu nation as a global force in the new millennium. For South Asians in the diaspora communities around the world the subcontinent is no longer home in any simple sense: most would call their new place of settlement home, particularly those born outside the subcontinent, who globally far outnumber those who have personally migrated. However, they are now able to inhabit a world where there are multiple reference points for perceived individual and group senses of belonging, and a variety of possible public identities. They are no longer bound by a single identity linked to the subcontinent or to their new homeland. In the lives of many the irony is that the more they have established 'home' abroad in the diaspora the more significant their linkages with other diaspora groups of South Asians and with the subcontinent have become. They have become 'global' in quite new ways of both perspective and action.

Conclusion

The aim of this book has been to introduce the reader to the history and experience of one of the largest movements of people in the modern world, namely out-migration from the subcontinent of South Asia from the nineteenth century to the present. Numerous flows of people out of the subcontinent have created a significant and very diverse South Asian diaspora spread through every continent. This diaspora has become important not only in the places where South Asians have settled, but also for the countries of the subcontinent from which they came. So the emphasis here has often been on India, Pakistan and Bangladesh as well as on the life of South Asians in the diaspora.

The first two chapters analysed the global and local environments that provided the opportunities and incentives for South Asians to travel such large distances overseas and to create permanent homes outside the subcontinent, even though most of them, at least among the earlier generations of migrants, clung to a 'myth of return' – a hope that one day they would return to their ancestral homelands. We first looked at the changing connections of South Asia with the wider world, and patterns of stability and movement among its people both within and outside the subcontinent, to understand why there developed an environment conducive to large-scale out-migration. We then turned to a description and analysis of the many and distinctive flows overseas, seeking to understand in more detail why people left their homes, where they came from, where they travelled to and why they went to those particular places. Clearly prior experiences, and sometimes specific problems or declining opportunities in the home region, often encouraged people to travel where there was thought to be new opportunity and the chance to better oneself and one's wider familial and kin group. Almost always migrants were prepared to work exceptionally hard, and often in harsh and unfamiliar situations, to achieve new prosperity and status. However, except in the unique circumstances of indentured labourers, it was rarely those at the bottom of South Asian societies, the very poor and most disadvantaged, who left for work abroad. Generally it was those with some resources and also the vision of a wider world sufficient to enable them to see what opportunities there might be elsewhere who made the journey overseas. Often they were people who had already experienced mobility themselves or in their families, at first between places on the subcontinent in search of work and land, or even beyond the homeland in the service of their imperial rulers before the British relinquished their rule of the subcontinent in 1947; and later after the subcontinent gained political independence as news of work and opportunities abroad spread rapidly by word of mouth among kin and friends, as well as by more formal recruitment mechanisms.

Migration was never just a matter of a journey, however large and significant a departure that was. It was an ongoing process, often over several generations. To pursue this understanding of migration the next three chapters took a thematic approach and looked at the tasks which migrants and their children and grandchildren have had to do in order to settle in new homelands and establish themselves as a lasting diaspora. The intention is that by highlighting important themes in the 'work' of becoming a successful diaspora, the reader will then be able to progress to the detailed and often complex literature on particular aspects of South Asian diaspora experience, and also more broadly in daily life to understand something of the life lived by South Asian neighbours and fellow citizens, and to comprehend and empathise with some of their concerns. It has been impossible here to give anything approaching total coverage of the history of the diaspora in all its different geographical locations, partly because of space. More crucially it would be difficult because there was so much diversity in the histories and experiences of South Asians overseas and the sources are so uneven in the information they provide. (For example it is far easier to hear the voices of the contemporary diaspora given the numerous types of written, oral, visual and electronic evidence available, compared with the illiterate indentured labourers who left few direct records of their experiences. Moreover, in modern polities where governments and their agencies are constantly monitoring performance and access in many areas of life in pursuit of equality policies, far more evidence is generated about the quantifiable aspects of diaspora life, ranging from actual numbers to housing circumstances, employment and unemployment among men and women, housing conditions and educational levels.) Not surprisingly diaspora life has yielded up many different experiences, created by the initially varied strands in the diaspora and by subsequent internal differentiations among diasporic groups. This is another reason why totally descriptive coverage would be impossible and a thematic approach is more illuminating.

Chapters 3 to 5 were arranged under three major conceptual themes. How do South Asians outside the subcontinent establish new homes, social networks and communities? How do they relate to the public space and life of their new homelands? What sort of connections do they keep or forge with their old homelands? Chapter 3 dealt with the broad contours of settlement in the diaspora, the business of establishing an economic base, creating new homes and social communities, reconstructing religious traditions and establishing sacred space. It also touched on some of the areas of concern and internal contest within diaspora groups which generate tensions, which at times have spilt over into public space, particularly understandings of gender, different generational priorities, and religious issues. What is clear is that this task of establishing new homes, social networks and wider communities is a process which must be undertaken in each generation of South Asians. Those born in the diaspora and educated alongside other ethnic groups, who speak the language of the host society fluently, often in contrast to the limited command of the new language by their parents' generation, are often not content or at ease in the tightly knit ethnic groups constructed by their parents, and may wish to live and work in different locations, branch out into new jobs, and extend their circle of friendships. Indeed this broadening of the diaspora's connections, and particularly the diversification of its economic base, is often essential to its continuing prosperity in changing circumstances. Younger women are very significant in this process. Not only are they increasingly becoming significant earners in their own right, thereby enhancing the economic success and stability of their families, as well as increasing their personal social leverage, but they also often wish to challenge understandings of gender brought from South Asia, in order to construct new public and private roles for themselves. All young South Asians have to negotiate cultural differences in the locations which are now their home, dealing with their parents and their assumptions about the good and proper life, but also facing out to a wider world where they have new connections, role models and opportunities. Of considerable significance is the way they respond to the religious traditions of their parents, and discern whether those traditions can provide them with meaning and guidance in their new homelands.

The discussion in Chapter 3 also indicated that in no diaspora location are South Asians a single South Asian community or ethnic minority. They are divided by national and regional places of origin; by South Asian language; by religious tradition and sectarian divisions within major religious tradition; by socio-economic status at the time of origin and by later internal socio-economic divergence. Among South Asians in UK, for example, there are people from India, Pakistan and Bangladesh; Hindus, Sikhs, Parsis, Muslims and Christians; followers of many different sectarian traditions within these major religions; speakers of Punjabi, Gujarati,

Hindi and Urdu; and the whole socio-economic range from highly educated lawyers and doctors and wealthy business people, through the self-employed and small business person and semi-skilled worker, to the school leaver with no educational qualifications who ends up unemployed, in prison or living on social security. It is no wonder that there is no homogeneous South Asian minority or community, even though the media sometimes portrays migrants and their children in this way. Nor is there one South Asian woman's experience, though again the media may portray the South Asian woman in the diaspora as oppressed by patriarchy, secluded and ill-educated. For every woman from a conservative family who fits this description there are South Asian women who go out to work, who increasingly control their own incomes, who are themselves educated and see that their daughters are educated, who are rising high in numerous professions and are also prepared to take a public stand on major issues, such as working conditions, treatment of women and human rights. This mirrors, of course, the changes also occurring on the subcontinent where women are now a force to be reckoned with in public and political life, as they have always been in the domain of the family.

Chapter 4 took the focus of discussion beyond the establishment of domestic and sacred space, and the creation of a dense network of social connections and relationships, to the wider stage of the public life of the countries where South Asians now live. In particular it looked at the meaning of belonging to a new national polity, and the extent to which migrants and their children have become participant citizens, contributing to and benefiting from the nation states in which they make their homes. It contrasted their experience in those areas where their ethnicity has made them the target of hostile ethnic nationalisms and in those where they have taken their places in more plural polities with more hospitable public understanding of the nation and national identity. It also indicated where South Asian groups have experienced potential and actual conflict with the public authorities or with the majority in the host societies, when cultural customs conflict with majority expectations and assumptions about what is right and wrong. It also examined the often contentious issues arising out of the emergence of new religious pluralisms in previously homogeneous societies. It noted particularly how very recently many Muslims have come to feel uneasy and at times threatened by the host society as well as by wider events in world politics. The eruption of terrorist violence against British society by Muslims of Pakistani descent in 2005 brought this problem to sharp and violent focus in public discourse and experience. The tragedy of death and destruction in London in July 2005 shows how vital it is to try to understand the lives and concerns of many of those in the diaspora, though of course most Muslims, even those from the same background as the young bombers, do not share either their religious view of the world or their determination to attack their own homelands.

Chapter 5 acknowledged that South Asians in the diaspora have identities created by many senses of belonging, that they are people who belong to several worlds, one of which is the subcontinent from which they or their ancestors came. Although South Asia is not home in any daily and lived experience, it is a point of personal and group reference, and it is a place with which many in the diaspora are still connected. So we examined many of these diverse connections between people in the diaspora and people in the old homeland. Ties of kinship have been strengthened by the development of modern forms of communication and travel, and so the experience of living abroad has not been an isolated one, with roots and connections with the subcontinent almost totally severed, as was the experience of indentured labourers in the nineteenth century. Now even relatively poor South Asians overseas travel back to the subcontinent, take their children there, and have a lively sense of belonging to families and wider kin groups which straddle national boundaries. Younger South Asians in the diaspora also keep in touch with the subcontinent and create virtual diaspora worlds through the electronic resources of the internet and e-mail. There is a considerable flow of goods and capital back to the subcontinent through diaspora economic connections. These are of macroeconomic significance in the national economies of South Asia, as well as having distinct effects on the local societies and economies of regions and villages from which migrants originally came. South Asians abroad also make charitable and religious investments in their old homelands, either through personal service or through the many organisations in the diaspora which act as conduits for donations of money on a regular basis or in times of crisis. Indeed, it is evident that even when South Asians are active citizens of the polities of their new homelands, they also seek to intervene in the public life of South Asia, partly in these regular ways but particularly where conflicts have erupted in the regions from which they came, as in Kashmir and Punjab. Indians in the later strands of the diaspora have been among the most active in demanding formal status in the public life of their old homeland, and they have also used diaspora money and influence to foster in the old homeland and abroad an image of India as a specifically Hindu state, aligning with one particular strand in Indian political and religious life.

An examination of the broad contours of and key themes in the experience of South Asians who have made up the many and varied strands in the modern diaspora suggests many ways in which the diaspora is of significance to those outside it and those who seek to understand it historically, as well as to those who live within it. Most immediately the diaspora is an aspect of the modern patterns of globalisation, the flows of people, goods, capital and ideas which have bound the world together in new ways in recent decades. All these distinctive flows can be seen in the experience of the diaspora. There have obviously been and still are major movements of people out of the subcontinent on a permanent basis, and fairly continuous movements to and fro between South Asian and diaspora locations, as kin and friends visit each other and travel to reinforce familial and cultural identities. The peripatetic grandparent who visits children in a number of diaspora locales to care for new grandchildren, the diaspora pilgrim or businessman returning to the subcontinent, the young South Asian student from Europe or America who nervously visits South Asia for the first time, are familiar sights at airports. Their journeys are symptomatic of continuing patterns of personal movement which straddle the globe and bind regions and countries together. Goods travel as South Asians take gifts back to families and friends still on the subcontinent, and as South Asian communities overseas import goods into their new homes to sustain their cuisine, dress and cultural observances, and as they spread a taste for South Asian food, jewellery, fabrics and clothes among the wider society in their new homes. Capital moves in various directions also. We have seen how East African Asians often were able to transfer some capital out of Africa in advance of their ejection, and to use it as a base for their new lives in England. From the start of the modern diaspora flows migrants have also sent significant quantities of capital back to their families and home regions, as well as making privileged investments more recently, as we noted in Chapter 5. Ideas, too, have moved in many directions along with the formation of the diaspora, particularly with the migration of religious traditions and the political ideas which flow from them. More worryingly, conflicts have also become more global in their implications as in the case of several South Asian regional conflicts which have generated great anguish in the diaspora as well as actual participation, and more recently in the political implications of a global Islamism.

The development of the South Asian diaspora has of course had a significant economic and demographic impact in many host societies. Of particular significance has been the ways in which significant minority groups have come to live in what were formerly homogeneous societies, thus creating plural societies for the first time, or have increased the complexity and diversity of existing plural societies. This has raised some of the most profound social and political issues of our time, particularly those of discrimination and equality. Ranging from the extreme end of anti-Indian public action in East Africa or Fiji, to the virtual exclusion of

Indians from political influence in Malaysia, to experiences of discrimination in employment and in daily encounters on the street in Britain, the South Asian experience allows us to consider the circumstances in which minorities are feared and disliked, and to examine the roots of social conflict as well as the possibilities of social cohesion. We can also consider through the South Asian experience the mechanisms by which discrimination and hostility can be combated, whether by migrants themselves or by public authorities in the host society. In particular the diaspora experience enables us to examine the efficacy of anti-discrimination laws and programmes in several modern polities such as the UK, Canada and the USA.

Of particular and perhaps unexpected importance at the turn of the new millennium is the specific issue of religious pluralism. Whereas scholars quite recently thought that religion would increasingly become a private matter in a context of the continuing secularisation of public life, we now see that religious pluralism is in many places a very public rather than a private matter, and of increasing public and political concern. The diaspora presence and experience has often been central to this. Host societies and polities where South Asians have settled have seldom had any difficulties about sharing public space with South Asian religious traditions. These have taken their place beside Judaism and the many strands within Christianity as part of a broad mosaic of religious observance and institutionalisation. But where minority religious beliefs spill over (often at the hands of a minority within a minority) into attempts to censor particular books or plays, or at the most extreme into violence against the host society itself, then the fact of religious pluralism raises moral, legal and political questions about the legitimate role of religion in the public sphere and the way religious difference should be handled.

However, the emergence of religious and cultural pluralism in new places as a result of South Asian migration does not only raise issues of potential and actual conflicts and their public management. It also points students of religion and the cultures which are often powerfully moulded by religious belief and practice to evidence of the way religious and cultural traditions have proved immensely adaptable. Like people they often travel well. Our examination of South Asians' experience in the diaspora has shown how they have retained yet often modified cultural traditions and religious observances to suit the new situations in which they live, and have discovered within those traditions the authority and strength to manage change. As we saw, parents often worry about how they will pass on their traditions and beliefs to their children and grandchildren, particularly when older mechanisms for transmission are weakened or no longer available. But they have often found new means even if this has meant significant innovation. The *mandirs* and *gurudwaras* which run classes for young people along the lines of older Christian Sunday schools are one example, as are the vacation camps for the young, and the discussion groups for the older. Websites offering religious guidance and the welcome for *gurus* and other holy persons who have an international ministry are yet further aspects of modern life pressed into the service and transmission of older traditions. Many groups of non-Muslims also change their patterns of observance to use the spaces of leisure opened up by the conventions of the host society, particularly using Sunday for new forms of congregational worship. However, issues of religious guidance, authority and particularly the ability to connect with the younger generation are urgent and sometimes contentious. This can be seen in communities as different as the Parsis, who struggle to preserve their religion without the guidance of an international authority which understands the pressure on a tiny, well-educated group which is well-integrated into wider modern society in the western world, and the conservative Muslims of Pakistani origin in Britain whose Imams often fail to tackle, or are linguistically and intellectually unable to tackle, critical problems of interpretation, guidance and global meaning, leaving younger people rudderless in a confusing world.

The experience of South Asians outside the subcontinent is also broadly significant because it contributes to our ideas about the range of identities open to people and the ways these are fashioned. In the mid to late twentieth century historians were greatly interested in questions relating to national identity – how people came to perceive of themselves as belonging to a nation, the predisposing circumstances and shared experiences which created imagined national identities, the political and material mechanisms by which such identities were spread and fostered, and the political implications of nationalism, particularly the assumption that its fruition was the nation state. This scholarly preoccupation reflected in large part the dominance of the nation state as a form of modern polity, the experience of some of the great political movements and crises in recent European history, as well as the development of colonial nationalisms around the world in opposition to European empires. However it is also clear that in a world marked by many aspects of globalisation there are a whole range of senses of belonging which are available. Some have roots which go back well before the idea of the nation, including the regionalisms which have often re-emerged as profound sources of political loyalty, such as the Celtic nationalisms within Britain or the regional loyalties of parts of Europe, or the identities which cross national boundaries with the resurgence of many forms of religious fundamentalism. Others are comparatively new, as in the case of new political identities across old national boundaries in Europe, or new social and business identities created by work within multinational business corporations, or participation in the modern worlds of universities with their international patterns of research and scholarly cooperation enabled by internet contact and rapid air travel.

Another life-changing experience which creates new senses of identity is long-distance migration and settlement outside an original familial homeland. Here the experiences of the South Asians we have studied are particularly interesting. Among the first generation of migrants there was often a persistent sense of the subcontinent as home, a feeling of loss and a wish to return some day, even though this became less of a practical reality as people put down social roots and grew older in their new homes. But among those born abroad in the disaspora there is a clear sense of the place of birth and residence as home in a practical and affective sense, the place where they go about their daily business of work and play, where they make friendships and in turn raise their own families, the place whose language is the one which they find their most natural means of communication, the environment in which they wish to succeed. The countries of the subcontinent remain a point of reference in many ways, marking out ethnic origin, being the source of culture and religion, though decreasingly of a well-known language. South Asians in the diaspora often think of themselves in composite and multiple terms, reflecting that experience of having more than one source of personal origin or means of self-identification. They are in their own eyes Asian-Americans, Fijian Indians, British-Pakistanis, British Muslims, Canadian Sikhs, for example, and may often identify fiercely with a particular city or town in the diaspora. They manage many different identities in combination and move with considerable ease in and between different public and private environments, at home in the diaspora but with a knowledge of ethnic and religious distinctiveness which marks them out from older members of the host society as well as other strands in the diaspora.

Moreover, an added dimension of their identity is the connection with other parts of the diaspora through ties of kinship, particularly among the wealthier and more educated who have been able to seize the opportunities of global migration and employment. Indians in Britain, for example, will often also have kin in the USA, Canada or Australia, who may have migrated there directly or gone on from East Africa or Britain to become 'thrice-migrants'. They will visit them whenever possible, and will look on this pan-diasporic society as the one from which to choose brides and grooms for their own immediate families. They have become in a quite new way transnational individuals and families, at home in the places where they have settled, put down strong roots and constructed supportive social and cultural networks, yet linked in many ways to the countries of familial origin, while at the same time recognising their connections with a wider diaspora. Their experiences and senses of self, and of belonging as well as rejection, tell us much about the profound changes occurring in the modern world.

Bibliography

Abella, M. I. 'Asian migrant and contract workers in the Middle East', in Cohen, R. (ed.) *The Cambridge Survey of World Migration*, Cambridge: Cambridge University Press, 1995: pp. 418–423

Ahmad, F., Modood, T. and Lissenburgh, S. *South Asian Women and Employment in Britain: The Interaction of Gender and Ethnicity*, London: Policy Studies Institute, 2003

Ansari, H. *'The Infidel Within'. Muslims in Britain since 1800*, London: Hurst, 2004

Anwar, M. 'The participation of Asians in the British political system', in Clarke, C., Peach, C. and Vertovec, S. (eds.) *South Asians Overseas. Migration and Ethnicity*, Cambridge: Cambridge University Press, 1990: Ch. 13

Anwar, M. *British Pakistanis: Demographic, Social and Economic Position*, University of Warwick: Centre for Research in Ethnic Relations, 1996

Anwar, M. *Between Cultures. Continuity and Change in the Lives of Young Asians*, London and New York: Routledge, 1998

Bains, J. and Johal, S. *Corner Flags and Corner Shops. The Asian Football Experience*, London: Victor Gollancz, 1998

Ballard, R. 'Migration and kinship: the differential effect of marriage rules on the processes of Punjabi migration to Britain', in Clarke, C., Peach, C. and Vertovec, S. (eds.) *South Asians Overseas. Migration and Ethnicity*, Cambridge: Cambridge University Press, 1990: Ch. 10

Ballard, R. (ed.) *Desh Pardesh. The South Asian Presence in Britain*, London: Hurst, 1994

Banks, M. 'Why Move? Regional and long distance migrations of Gujarati Jains', in Brown, J. M. and Foot, R. (eds.) *Migration: The Asian Experience*, Houndmills and London: MacMillan, 1994: Ch. 6

Basran, G. S. and Bolaria, B. S. *The Sikhs in Canada. Migration, Race, Class and Gender*, New Delhi: Oxford University Press, 2003

Bates, C. (ed.) *Community, Empire and Migration. South Asians in Diaspora*, Basingstoke: Palgrave, 2001

Baumann, G. *Contesting Culture. Discourses of Identity in Multi-ethnic London*, Cambridge: Cambridge University Press, 1996

Bayly, C. A. *The New Cambridge History of India II. 1 Indian Society and the Making of the British Empire*, Cambridge: Cambridge University Press, 1988

Bayly, S. *The New Cambridge History of India IV.3. Caste, Society and Politics in India from the Eighteenth Century to the Modern Age*, Cambridge: Cambridge University Press, 1999

Beall, J. 'Women under indenture in colonial Natal, 1860–1911', in Clarke, C., Peach, C and Vertovec, S. (eds.) *South Asians Overseas. Migration and Ethnicity*, Cambridge: Cambridge University Press, 1990: Ch. 2

Bhachu, P. 'New cultural forms and transnational South Asian women: culture, class, and consumption among British South Asian women in the diaspora', in van der Veer, P. (ed.) *Nation and Migration. The Politics of Space in the South Asian Diaspora*, Philadelphia: University of Pennsylvania Press, 1995: Ch. 9

Bhachu, P. *Twice Migrants. East African Sikh Settlers in Britain*, London and New York: Tavistock Publications, 1985

Bhana, A. and Bhana, S. 'An exploration of the psycho-historical circumstances surrounding suicide among indentured Indians, 1875–1911', in Bhana, S. (ed.) *Essays on Indentured Indians in Natal*, Leeds: Peepal Tree, 1991: pp. 137–188

Bhana, S. (ed.) *Essays on Indentured Indians in Natal*, Leeds: Peepal Tree, 1991

Bhana, S. and Brain, J. *Setting Down Roots. Indian Migrants in South Africa 1860–1911*, Johannesburg: Wiwatersrand University Press, 1990

Bhardwaj, A. 'Growing up young, Asian and female in Britain: a report on self-harm and suicide', *Feminist Studies*, vol. 68, No. 1 (2001), pp. 52–67

Bhatt, C. and Mukta, P. (eds.) Special issue on Hindu nationalism and the South Asian diaspora, *Ethnic and Racial Studies*, Vol. 23, No. 3 (May, 2000)

Brah, A. 'Women of South Asian origin in Britain: issues and concerns', *South Asia Research*, vol. 7, No. 1 (May 1987), pp. 39–54

Brah, A. *Cartographies of Diaspora. Contesting Identities*, London and New York: Routledge, 1996

Braziel, J. E. and Mannur, A. (eds.) *Theorizing Diaspora. A Reader*, Oxford: Blackwell Publishing, 2003

Brereton, B. *A History of Modern Trinidad 1783–1962*, Kingston, Jamaica and London: Heinemann, 1981

Brown, J. M. and Foot, R. (eds.) *Migration: The Asian Experience*, Houndmills and London: MacMillan, 1994

Brown, Judith M. *Nehru. A Political Life*, New Haven and London: Yale University Press, 2003

Brown R. A. 'The Indian political elite in Malaysia', in Sandhu, K. S. and Mani, A. (eds.) *Indian Communities in Southeast Asia*, Singapore: Times Academic Press, 1993: Ch. 9

Burghart, R. (ed.) *Hinduism in Great Britain. The Perpetuation of Religion in an Alien Cultural Milieu*, London and New York: Tavistock Publications, 1987

Butalia, U. *The Other Side of Silence. Voices from the Partition of India*, New Delhi: Viking, Penguin Books India, 1998

Carter, M. *Lakshmi's Legacy. The Testimonies of Indian Women in 19th Century Mauritius*, Stanley, Rose-Hill, Mauritius: Editions de L'Ocean Indien, 1994

Cell, J. W. *Hailey. A Study in British Imperialism 1872–1969*, Cambridge: Cambridge University Press, 1992

Census Of India, 1911 Volume 1. India. Part 1 – Report (by E. A. Gait), Calcutta: Government of India, 1913

Census Of India, 1921 Volume 1. India. Part 1 – Report (by J. T. Marten), Calcutta: Government of India, 1924

Census of UK, 1991, London: Office for National Statistics

Census of UK, 2001, London: Office for National Statistics

Chakrabarty, D. *Rethinking Working-Class History. Bengal 1890–1940*, Princeton: Princeton University Press, 1989

Chohan, S.S. 'Punjabi Religion among the South Asian Diaspora in Britain: the role of the *Baba*', in Jacobsen, K. A. and Kumar, P. P. (eds.) *South Asians in the Diaspora. Histories and Religious Traditions*, Leiden and Boston: Brill, 2004: pp. 393–414

Clarke, C., Peach, C. and Vertovec, S. (eds.) *South Asians Overseas. Migration and Ethnicity*, Cambridge: Cambridge University Press, 1990

Clarke, C. G. *East Indians in a West Indian Town. San Fernando, Trinidad, 1930–70*, London: Allen and Unwin, 1986

Cohen, R. *Global Diasporas. An Introduction*, London and Washington: University College London Press and University of Washington Press, 1997

Cohen, R. (ed.) *The Cambridge Survey of World Migration*, Cambridge: Cambridge University Press, 1995

Connell, J. and Raj, S. 'A passage to Sydney', in Lal, B. V. (ed.) *Bittersweet the Indo-Fijian Experience*, Canberra, Australian National University: Pandanus Books, 2004: Ch. 18

Crook, W. *The North-Western Provinces of India. Their History, Ethnology and Administration*, London: Methuen, 1897

Dabydeen, D. and Samaroo, B. (eds.) *Across the Dark Waters. Ethnicity and Indian Identity in the Caribbean*, Houndmills and London: MacMillan, 1996

Daniels, R. 'The Indian diaspora in the United States', in Brown, J. M. and Foot, R. (eds.) *Migration: The Asian Experience*, Houndmills and London: MacMillan, 1994: Ch. 4

Darling, M. *The Punjab Peasant in Prosperity and Debt*, 1925, reprinted with a new introduction by C. J. Dewey, New Delhi: Manohar, 1977

Davis, K. *The Population of India and Pakistan*, Princeton: Princeton University Press, 1951; reissued 1968, Russell and Russell

Department for Education and Skills (UK) *Ethnicity and Education: The Evidence on Minority Ethnic Pupils*, 2005

Diesel, A. and Maxwell, P. *Hinduism in Natal. A Brief Guide*, Pietermaritzburg: University of Natal Press, 1993

Diesel, A. 'The Ramakrishna Sarada Devi Ashram for women in South Africa', *Journal of Contemporary Religion*, Vol. 11, No. 2 (1996), pp. 169–184

Diesel, A. 'Hinduism in KwaZulu-Natal, South Africa', in Parekh, B. Singh, G. and Vertovec, S. (eds.) *Culture and Economy in the Indian Diaspora*, London and New York: Routledge, 2003: Ch. 2

Dusenbery, V. A. 'A Sikh diaspora? Contested identities and constructed realities', in van der Veer, P. (ed.) *Nation and Migration. The Politics of Space in the South Asian Diaspora*, Philadelphia: University of Pennsylvania Press, 1995: Ch. 1

Dwyer, R. 'The Swaminarayan movement', in Jacobsen, K. A. and Kumar, P. P. (eds.) *South Asians in the Diaspora. Histories and Religious Traditions*, Leiden and Boston: Brill, 2004: pp. 180–199

Eade, J. *The Politics of Community. The Bangladeshi Community in East London*, Aldershot: Avebury, 1989

Eade, J. 'Bangladeshi community organization and leadership in Tower Hamlets, East London', in Clarke, C., Peach, C. and Vertovec. S. (eds.) *South Asians Overseas. Migration and Ethnicity*, Cambridge: Cambridge University Press, 1990: Ch. 14

Eade, J. 'The political construction of class and community. Bangladeshi political leadership in Tower Hamlets, East London', in Werbner, P. and Anwar, A. (eds.) *Black and Ethnic Leadership in Britain. The Cultural Dimensions of Political Action*, London and New York: Routledge, 1991: Ch. 3

Ellis, P. and Khan, Z. 'Political allegiances and social integration: the British Kashmiris', in Weil, S. (ed.) *Roots and Routes. Ethnicity and Migration in Global Perspective*, Jerusalem: Magnes Press, 1999: pp. 119–134

Fisher, M. *Counterflows to Colonialism. Indian Travellers and Settlers in Britain 1600–1857*, Delhi: Permanent Black, 2003

Forbes, G. *The New Cambridge History of India IV.2. Women in modern India*, Cambridge: Cambridge University Press, 1996

Freund, B. *Insiders and Outsiders. The Indian Working Class of Durban, 1910–1990*, Portsmouth N.H., Pietermaritsburg & London: Heinemann, University of Natal Press and James Curry, 1995

Frykenberg, R. E. (ed.) *Pandita Ramabai's America. Conditions of Life in the United States*, Grand Rapids and Cambridge: William B. Eerdmans, 2003

Gandhi, M. K. *An Autobiography. The Story of My Experiments with Truth*, first pub. 1927: paperback ed., London: Jonathan Cape, 1966

Gardner, K. *Global Migrants, Local Lives. Travel and Transformation in Rural Bangladesh*, Oxford: Clarendon Press, 1995

Gibson, M. A. 'Punjabi orchard farmers: an immigrant enclave in rural California', *International Migration Review*, Vol. 22, No. 1 (Spring 1988), pp. 28–50

Gillespie, M. *Television, Ethnicity and Cultural Change*, London and New York: Routledge, 1995

Gillion, K. *The Fiji Indians. Challenge to European Dominance 1920–1946*, Canberra: Australian National University Press, 1977

Gilmartin, D. 'Migration and modernity: the state, the Punjabi village, and the settling of the canal colonies', in Talbot, I. and Thandi, S. (eds.) *People on the Move. Punjabi Colonial and Post-Colonial Migration*, Karachi: Oxford University Press, 2004: Ch. 1

Gopal, S. (ed.) *Anatomy of a Confrontation. The Babri Masjid-Ramjanmabhumi Issue*, New Delhi: Penguin Books India, 1991

Greaves, R. A. 'The worship of Baba Balaknath', *International Journal of Punjab Studies*, Vol. 5, No. 1 (1998), pp. 75–85

Gregory, R. G. *India and East Africa. A History of Race Relations within the British Empire 1890–1939*, Oxford: Clarendon Press, 1971

Gupta, A. 'India and the Asians in East Africa', in Twaddle, M. (ed.) *Expulsion of a Minority. Essays on Ugandan Asians*, London: Athlone Press, 1975: Ch. 9

Halsey, A. H. and Webb, J. (eds.) *Twentieth-Century British Social Trends*, Houndmills, London and New York: MacMillan and St. Martin's Press, 2000

Hansen, R. *Citizenship and Immigration in Post-war Britain. The Institutional Origins of a Multicultural Nation*, Oxford: Oxford University Press, 2000

Hansen, T. B. *The Saffron Wave. Democracy and Hindu Nationalism in Modern India*, Princeton: Princeton University Press, 1999

Harvey, J. 'Naraini's story', in Lal, B. V. (ed.) *Chalo Jahaji on a Journey through Indenture in Fiji*, Canberra & Suva: Australian National University & Fiji Museum, 2000: Ch. 18

Hasan, M. (ed.) *India's Partition. Process, Strategy and Mobilization*, New Delhi: Oxford University Press, 1994

Hasan, M. (ed.) *Inventing Boundaries. Gender, Politics and the Partition of India*, New Delhi: Oxford University Press, 2000

Hazareesingh, K. *History of Indians in Mauritius*, London & Basingstoke: MacMillan, revised ed., 1977

Helweg, A. W. *Sikhs in England. The Development of a Migrant Community*, Delhi: Oxford University Press, 1979

Helweg A. W. and Helweg, U. M. *An Immigrant Success Story. East Indians in America*, Philadelphia: University of Pennsylvaniaia Press, 1990

Hinnells, J. R. 'The modern Zoroastrian diaspora', in Brown, J. M. and Foot, R. (eds.) *Migration: The Asian Experience*, Houndmills and London: MacMillan, 1994: Ch. 3

Hooker, R. and Sargant, J. (eds.) *Belonging To Britain: Christian Perspectives on Religion and Identity in a Plural Society*, London: Council of Churches for Britain and Ireland (CCBI) Publications, c. 1991

Islam, M. 'Bangladeshi migration: an impact study', in Cohen, R. (ed.) *The Cambridge Survey of World Migration*, Cambridge: Cambridge University Press, 1995: pp. 360–366

Jacobsen, K. A. and Kumar, P. P. (eds.) *South Asians in the Diaspora. Histories and Religious Traditions*, Leiden and Boston: Brill, 2004

Jacobson, J. *Islam in Transition. Religion and Identity among British Pakistani Youth*, London and New York: Routledge, 1998

Jagpal, S. S. *Becoming Canadians. Pioneer Sikhs in their Own Words*, Madeira Park and Vancouver: Harbour Publishing, 1994

Jain, P. C. 'Culture and economy in an 'incipient' diaspora: Indians in the Persian Gulf region', in Parekh, B., Singh, G. and Vertovec, S. (eds.) *Culture and Economy in the Indian Diaspora*, London and New York: Routledge, 2003: Ch. 5

Jain, R. K. 'Culture and economy: Tamils on the plantation frontier in Malaysia revisited, 1998–1999', in Parekh, B., Singh, G. and Vertovec, S. (eds.) *Culture and Economy in the Indian Diaspora*, London & New York: Routledge, 2003: Ch. 3

Jeffery, P. *Migrants and Refugees. Muslim and Christian Families in Bristol*, Cambridge: Cambridge University Press, 1976

Jensen, J. M. *Passage from India. Asian Indian Immigrants in North America*, New Haven and London: Yale University Press, 1988

Jones, K. W. *The New Cambridge History of India. III.1. Socio-religious Reform Movements in British India*, Cambridge: Cambridge University Press, 1989

Junghare, I. Y. 'The Hindu religious tradition in Minnesota', in Jacobsen, K. A. and Kumar, P. P. (eds.) *South Asians in the Diaspora. Histories and Religious Traditions*, Leiden and Boston: Brill, 2004: pp. 149–160

Karatani, R. *Defining British Citizenship. Empire, Commonwealth and Modern Britain*, London and Portland, Or.: Frank Cass, 2003

Kessinger, T. G. *Vilyatpur 1848–1968. Social and Economic Change in a North Indian Village*, Berkeley, Los Angeles and London: University of California Press, 1974

Khandelwal, M. S. 'Indian immigrants in Queens, New York City; patterns of spacial concentration and distribution, 1965–1990', in van der Veer, P. (ed.) *Nation and Migration. The Politics of Space in the South Asian Diaspora*, Philadelphia:University of Pennsylvania Books, 1995: Ch. 7

Knerr, B. 'South Asian countries as competitors on the world labour market', in Clarke, C., Peach, C. and Vertovec, S. (eds.) *South Asians Overseas. Migration and Ethnicity*, Cambridge: Cambridge University Press, 1990: Ch. 8

Knott, K. 'Hindu temple rituals in Britain: the re-interpretation of tradition', in Burghart, R. (ed.), *Hinduism in Great Britain. The Perpetuation of Religion in an Alien Cultural Milieu*, London and New York: Tavistock Publications, 1987: Ch. 9

Kudaisya, M. M. *The Life and Times of G. D. Birla*, New Delhi: Oxford University Press, 2003

Kumar, D. and Desai, M. (eds.) *The Cambridge Economic History of India. Volume 2: c.1757–1970*, Cambridge: Cambridge University Press, 1983

Kumar, V. 'Goodbye to Paradise', in Lal, B. V. (ed.) *Bittersweet the Indo-Fijian Experience*, Canberra, Australian National University: Pandanus Books, 2004: Ch. 19

Kuper, J. 'The Goan community in Kampala', in Twaddle, M. (ed.) *Expulsion of a Minority. Essays on Ugandan Asians,* London: Athlone Press, 1975: Ch. 4

Kurien, P. 'Religion, ethnicity and politics: Hindu and Muslim Indian immigrants in the United States', *Ethnic and Racial Studies*, Vol. 24, No. 2 (March 2001), pp. 263–293

Lal, B. V. (ed.) *Chalo Jahaji on a Journey through Indenture in Fiji* Canberra and Suva: Australian National University and Fiji Museum, 2000; Ch. 11, 'Kunti's Cry'

Lal, B. V. (ed.) *Bittersweet the Indo-Fijian Experience,* Canberra, Australian National University: Pandanus Books, 2004

Lall, M. C. *India's Missed Opportunity. India's Relationship with the Non-Resident Indians*, Aldershot: Ashgate, 2001

Lele, J. 'Indian diaspora's long-distance nationalism: the rise and proliferation of 'Hindutva' in Canada', in Varma, S. J. and Seshan, R. (eds.) *Fractured Identity. The Indian Diaspora in Canada,* Jaipur and New Delhi: Rawat Publications, 2003: Ch. 3

Lemon, A. 'The political position of Indians in South Africa', in Clarke, C., Peach, C. and Vertovec, S. (eds.) *South Asians Overseas. Migration and Ethnicity,* Cambridge: Cambridge University Press, 1990: Ch. 6

Leonard, K. I. *Making Ethnic Choices. California's Punjabi Mexican Americans,* Philadelphia: Temple University Press, 1995

Lessinger, J. 'Indian immigrants in the United States: the emergence of a transnational population', in Parekh, B., Singh, G. and Vertovec, S. (eds.) *Culture and Economy in the Indian Diaspora,* London & New York: Routledge, 2003: Ch. 8

Lewis, P. 'Being Muslim and being British. The dynamics of Islamic reconstruction in Bradford', in Ballard, R. (ed.) *Desh Pardesh. The South Asian Presence in Britain,* London: Hurst, 1994: pp. 58–87

Lewis, P. *Islamic Britain. Religion, Politics and Identity among British Muslims: Bradford in the 1990s,* London and New York: Tauris, 1994

Marett, V. 'Resettlement of Ugandan Asians in Leicester', *Journal of Refugee Studies,* Vol. 6, No. 3 (1993), pp. 248–259

Marshall, P. J. *Problems of Empire: Britain and India 1757–1813,* London: George Allen and Unwin Ltd., 1968

Marshall, P. J. *The New Cambridge History of India II.2. Bengal. The British Bridgehead. Eastern India 1740–1828,* Cambridge: Cambridge University Press, 1997

Marshall, P. J. 'The British in Asia: trade to dominion, 1700–1765', in his ed. *The Oxford History of the British Empire Volume II. The Eighteenth Century,* Oxford: Oxford University Press, 1998: Ch. 22

Mayer, A. C. *Peasants in the Pacific. A Study of Fiji Rural Society,* London: Routledge, 1988; reprinted & augmented 1961 edition

McDonald, M. 'Rituals of motherhood among Gujarati women in East London', in Burghart, R. (ed.), *Hinduism in Great Britain. The Perpetuation of Religion in an Alien Cultural Milieu,* London and New York: Tavistock Publications, 1987: Ch. 3

Menski, W. 'Legal pluralism in the Hindu marriage', in Burghart, R. (ed.), *Hinduism in Great Britain. The Perpetuation of Religion in an Alien Cultural Milieu,* London & New York: Tavistock Publications, 1987: Ch. 10

Metcalf, T. R. *Forging the Raj. Essays on British India in the Heyday of Empire,* New Delhi: Oxford University Press, 2005

Michaelson, M. 'Domestic Hinduism in a Gujarati trading caste', in Burghart, R. (ed.) *Hinduism in Great Britain. The Perpetuation of Religion in an Alien Cultural Milieu,* London and New York: Tavistock Publications, 1987: Ch. 2

Moon, P. *Divide and Quit,* Berkeley and Los Angeles: University of California Press, 1962

Morris, M. D. *The Emergence of an Industrial Labor Force in India. A Study of the Bombay Cotton Mills, 1854–1947,* Berkeley and Bombay: University of California Press and Oxford University Press, 1965

Murphy, A. 'Mobilizing *seva* ('service'): modes of Sikh diaspora action', in Jacobsen, K. A. and Kumar, P. P. (eds.) *South Asians in the Diaspora. Histories and Religious Traditions,* Leiden and Boston: Brill, 2004: pp. 337–372

Muzaffar, C. 'Political marginalization in Malaysia', in Sandhu, K. S. and Mani, A. (eds.), *Indian Communities in Southeast Asia,* Singapore: Times Academic Press, 1993: Ch, 8

Narayanan, V. 'Creating the South Indian 'Hindu' experience in the United States', in Williams, R. B. (ed.) *A Sacred Thread. Modern Transmission of Hindu Tradition in India and Abroad,* Chambersburg: Anima, 1992: Ch. 7

Nave, A. 'Nested identities: ethnicity, community and the nature of group conflict in Mauritius', in Bates, C. (ed.) *Community, Empire and Migration. South Asians in Diaspora,* Basingstoke: Palgrave, 2001: Ch. 3

Nayyar, D. *Migration, Remittances and Capital flows. The Indian Experience,* Delhi: Oxford University Press, 1994

Nayyar, D. *Governing Globalization. Issues and Institutions,* Oxford: Oxford University Press, 2002

Nehru, J. *An Autobiography,* London: Bodley Head 1936

Nesbitt, E. 'Celebrating and learning in community: the perpetuation of values and practices among Hindu Punjabi children in Coventry, UK', *Indo-British Review. A Journal of History,* Vol. XXI, No. 1 (not dated), pp. 119–131

Northrup, D. *Indentured Labor in the Age of Imperialism 1834–1922,* Cambridge: Cambridge University Press, 1995

Omissi, D. *The Sepoy and the Raj. The Indian Army, 1860–1940*, Houndmills and London: MacMillan, 1994

Omissi, D. *Indian Voices of the Great War. Soldiers' Letters, 1914–18,* Houndmills, London and New York: MacMillan and St. Martin's Press, 1999

Oxford University, *Undergraduate Admissions Statistics 2005 Entry,* Oxford: December 2005

Pandit, V. L. *The Scope of Happiness. A Personal Memoir,* London: Weidenfeld and Nicolson, 1979

Parekh, B. *Some Reflections on the Indian Diaspora,* London: British Organisation of People of Indian Origin (BOPIO), 1993

Parekh, B., Singh, G. and Vertovec, S. (eds.) *Culture and Economy in the Indian Diaspora,* London and New York: Routledge, 2003

Porter, A. N. (ed.) *Atlas Of British Overseas Expansion,* London: Routledge, 1991

Porter, A. N. (ed.) *The Oxford History of the British Empire. Volume III. The Nineteenth Century,* Oxford: Oxford University Press, 1999

Puthucheary, M. 'Indians in the public sector in Malaysia', in Sandhu, K. S. and Mani, A. (eds.) *Indian Communities in Southeast Asia,* Singapore: Times Academic Press, 1993: Ch. 13

Ramesar, M. S. 'The Repatriates', in Dabydeen, D. and Samaroo, B. (eds.) *Across the Dark Waters. Ethnicity and Indian Identity in the Caribbean,* Houndmills and London: MacMillan, 1996: Ch. 9

Raymer, S. 'Doctors help fill US health care needs', *YaleGlobal online*, Yale Center for the Study of Globalization, February 16 2004: www.yaleglobal.yale.edu

Robinson, F. (ed.) *The Cambridge Encyclopedia of India, Pakistan, Bangladesh, Sri Lanka, Nepal, Bhutan and the Maldives,* Cambridge: Cambridge University Press, 1989

Robinson, V. 'Boom and gloom: the success and failure of South Asians in Britain', in Clarke, C., Peach, C. and Vertovec, S. (eds.) *South Asians Overseas. Migration and Ethnicity,* Cambridge: Cambridge University Press, 1990: Ch. 12

Robinson, V. 'Marching into the middle classes? the long-term resettlement of East African Asians in the UK', *Journal of Refugee Studies,* Vol. 6, No. 3 (1993), pp. 230–247

Robinson, V. 'The migration of East African Asians to the UK', in Cohen, R. (ed.) *The Cambridge Survey of World Migration*, Cambridge: Cambridge University Press, 1995: pp. 331–336

Runnymede Trust, *Black and Ethnic Minority Young People and Educational Disadvantage,* London: 1997

Runnymede Trust, *Islamophobia:A Challenge for Us All,* London: 1997

Sandhu, K. S. and Mani, A. (eds.) *Indian Communities in Southeast Asia,* Singapore: Times Academic Press, 1993

Shaw, A. 'The Pakistani community in Oxford', in Ballard, R. (ed.) *Desh Pardesh. The South Asian Presence in Britain,* London: Hurst, 1994: pp. 35–57

Shaw, A. *Kinship and Continuity. Pakistani Families in Britain,* Amsterdam: Harwood Academic Publishers, 2000

Solomos, J. *Race and Racism in Contemporary Britain,* Houndmills and London: MacMillan, 1989

Sorabji, C. *India Calling,* 1934; new edn. by C. Lokuge, New Delhi: Oxford University Press, 2001

Strizhek, E. F. 'The Ugandan Asian expulsion: resettlement in the USA', *Journal of Refugee Studies,* Vol. 6, No. 3 (1993), pp. 260–264

Stopes-Roe, M. and Cochrane, R. *Citizens of This Country: The Asian British,* Clevedon and Philadelphia: Multilingual Matters Ltd., 1990

Symonds, R. *Oxford and Empire. The Last Lost Cause?* Oxford University Press and MacMillan, 1986; revised paperback edn., Oxford: Clarendon Press, 1991

Talbot, I. *Freedom's Cry. The Popular Dimension in the Pakistan Movement and Partition Experience in North-West India,* Karachi: Oxford University Press, 1996

Talbot, I. and Thandi, S. (eds.) *People on the Move. Punjabi Colonial and Post-Colonial Migration,* Karachi: Oxford University Press, 2004

Tan, T. Y. and Kudaisya, G. *The Aftermath of Partition in South Asia,* London and New York: Routledge, 2000

Tandon, P. *Punjabi Century 1857–1947,* London: Chatto and Windus, 1963

Tatla, D. S. 'Sikh free and military migration during the colonial period', in Cohen, R. (ed.) *The Cambridge Survey of World Migration,* Cambridge: Cambridge University Press, 1995: pp. 69–73

Tatla, D. S. 'Rural roots of the Sikh diaspora', in Talbot, I. and Thandi, S. (eds.) *People on the Move. Punjabi Colonial and Post-Colonial Migration,* Karachi: Oxford University Press, 2004: Ch. 5

Tatla, D. S. *The Sikh diaspora. The Search for Statehood,* London: University College London Press, 1999

Thandi, S. '*Vilayati Paisa*: some reflections on the potential of diaspora finance in the socio-economic development of Indian Punjab', in Talbot, I. and Thandi, S. (eds.) *People on the Move. Punjabi Colonial and Post-Colonial Migration,* Karachi: Oxford University Press, 2004: Ch. 11

Thapar, R. 'Imagined religious communities? Ancient history and the modern search for a Hindu identity', *Modern Asian Studies,* Vol. 23, Part 2 (May 1989), pp. 209–231

Thapar, R. 'A historical perspective on the story of Rama', in Gopal, S. (ed.) *Anatomy of a Confrontation. The Babri Masjid-Ramjanmabhumi Issue*, New Delhi: Penguin Books India, 1991: pp. 141–163

Thompson A. and Begum, R. *Asian 'Britishness'. A Study of First Generation Asian Migrants in Greater Manchester*, London: Institute for Public Policy Research, 2005

Tinker, H. *A New System of Slavery. The Export of Indian Labour Overseas 1830–1920*, London: Oxford University Press, 1974

Tinker, H. *Separate and Unequal. India and the Indians in the British Commonwealth 1920–1950*, London: C. Hurst and Co., 1976

Tinker, H. *The Banyan Tree. Overseas Emigrants from India, Pakistan and Bangladesh*, Oxford: Oxford University Press, 1977

Tinker, H. *The Ordeal of Love. C. F. Andrews and India*, Delhi: Oxford University Press, 1979

Tomlinson, B. R. 'Economics and Empire: the periphery and the imperial economy', in Porter, A. N. (ed.) *The Oxford History of the British Empire. Volume III. The Nineteenth Century*, Oxford: Oxford University Press, 1999: Ch. 3

Twaddle, M. (ed.) *Expulsion of a Minority. Essays on Ugandan Asians*, London: Athlone Press, 1975

van der Burg, C. J. G. 'The Hindu diaspora in the Netherlands: halfway between local structures and global ideologies', in Jacobsen, K. A. and Kumar, P. P. (eds.) *South Asians in the Diaspora. Histories and Religious Traditions*, Leiden and Boston: Brill, 2004: pp. 97–115

van der Veer, P. (ed.) *Nation and Migration. The Politics of Space in the South Asian Diaspora*, Philadelphia: University of Pennsylvania Press, 1995

Van Hear, N. *New Diasporas. The Mass Exodus, Dispersal and Regrouping of Migrant Communities*, London and Seattle: University College London Press and University of Washington Press, 1998

Varma, S. J. and Seshan, R. (eds.) *Fractured Identity. The Indian Diaspora in Canada*, Jaipur and New Delhi: Rawat Publications, 2003

Vertovec, S. *Hindu Trinidad. Religion, Ethnicity and Socio-Economic Change*, London and Basingstoke: MacMillan, 1992

Vertovec, S. *The Hindu Diaspora. Comparative Patterns*, London: Routledge, 2000

Visram, R. *Ayahs, Lascars and Princes. Indians in Britain 1700–1947*, London: Pluto Press, 1986

Voigt-Graf, C. 'Indians at home in the Antipodes', in Parekh, B., Singh. G. and Vertovec, S. (eds.) *Culture and Economy in the Indian Diaspora*, London and New York: Routledge, 2003: Ch. 7

Warrier, S. 'Gujarati Prijapatis in London. Family roles and sociability networks', in Ballard, R. (ed.) *Desh Pardesh. The South Asian Presence in Britain*, London: Hurst, 1994: pp. 191–212

Washbrook, D. 'India, 1818–1860: the two faces of colonialism', in Porter, A. N. (ed.) *The Oxford History of the British Empire. Volume III. The Nineteenth Century*, Oxford: Oxford University Press, 1999: Ch. 18

Weil, S. (ed.) *Roots and Routes. Ethnicity and Migration in Global Perspective*, Jerusalem: Magnes Press, 1999

Werbner, P. 'The fiction of unity in ethnic politics. Aspects of representation and the state among British Pakistanis', in Werbner, P. and Anwar, M. (eds.) *Black and Ethnic Leadership in Britain. The Cultural Dimensions of Political Action,* London and New York: Routledge, 1991: Ch. 4

Werbner, P. 'Renewing an industrial past: British Pakistani entrepreneurship in Manchester', in Brown, J. M. and Foot, R. (eds.) *Migration: The Asian Experience,* Houndmills & London: MacMillan, 1994: Ch. 5

Werbner, P. 'Murids of the Saint: migration, diaspora and redemptive sociality in Sufi regional and global cults', in Talbot, I. and Thandi, S. (eds.) *People on the Move. Punjabi Colonial and Post-Colonial Migration,* Karachi: Oxford University Press, 2004: Ch. 11

Werbner, P. *The Migration Process. Capital, Gifts and Offerings among British Pakistanis,* New York, Oxford and Munich: Berg, 1990

Werbner, P. and Anwar, M. (eds.) *Black and Ethnic Leadership in Britain. The Cultural Dimensions of Political Action,* London and New York: Routledge, 1991

White, B.-S. *Turbans and Traders. Hong Kong's Indian Communities.* Hong Kong: Oxford University Press, 1994

Williams, R. B. (ed.) *A Sacred Thread. Modern Transmission of Hindu Tradition in India and Abroad,* Chambersburg: Anima, 1992

Williams, R. B. *Religions of Migrants from India and Pakistan. New Threads in the American Tapestry,* Cambridge: Cambridge University Press, 1988

WEB SITES

WEBSITES RUN BY GOVERNMENTS

www.statcan.ca (Census of Canada, 2001 statistics)
www.statistics.gov.uk/census 2001 (Census of the UK, 2001)
www.cre.gov.uk (Commission for Racial Equality, UK)
www.parliament.uk (UK Parliament website)
www.dfes.org.uk (UK Department for Education and Science)
www.homeoffice.gov.uk (UK Home Office)
www.missdorothy.com (site run by the UK government to aid those in danger of forced marriage)
www.cia.gov/cia/publications/factbook (CIA World Factbook)
www.movinghere.org.uk (a website on migration into the UK which is independent but involves many public bodies)

WEBSITES OF FORMAL ORGANISATIONS AND CHARITIES

www.ashianahelp.org.uk
www.hinducounciluk.org.uk
www.maitri.org
www.refuge.org.uk
www.runnymedetrust.org
www.sawnet.org
www.swaminarayan-baps.org.uk

DIASPORA WEBSITES

www.redhotcurry.com
www.punjabi-marriage.com
www.rekha.com
www.sulekha.com

Index